Readers looking for a fresh take on higher education in the postwar period will delight in this book. With thoughtful contributions and deft framing, this stimulating volume offers new insights on higher education's recent past.

Christopher P. Loss, *Associate Professor of Public Policy and Higher Education and History, Vanderbilt University*

The quarter century from 1945 to 1970 stands out as important and exciting for the development of American higher education. Three outstanding historians have collaborated as editors and authors, along with additional stellar contributing authors, to provide an anthology that is a model of thoughtful scholarship.

John R. Thelin, *University Research Professor, University of Kentucky and author of American Higher Education: Issues and Institutions (Routledge, 2017)*

AMERICAN HIGHER EDUCATION IN THE POSTWAR ERA, 1945–1970

After World War II, returning veterans with GI Bill benefits ushered in an era of unprecedented growth that fundamentally altered the meaning, purpose, and structure of higher education. This volume explores the multifaceted and tumultuous transformation of American higher education that occurred between 1945 and 1970, while examining the changes in institutional forms, curricula, clientele, faculty, and governance. A wide range of well-known contributors cover topics such as the first public university to explicitly serve an urban population, the creation of modern-day honors programs, how teachers colleges were repurposed as state colleges, the origins of faculty unionism and collective bargaining, and the dramatic student protests that forever changed higher education. This engaging text explores a critical moment in the history of higher education, signaling a shift in the meaning of a college education, the concept of who should and who could obtain access to college, and what should be taught.

Roger L. Geiger is Distinguished Professor of Higher Education Emeritus at the Pennsylvania State University, USA.

Nathan M. Sorber is Assistant Professor of Higher Education and Director of the Center for the Future of Land-Grant Universities at West Virginia University, USA.

Christian K. Anderson is Associate Professor of Higher Education at the University of South Carolina, USA.

PERSPECTIVES ON THE HISTORY OF HIGHER EDUCATION SERIES

Editors
Roger L. Geiger
Pennsylvania State University
Nathan M. Sorber
West Virginia University
Christian K. Anderson
University of South Carolina

Editorial board
Katherine Reynolds Chaddock, *University of South Carolina*
Marybeth Gasman, *University of Pennsylvania*
Peter Dobkin Hall, *Baruch College, City University of New York*
Jurgen Herbst, *University of Wisconsin-Madison*
Philo Hutcheson, *University of Alabama*
W. Bruce Leslie, *State University of New York, College at Brockport*
David B. Potts, Tacoma, Washington
John Thelin, *University of Kentucky*
Harold S. Wechsler, Former Editor, *New York University*
Roger L. Williams, *The Pennsylvania State University*

Volume 19 – History of Higher Education Annual
1999
Roger L. Geiger

Volume 18 – History of Higher Education Annual
1998
Roger L. Geiger

Volume 17 – History of Higher Education Annual
1997
Roger L. Geiger

Volume 16 – History of Higher Education Annual
1996
Roger L. Geiger

AMERICAN HIGHER EDUCATION IN THE POSTWAR ERA, 1945–1970

Edited by
Roger L. Geiger,
Nathan M. Sorber, and
Christian K. Anderson

NEW YORK AND LONDON

First published 2018
by Routledge
711 Third Avenue, New York, NY 10017

and by Routledge
2 Park Square, Milton Park, Abingdon, Oxon, OX14 4RN

Routledge is an imprint of the Taylor & Francis Group, an informa business

© 2018 Taylor & Francis

The right of Roger L. Geiger, Nathan M. Sorber, and Christian K. Anderson to be identified as the authors of the editorial material, and of the authors for their individual chapters, has been asserted in accordance with sections 77 and 78 of the Copyright, Designs and Patents Act 1988.

All rights reserved. No part of this book may be reprinted or reproduced or utilized in any form or by any electronic, mechanical, or other means, now known or hereafter invented, including photocopying and recording, or in any information storage or retrieval system, without permission in writing from the publishers.

Trademark notice: Product or corporate names may be trademarks or registered trademarks, and are used only for identification and explanation without intent to infringe.

Library of Congress Cataloging in Publication Data
A catalog record for this book has been requested

ISBN: 978-1-138-09619-6 (hbk)
ISBN: 978-1-4128-6559-3 (pbk)
ISBN: 978-1-315-10431-7 (ebk)

Typeset in Bembo
by Wearset Ltd, Boldon, Tyne and Wear

CONTENTS

Preface ix

1 Introduction: American Higher Education in the Postwar Era, 1945–1970 1
 Roger L. Geiger

2 The Surprising History of the Post-World War II State Teachers College 23
 W. Bruce Leslie and Kenneth P. O'Brien

3 "Education for Citizenship ... Is Too Important to Leave to Chance": John Allen and the University of South Florida, 1956–1970 50
 Charles Dorn

4 The Reinvention of Honors Programs in American Higher Education, 1955–1965 79
 Julianna K. Chaszar

5 Collective Bargaining and College Faculty: Illinois in the 1960s 116
 Timothy Reese Cain

| 6 | Brave Sons and Daughters True: 1960s Protests at "The Fundamentalist Harvard"
Adam Laats | 146 |
| 7 | The Student Protest Movement in the *1968 Era* in Three Acts: Inception, Confrontations, and Legacies
Roger L. Geiger | 170 |

Notes on Contributors   *201*
Index   *203*

PREFACE

The editors of *Perspectives on the History of Higher Education* are pleased to present *American Higher Education in the Postwar Era, 1945–1970*, the thirty-second volume in the series. Originally named the *History of Higher Education Annual*, the series was founded in 1981 as the sole national journal of higher education history under the editorship of Edwin D. Duryea of the State University of New York-Buffalo. Early contributors included prominent scholars such as Jurgen Herbst, Walter Metzger, Laurence R. Veysey, and David Potts. The *Annual* was thereafter hosted by the University of Rochester under the editorship of Harold S. Wechsler, and through the remainder of the 1980s, Wechsler introduced the scholarship of a new generation of education historians—Roger L. Geiger, Lynn Gordon, Ellen Condliffe Lagemann, and Wayne Urban. In 1992, the *Annual* moved to Pennsylvania State University with Roger L. Geiger as editor, and in 2004, it was rechristened as *Perspectives*.

Over the last 35 years, the *Annual/Perspectives* has had a significant influence on the historiography of colleges and universities, transforming the way scholars understand the changes, continuities, and contexts of higher education. Contributors have expanded our knowledge of college students, faculty, governance, leadership, policy, and organizations, have explicated changing dynamics of the core missions of teaching, research and service, and addressed how higher education history has been mediated by region, class, gender, and race. In the 1980s and 1990s, *Annual/Perspectives* became a place for authors to challenge traditional interpretations of higher education history. Often referred to as the revisionist movement, these scholars had the most dramatic influence on conceptions of higher education in the antebellum era, countering the consensus conclusion of high failure rate of colleges—the so-called "great retrogression"—and the limited appeal of narrow classical colleges. Instead, the revisionists presented a more vigorous and socially responsive higher education landscape in the nineteenth century with women's colleges, schools of useful knowledge, multipurpose colleges, scientific schools, polytechnics, and innovative classical colleges. In recent years, *Perspectives* engaged with underdeveloped areas of the historiography through thematic volumes, including books on higher education in the South, the land-grant college movement, higher education for African-Americans before the Civil Rights Era, higher education leadership, and the shaping of the American academic profession. The far-reaching historiographical impact of *Annual/Perspectives* is most evident in Roger L. Geiger's comprehensive history, *The History of American Higher Education: Learning and Culture from the Founding to World War II*.

This volume of *Perspectives* continues this tradition by exploring the multifaceted and tumultuous transformation of American colleges and universities after World War II. The authors illustrate how the postwar era was a period of dramatic and fundamental change in higher education. Burgeoning student demand and rapid enrollment growth altered purposes and forms, and recast the relationship between higher education and federal and state governments. The six studies by W. Bruce Leslie and Kenneth P. O'Brien, Charles Dorn, Julianna K. Chaszar, Timothy Reese Cain, Adam Laats, and Roger L. Geiger address important, and in some cases neglected trends that epitomize the era, including the arrival of faculty unionism, the conversion of teachers colleges into regional universities, the rapid ascent of urban-serving universities, the rise of honors colleges, and student activism. In sum, the chapters reveal decisive break with the stability of preceding decades and the emerging foundations of contemporary higher education.

Starting with the present edition, *Perspectives* will be published by Routledge. The editors are excited with this opportunity to preserve *Perspectives* as an outlet for established and budding scholars to introduce major historical works. Indeed, one of the legacies of this series is the number of volumes that contain the nascent ideas and arguments of celebrated books in the field. In the early years, Roger L. Geiger refined his ideas on research universities, Lester F. Goodchild's article on Jesuit higher education presaged his work on Catholic Universities, and Lynn D. Gordon polished material that would contribute to her book *Gender and Higher Education*. Margaret A. Nash introduced ideas on women's higher education in the nineteenth century, Roger Williams inaugurated his revision of land-grant college history that would guide *Origins of Federal Support*, and Mary Beth Gasman authored work on the United Negro College Fund that would be developed into her important book on the subject. Over the last decade, several books were published that began as articles in *Perspectives*, including: Daniel A. Clark's *Creating the College Man*, Timothy Reese Cain's *Establishing Academic Freedom*, Marc Van Overbeke's *The Standardization of American Schooling*, A. J. Angulo's *William Barton Rogers and the Idea of MIT*, Katherine Chaddock Reynolds' *The Multi-Talented Mr. Erskine: Shaping Mass Culture through Great Books and Fine Music,* and Timothy J. Williams' *Intellectual Manhood: University, Self, and Society in the Antebellum South.* This trend continues with the current volume, as Adam Laats furthers ideas introduced in *The Other School Reformers: Conservative Activism in American Education,* and finally in his introduction and concluding chapter, Roger L. Geiger expands on material that will appear in his future volume of the *History of American Higher Education Since 1945.*

1

INTRODUCTION

American Higher Education in the Postwar Era, 1945–1970

Roger L. Geiger

The Postwar Era of American higher education, from 1945 to 1970, can be characterized by no single feature other than rapid and continual change along a multitude of dimensions. In this respect it differed from the comparative stability of the period that followed. The Postwar Era in many ways opened a new chapter in the long history of American higher education. It was separated from the past by two monumental hiatuses. During World War II, the campuses were emptied of regular male students, as well as a good share of professors, and they assumed a variety of war-related tasks. Then, a tidal wave of veterans inundated campuses to study under the terms of the 1944 Serviceman's Readjustment Act—the GI Bill. The late 1940s were turbulent times in American politics and economy as well as higher education. For colleges and universities, fundamental issues were raised about who should attend and what they should be taught. After 1950, a conservative consensus congealed over both American society and higher education. Americans embraced an apotheosis of the "American Way of Life," which encompassed, among other things, economic prosperity, a growing middle class, and rising college enrollments. All these features accelerated after 1960, but now increasingly accompanied by an advancing liberal tide that challenged 1950s complacency. In the last half of the decade, these challenges turned increasingly negative, rejecting fundamental features of American society, especially on university campuses, and culminating in the most prolonged and violent protests that the academy ever endured.

This volume cannot attempt a full account of this tumultuous quarter-century. Rather, these six studies examine and clarify developments that played various roles in this history—some central, some representative of larger trends, and some hitherto neglected. This introductory chapter summarizes the intense exchanges immediately after the war over who should go to college and what they should be expected to learn there. The chapters by Bruce Leslie and Kenneth O'Brien and Charles Dorn address two important dimensions of this issue, the increased supply of higher education that made possible the great postwar expansion. The teachers colleges that were incorporated into the State University of New York (SUNY) were representative of nearly 200 like institutions that made an eventual transition to full state colleges and often regional universities. The authors show how Brockport State Teachers College provided students of limited means and mobility access to both a quasi-liberal education and teaching careers. It served, above all, students who were the first in their families to attend college. The same can be said for the subsequent proliferation and expansion of public urban universities. Charles Dorn's depiction of the University of South Florida—the first public university created expressly to serve an urban clientele—reveals the cross-purposes of university conceptions of a liberal education and the careerist motivations of commuting urban students.

The creation of modern honors programs in the 1950s is depicted here for the first time by Julianna Chaszar. Whereas previous honors had allowed small numbers of juniors or seniors to work on individual projects, the new programs provided selected incoming "superior students" with special classes and programs. The prophet of this movement was Joseph Cohen, a philosophy professor at the University of Colorado. He obtained foundation support to establish the Inter-University Committee on the Superior Student (ICSS) in order to promote this vision of "general honors." These programs were explicitly intended to address the challenge of heterogeneous students in growing state universities. As such, they proved a strategic and timely adaptation to the great expansion of American higher education.

The rise of faculty unionism was a major development of the late 1960s. Timothy Cain's study of its emergence in Illinois highlights the tentative and fragmentary origins of what proved to be an inexorable movement. In the four cases he analyzes, postsecondary unionism developed directly out of preceding teachers unions. In only one case, however, were these origins translated into a militant organization of higher education faculty. In the others, faculty sought some degree of separation from the lower schools by associating with the American Association of University Professors (AAUP). Ironically, the relationship with Bellville Junior College proved instrumental in leading the AAUP to embrace collective bargaining.

Adam Laats explores a different dimension of higher education by investigating how evangelical institutions and specifically Wheaton College reacted to the protests of the 1960s. These schools had to come to terms, on one hand, with comparatively moderate requests for relaxation of strict codes of behavior, lifting of censorship, and greater racial accommodations. On the other hand, they faced intense pressure both to uphold the standards expected by the evangelical community and to defend themselves against criticism from more rigid fundamentalists. The alternatives of too much or too little liberalism were argued with vehemence in the 1960s, so that Wheaton's dilemma illuminates the turmoil of this entire sector of higher education.

The student protests of the 1960s escalated to violent confrontations at many campuses from spring 1968 through spring 1970—the "1968 Era." The final chapter by Roger L. Geiger provides a chronology of the radicalization of the New Left during the 1960s and describes the most egregious campus rebellions that occurred in this final stage. These outbursts expressed an extreme rejection of the American way of life, which had undergirded the growth of higher education through the Postwar Era. Although these confrontations essentially failed as protests, the 1968 Era signaled a turning point for higher education and for the nation generally. The New Left hostility to bourgeois values and national ideals persisted among significant groups, manifested in numerous causes, but it has been represented most prominently on campuses by the self-proclaimed Academic Left.

The remainder of this chapter will relate these topics to more general developments in American higher education in the Postwar Era. Some important facets of this vast history are not addressed, such as the impact of McCarthyism, the enormous growth of university research and graduate education, and the struggle for desegregation in the North as well as the South.[1] But an underlying thread connecting these six studies is the narrative on the meaning of a college education: the perpetual quest to define who should and who could obtain access to college and what they would be taught there.

General and Liberal Education

Defining the nature and role of liberal education was the unfinished business of American higher education between the wars. With the coming of mass higher education after World War I, some reformers attempted to counter this trend by rekindling the spirit of liberal education, while other prophets and their projects tended to embrace inclusiveness, advocating practices that claimed to enhance the educational experiences of all students. By the 1930s, these innovators preferred the term general education, in keeping with a view that the first two years of college should be oriented toward common learning. The majority of colleges, judging from the official publications of institutional associations, still identified with liberal education, however defined. Depictions of liberal and general education overlapped considerably, and both camps harbored contradictory interpretations. Often the same language was used for entirely different purposes, and each often invoked "baskets" of attributes.[2] But beneath this confusion lay the crucial issue of the future direction of undergraduate education and the nature of American collegiate education. The war raised the ideological stakes attached to these issues.

What liberal and general education had in common was aversion to "specialization" and "vocationalism," two of the most prominent trends of the interwar years.[3] Specialization was the pejorative term for the relentless advance of academic knowledge, coupled with the elective system that allowed students to choose most of their own courses. Critics acknowledged this reality, but argued that esoteric academic knowledge had little relevance for collegians in the first two years of general education, or even in a four-year bachelor's course. Similar arguments sought to locate the study of practical fields for specific careers after general education. What they favored was the desirability of common learning to overcome the fragmentation of the elective system. However, curricular reformers faced the hurdle of existing practice. Many colleges equated liberal education with the mastery of advanced knowledge in academic disciplines and were striving to extend their capacity to teach such knowledge. However, in 1940 less than 40 percent of bachelor's degrees were awarded in the liberal arts and sciences, about the same number conferred in education and business.[4] Despite an outpouring of writing on liberal and general education, American higher education was primarily engaged in teaching the disciplines and professions.

The Postwar Era saw the appearance of three major reports that addressed these curricular issues, but extended beyond them to the nature of higher education and who would attend. Each was influential in its own way; and each contradicted rival positions, explicitly or implicitly. The Harvard Red Book, *General Education in a Free Society*, was as concerned about the intellectual foundations of a democratic society as the curriculum of Harvard College. The President's Commission's *Higher Education for American Democracy* championed approaches that the Harvard Committee had specifically rejected. The Commission on Financing Higher Education was formed in reaction to the President's Commission report, and encompassed far more than finances. It expressed a consensus among those institutions whose interests had been ignored and was far more defensive toward the status quo.

The Harvard Red Book had a diffuse but pervasive influence on American higher education. This influence is often ascribed to the prestige of Harvard and widespread publicity. These things could not have hurt; but its basic message resonated with the zeitgeist, circa 1945, and answered some of the charges against liberal education.[5] First, in seeking to strengthen national unity, it proposed an approach to common learning that encompassed all Americans. The focus was on general education in the high school, where it outlined an academic curriculum that would address the needs of both those who would advance to further education and the majority of those who would not. Second, for higher education, the report democratized the liberal arts by emphasizing the development of judgment and understanding as being prior to the advanced specialized knowledge that critics had stigmatized. Taught in this manner early in the college curriculum, basic arts and sciences subjects might provide a common intellectual foundation for all students.

The Red Book thus articulated a novel and democratic purpose for the liberal arts. It supplied an important voice in the movement to strengthen secondary education, but colleges and universities generally were concerned with providing all students with a common core of learning and instilling an ideological foundation for democratic citizenship. Almost every institution established some kind of required course in the Western heritage. And for the next 20 years, colleges and universities devised countless approaches to introductory liberal arts sequences. Ironically, at Harvard the general education curriculum was adopted by the faculty but soon vitiated. President Conant attempted to lead in 1947 by offering a foundational course in "The Growth of Experimental Science," but Harvard scientists were among the first to reject this approach and defend traditional introductory courses. Regardless, *General Education in a Free Society* contributed to upholding the sacrosanct status of the liberal arts in postwar American higher education.

The President's Commission on Higher Education adopted democracy and general education as its themes, but interpreted them quite differently from the Harvard committee. Adopting the progressive goals that the latter had rejected, it envisioned an idealistic reshaping of American society, declaring that the primary purpose of education should be to instill the democratic ideal in citizens in order to transform society into a higher form of democratic community. Thus, for colleges and universities, "education for democratic living … should become … a primary aim of all classroom teaching and, more important still, of every phase of campus life." The Commission adopted (without identifying) John Dewey's notion of *general education*: "nonspecialized and nonvocational learning which should be the common experience of all educated men and women." By this the report meant achieving, among other things, "satisfactory emotional and social adjustment," and "attitudes basic to a satisfying family life." Remarkably, all the usual functions of higher education were subordinated to this conception of general education for democracy. Manpower considerations were barely mentioned, and vocational training was less important than a healthy orientation toward work. Social mobility was potentially harmful to community unity; in fact, "through education society should come to recognize the equal dignity of all kinds of work, and so erase distinctions based on occupational castes." Specialized (disciplinary) knowledge was described as the bane of the college curriculum, and liberal education dismissed as "aristocratic."[6]

More positively, *Higher Education for American Democracy* forcefully advocated expansion of higher education. Using data from the Army General Classification Test that had been administered to ten million inductees, it concluded that "at least 49 percent of our population has the mental ability to complete 14 years of schooling"; and "at least 32 percent [could] complete an advanced liberal or specialized professional education."[7] The two-year students could be accommodated in community colleges, a term it substituted for junior colleges. And it challenged contemporary mores by condemning discrimination against Jewish and Negro students. The President's Commission also proposed federal support for general and capital expenditures, but only for state institutions—a stipulation that alienated the hard-pressed private sector. Justifying federal financing and influence for higher education had been a principal goal in forming the Commission, but such an initiative was a dead letter politically as the Cold War hardened at the end of the decade.

The President's Commission is sometimes considered prescient for advocating a dramatic expansion of higher education enrollment, an important role for community colleges, and a prominent federal financial role. Yet, all these developments occurred later for reasons that were unconnected with the Commission's report. Its Deweyan life skills curriculum was never taken seriously among colleges, and was soon attacked in the lower schools (as noted by Bruce Leslie and Kenneth O'Brien). Hostility to liberal arts, academic disciplines, and the advancement of knowledge were in fact profoundly at odds with the nature of American higher education. Besides dismissing the private sector, its views were antithetical to the research universities. So much so that it galvanized an official response.

The Commission on Financing Higher Education (CFHE) began to take shape in November 1947, the date of the first publication from the President's Commission. Organized under the Association of American Universities and funded by the Rockefeller Foundation and the Carnegie Corporation, the CFHE represented the research universities, and included Paul Buck and the presidents of Johns Hopkins, Caltech, Stanford, and Brown. The CFHE produced three types of reports in 1952. The Commission's large staff documented the realities of American higher education in eight studies and technical papers. These were condensed by John Millett in *Financing Higher Education in the United States*—a compendium of the state of higher education at the start of the 1950s. These findings were digested into policy statements in the Commission report, *Nature and Needs of Higher Education*.[8] Although finance received the greatest attention, the CFHE addressed the same issues as the President's Commission, factually in the staff reports and ideologically in *Nature and Needs*.

This dichotomy was most salient for the question of who should go to college. The staff report by Byron Hollinshead used existing studies to recommend that colleges should serve the top 25 percent in intelligence, with perhaps another 10 percent attending junior colleges. However, data clearly showed that less than half of these students actually enrolled, and that attendance was strongly influenced by social class. And this only pertained to White students, since the inferior education received by Blacks made their situation far worse. Assertions of equality of opportunity, Hollinshead observed, were "more demagogic than rational."[9] However, in *Nature and Needs* the Commission asserted:

> our colleges and universities enroll a wide representation of American youth.... They promote ... the ideal of the classless society and of careers open to talent. Colleges and universities are among the least discriminatory institutions of American society in so far as race, religion, and nationality are concerned.[10]

This facile optimism reflected contemporary thinking about education under the emerging Cold War mentality.

In other respects, the Commission expressed views prevailing among the leading universities and the American Association of Universities (AAU). Contra the President's Commission, it lauded the value of diversity provided by a vigorous private sector. It considered current federal programs for higher education to be sufficient, and feared that greater federal involvement would lead to federal control—a development explicitly encouraged by the President's Commission. It differed most radically in matters of curriculum, where the CFHE endorsed the Harvard report's conception of general education as a preliminary base of common learning, but idealized a traditional conception of liberal education as a higher form of learning, fundamental to a free society. Individual freedom was the touchstone, best achieved through the "understanding of man's cultural heritage, an appreciation of the great ennobling sentiments and thoughts of philosophers and scholars, [and] a grasp of the ways in which man's knowledge has accumulated and how it advances." The CFHE thus offered a synthesis of general and liberal education that was perhaps superficial in a philosophical sense, but it privileged the liberal learning that colleges and universities now embraced, and it rationalized that position for contemporaries by identifying liberal education, and the institutions that purveyed it, with freedom.[11]

The copious materials gathered by the CFHE documented conditions in American higher education at the beginning of the 1950s, but the Commission's message provided another kind of documentation. Funded by two great foundations, organized by the club of research universities, with membership including university and corporate leaders, the Commission spoke for the higher education establishment at the onset of the Cold War. The iterations of *free society* and *freedom* in higher education echoed the identification of the United States as leader of the "Free World." The Panglossian assumption about a classless society and absence of discrimination reflected a conscious or unconscious absorption of the preferred self-image of American society, and possibly self-censorship against acknowledging social maladies even to the extent that the President's Commission had. The focus on traditional undergraduate education in the liberal arts elevated and in a sense rehabilitated the central historical function of American higher education. *Nature and Needs*, in sum, sanctified the status quo. It identified possible threats to this fundamentally sound system, but pointed the way for private actors—not the federal government—to meet these challenges and further strengthen this system. The writings of the CFHE thus signify a transition from the tumultuous postwar debates over the roles and direction of American higher education to the emerging consensus on the "American way of life." Higher education in the 1950s would become increasingly central to that American way of life.

Demand for and Supply of College Education

The proportion of 18–21-year-olds enrolled as undergraduates reached 15 percent at the beginning of the 1940s. In 1951, after the GIs had left, it was 24 percent; and in 1961, 33 percent. This was *before* the baby-boom cohorts would more than double enrollments in the 1960s. American higher education was inherently expansive in the Postwar Era. The experts who initially pondered who should go to college found much room for improvement. The odds of attending college were determined largely by social and economic factors. A 1949 study found that 60 percent of high school graduates from the highest income quintile applied immediately to college, versus 20 percent from the lowest two quintiles. Students from wealthy families (>$9,000) in the lower half of their graduating class were more likely to attend than poorer students (<$5,000) in the top quarter. But American education was not a caste system. Blue-collar workers and farmers, comprising almost two-thirds of families, produced 39 percent of college graduates. Moreover, except for farmers, once a student enrolled in college, chances of graduation were nearly the same regardless of father's occupation.[12]

Contemporaries were less concerned with social inequity than with innate intelligence. The Harvard Red Book, the President's Commission, and the CFHE all assumed a kind of IQ determinism, so that college should serve the most intelligent 25 or 32 percent of the age group. Psychologists demonstrated a linear relationship between IQ of college students and their probability of graduating. A score of 110, or approximately the 75th percentile, seemed to mark the tipping point between a majority who graduated and a majority who dropped out.[13] However, among that top quarter of ability, just two-fifths attended college. A similar proportion graduated from high school but did not continue, and one-fifth dropped out of high school, many by the 10th grade. Cost of attendance was one significant factor. Contemporary studies indicated that one-third of the high school graduates not going to college would do so if they could afford it.[14] American society in the late 1940s still reflected the penury of the Depression. The Harvard Red Book had noted that a year of public high school entailed $90 in expenses, more than many working-class households could afford. The cost of a year at a residential college, circa 1950, ranged from $600 (public) to $1,500 (private).[15] Given these initial conditions, how can the expansion of the 1950s be explained?

Essentially, the growing prosperity of American society boosted social demand for higher education. Whereas an estimated 17 percent of families had sufficient incomes to afford a residential college education for a child in 1940, a decade later 30 percent did, and this figure continued to rise. The middle class, estimated to constitute 40 percent of the population, believed in "the individual's responsibility for his own status," and they were driven "to the greatest exertions of effort."[16] Their numbers grew in the 1950s from the increase in white-collar occupations and the burgeoning suburbs. By 1956, white-collar workers outnumbered blue-collars for the first time, and 60 percent of Americans achieved what the government defined as a middle-class standard of living.[17] For middle-class Americans, new or old, nothing exemplified the American way of life better than sending sons and daughters to college.

These new students, overwhelmingly the first in their families to go to college, needed places to attend. Such students and their families sensed a cultural gulf between their situations and the image of a traditional college with its wealthier clientele. They felt more comfortable with opportunities that were local, somewhat familiar, and more affordable. They tended to find such places at teachers colleges, urban universities, community colleges, and branch campuses. The supply of locally available places of study at these kinds of institutions accounted for a good deal of the expansion of the 1950s and even more so in the 1960s. In the 1950s, for the most part, this expansion largely took place in existing institutions; in the 1960s, it was augmented by the creation and transformation of new public institutions. The chapter in this volume by Bruce Leslie and Kenneth O'Brien provides an example of the former in the New York State Teachers College at Brockport. Charles Dorn describes an example of the latter in the case of the University of South Florida.

The burgeoning postwar supply of "local" college places cannot be measured with any precision since the categories themselves are vague and unstable.[18] Dongbin Kim and John Rury have estimated that the proportion of beginning students who lived at home with parents, and thus attended locally, comprised 35 percent in 1960, compared with 40 percent in college residences.[19] Two-year colleges grew by 66 percent in the 1950s, but that was less than the public sector as a whole (86 percent). Their take-off came later. Urban universities defined themselves by membership in the Association of Urban Universities, but were otherwise a heterogeneous category, confounded in part with branch campuses. Many state universities enlarged their educational role after the war by establishing branch campuses. Michigan responded to overtures from Flint and Dearborn; Indiana moved into Indianapolis; Illinois into Chicago; Purdue into Fort Wayne; Minnesota into Duluth. Teachers colleges were a shrinking category that faded away in the 1960s, but Leslie and O'Brien are correct to underline their persistence into that decade and their role in widening opportunity. In 1940 the average teachers college had fewer than 700 students, but in 1965 more than 3,500.[20] The transformation of teachers colleges into state colleges and universities was a prolonged process, starting in Ohio and California in the 1930s and concluding in Oregon in the 1980s. However, as at Brockport, most consequential changes occurred in the first half of the 1960s, and nomenclature did not always reflect curriculum. They contributed to enrollment growth in the 1950s chiefly as teachers colleges, and their character was slow to change before 1965, but rapid after that date.

No doubt most Brockport students would have given the same reason for attending that a 1950s Ball State Teachers College student did: "It was close to home; it was a choice of going to Ball State or not going at all."[21] Indeed, the information Leslie and O'Brien gleaned from alumni matches that gathered from a 1955 survey of students at Ball State. The country's 200 teachers colleges were quite similar. Predominately first-generation, students chose to enroll in these institutions after learning of them from friends or relatives, thus receiving some assurance of social compatibility. Affordability was essential too. Since room and board was the chief expense, commuting made attendance possible for many. Given these reasons for attendance, it seems that graduates became teachers as much because of the institution they attended as choosing the institution in order to become teachers. Ball State conferred bachelor's degrees in 1963, but they were outnumbered by education degrees five to one. Brockport conferred only education degrees until 1965. Despite these insular characteristics, students also sought to create and experience American collegiate life. Leslie and O'Brien describe how this powerful imagery shaped extracurricular life at Brockport, and the same was true for other teachers colleges.[22] This embrace of collegiate life suggests that these students sought something more than good jobs, although career expectations were axiomatic; they also sought the social distinction of being a college graduate. For that, the college experience took precedence over the college curriculum, which is perhaps one reason why teachers colleges were slow to change before the 1960s.

Presidents and faculty at teachers colleges were, by training and outlook, habituated to their roles. Almost all these institutions were, explicitly or implicitly, part of state systems, and usually governed by state boards of education. Where these systems were part of K-12 education, as in New Jersey, modernization was virtually impossible until that impasse was overcome. Even then, restrictions of various sort were the rule.[23] Brockport (and its SUNY sisters) experienced both effects. Included in the SUNY system in 1948, they were saddled with the stipulation that they could not teach liberal arts subjects for a decade. However, the commitment to academic advancement also came from SUNY in the 1960s. The replacement of Brockport's beloved, old-style president in 1965 (Leslie and O'Brien call it "brutal") came with a mandate for the liberal arts. However, internal dynamics were generally also at work in teachers colleges. As more arts and sciences faculty were hired (part of the movement away from elementary education) the balance of faculty commitments shifted away from teacher preparation. As non-education curricula were added, enrollments in such courses soared, tilting the balance further.

The pace of transition to liberal arts and graduate education, once underway, accelerated in the latter 1960s. Brockport's transformation was particularly abrupt, but representative of the former teachers colleges.[24] Still basically a teachers college until 1965, three years later it had embraced the identity of a public liberal arts college. Perhaps most remarkable—at Brockport and throughout the country—such transformations bore little relation to local demand, but rather were propelled by state-level policies and the academic ambitions of faculties, filled with new hires. These institutions continued to serve a largely local clientele, mostly first-generation attendees, but now for the first time they were generously funded by state legislatures. Enrollments at the former state teachers colleges mushroomed. By 1967 they enrolled 42 percent of students in public, four-year institutions. Aspirations, Leslie and O'Brien note, outpaced even curricular and enrollment growth. As institutions abruptly embraced the ideal of a liberal arts college, faculty identified with their disciplines rather than local communities. University status was the holy grail for institutions that had not yet been so blessed. Only a handful of these institutions attained the doctoral status that Brockport briefly dreamed of—Northern and Southern Illinois, Western Michigan, Kent State, Bowling Green and Ball State. By 1968, the demands of the California State Colleges for something close to parity in salaries, research opportunities, and doctoral programs threatened the 1960 Master Plan. However, the lofty aspirations and enrollment projections of the late 1960s went largely unfulfilled. Most of these institutions were subsumed by the Carnegie Commission under the rubric of "comprehensive colleges and universities" in 1971, where they have remained.[25]

State-sponsored urban universities provided much of the additional supply of higher education in the 1960s. The University of South Florida (USF) grew from 2,000 to 18,000 students in the decade, compared with 36,000 in the entire state in 1954! The relatively late efflorescence of such institutions is evident from USF's claim to be the first four-year public university created *de novo* in the twentieth century. In this respect, USF and its founding president, John Allen, had considerable freedom in designing the institution. This was seldom the case for other public urban universities. Unlike Tampa, older cities were thick with institutions of higher education, private or municipal. For decades they had been acquired or combined in order to meet fiscal or enrollment needs. Only in the 1960s did states tend to assume responsibility for these institutions as part of overall provision of public higher education. In Ohio, for example, from 1964 to 1967 municipal universities in Cincinnati and Akron, and private universities (former YMCA schools) in Cleveland and Youngstown, were made into state universities. As they adapted to their missions, they were buffeted by the politics of higher education and affected by the overweening stature of the liberal arts paradigm.

President Allen's original vision of a liberal arts core to provide "education for citizenship" was in the tradition of the Harvard Red Book and the ideal sanctioned by the CFHE. As honored as that ideal was among traditional colleges and universities, it presented two kinds of difficulties for these local-serving institutions. A heavy dose of introductory liberal arts, as at USF, ill-suited their first-generation, career-minded clientele. By delaying access to professional courses, the liberal arts core presented an obstacle to retention, especially for marginal or culturally disadvantaged students.[26] Conversely, withholding the ability to offer the liberal arts paradigm was sometimes used politically to prevent new institutions from competing with established institutions, as had been the case with the SUNY teachers colleges. This also occurred at the future Georgia State University. In educationally underserved Atlanta, it struggled to escape from the domination of the University of Georgia and the Georgia State System. When it became a separate institution in 1959, it was dubbed the State College of Business Administration and forbidden to teach upper-division liberal arts courses. It took another decade to obtain its current title and a degree of curricular freedom.[27] A third negative example might be drawn from SUNY's commitment to elevate Buffalo into a research university. The new institution made no effort to serve the local urban population, as the former private university had done, with consequences that can be seen in Chapter 7.

American higher education in the "golden age" of the 1960s was initially resistant to the notion of an urban service university, despite many existing examples. The one academic leader who championed this model was David Dodds Henry, who had presided over a notable exemplar in Wayne University, a vintage urban institution cobbled together in the interwar years from various professional schools.[28] In 1955 Henry assumed the presidency of the University of Illinois, which faced a huge urban challenge in Chicago, where the university had established a branch campus for GIs at the Navy Pier. The nation's second largest city possessed no public university and just two locally controlled teachers colleges (see Chapter 5, this volume). Enrollments continued to grow at the Naval Pier after the GIs departed, along with political pressure from Mayor Richard Daley—which was met with opposition in Urbana and downstate Illinois. Henry navigated these troubled waters for a decade. A new campus for some 11,000 students was opened at Chicago Circle in 1965, finally offering a full undergraduate curriculum. During this process, Henry articulated the mission of an urban university, "a special obligation to respond to the immediate educational needs of the community in which it is set."[29]

Henry's contention that a public urban university should first and foremost focus on access and service was largely met with apathy in the mid-1960s, the heyday of the "academic revolution." Faculty at Chicago Circle and elsewhere, fresh from Ph.D. programs, placed their highest priorities on research and graduate education—and so did policymakers in the higher education community. The latter favored the notion that university research could address urban problems in the way that land-grant universities had benefited agriculture. The Ford Foundation awarded $4.5 million to eight universities (1959–1966) for "urban extension experiments," and urban extension was written into Title I of the 1965 Higher Education Act. In expanding the University of California, Clark Kerr sought to have the Irvine campus specialize in applied social science research of this kind. Subsequently, as head of the Carnegie Commission, Kerr called for the creation of 67 urban-grant universities, "where the city itself and its problems would become the animating focus."[30] All these initiatives, actual or contemplated, essentially flopped. It seems that providing farmers with information useful for growing crops was different from telling politicians how to run their cities. This episode nonetheless illustrates the enthusiasm as well as the illusions surrounding the huge expansion of urban universities in the 1960s. Ultimately, urban-serving universities, like USF, tended to conform to Henry's model under constituent pressure and market forces. They substantially augmented the supply of higher education, without necessarily precluding research.

The Quality Imperative

The concern for quality is ubiquitous in higher education, but there is often little relation between rhetoric and reality. Moreover, a discrepancy between general trends and the efforts of a dedicated minority of individuals and institutions is common. The concern for quality in the 1950s began as an undercurrent, but rose to a national imperative.

Colleges had little choice but to cut corners in order to instruct and graduate the surge of GIs. Wishing to revert to the *status quo ante* after 1950, they were instead confronted by what *Time* magazine dubbed "the Silent Generation"—students characterized by indifference toward academics and apathy toward school spirit. As Julianna Chaszar relates, the situation elicited some positive efforts, including Advanced Placement Exams and National Merit Scholarships. But a battle raged in the schools (and teachers colleges) among "progressive educators," advocating life adjustment curricula, and critics demanding more academic instruction. Seemingly unrelated, each year brought more smart students into the colleges. Whereas 40 percent of the top tested quarter of students went to college in the 1940s, 50 percent attended after 1950, and 67 percent by 1960.[31]

Clearly, some school districts reacted to criticism with such innovations as college preparatory tracks in high schools and special programs for talented and gifted students, as well as a general upgrading of curricula.[32] An increased emphasis on college-going was also evident. These efforts were redoubled after the panic over the Soviet launch of Sputnik in 1957. Although diffuse, such measures had an apparent impact, especially on students with the highest tested abilities. A synthesis of studies of student aptitude concluded, "in the 1950s and 1960s … the percentage of students continuing to college rose sharply in the upper IQ brackets and more slowly in the lower ones."[33] In the first class of National Merit finalists and semi-finalists (1957), 96 percent entered college. Selective private colleges responded to more and better applicants by expanding enrollments moderately and raising the admissions bar throughout this period.[34] Public universities reacted by establishing a new form of honors program.

The new form was called general honors and referred to special courses for "superior students" beginning with freshman and sophomore classes. Chaszar summarizes the former practice of offering special honors arrangements, usually in specific departments, to juniors and/or seniors who had proved their mettle as underclassmen. These programs had been pioneered and promoted by Frank Aydelotte at Swarthmore, but engaged relatively few students elsewhere. General honors were particularly attractive to growing state universities which, according to Joseph Cohen, had a responsibility for "a great outpouring of able students from the high schools which the private sector cannot begin to absorb." Cohen was the entrepreneur, and ICSS the vehicle, for introducing this innovation, which addressed the increasing pressures, internal and external, on state universities to enhance quality. The ICSS welcomed the participation of private colleges too, and large numbers were drawn to the honors bandwagon. But Cohen admitted that "our program has been dominated by a concern for four year tax-supported institutions," and it was perceived as such. *Time* reported in 1960, "impressive honors programs have spread to 87 public campuses under the influence of the Carnegie-financed Inter-University Committee on the Superior Student."[35]

The ICSS never hazarded a definition of the "superior student." Clearly, state universities were enrolling ever increasing numbers of high-ability students in the Postwar Era, but reliable data are lacking for either the magnitude or the criteria for such students.[36] Still, Chaszar notes that Michigan complained that it was losing such students to private colleges, and Penn State University did as well. The best evidence of the evolution of attendance patterns has been provided by economist Caroline Hoxby's model of what she terms "the resorting of American higher education" after 1950. The factors driving this resorting were the increasing mobility of students (geographical integration) and the increasing availability of information about students and institutions. Under these conditions, high-ability students tended to seek places in colleges that provided the greatest education resources. Such students were themselves a resource, producing positive peer effects on fellow students. These dynamics caused differences in average student ability to become greater *across* institutions, but to decrease *within* institutions—in other words, the rich got richer and the poor poorer.[37]

Hoxby's model accurately depicts the evolution of the private sector in the Postwar Era and particularly since 1980. Private colleges are smaller, more variable, and more subject to market forces. The public sector traced the same pattern, in somewhat more muted form, but exhibited little change from 1966 to 1971 (the earliest period in which SAT scores were reported). However, Hoxby underestimated the attraction of public research universities, in particular, predicting a migration of superior students from public to private elite institutions. But she in fact noted that an honors college (or program) can lessen the disadvantage of public universities.[38] Honors programs counteract two critical factors by increasing the educational resources devoted to honors students and enhancing peer effects in an honors cohort. In addition, recognition should be accorded for the immense volume of learning resources offered by public research universities to those willing and able to make use of them. The only study that counted actual superior students (those attaining 700s verbal or quantitative SAT scores in 2000), found virtually equal numbers at public and private research universities.[39] Thus, Hoxby provides a theoretical explanation for how the reinvention of honors education depicted by Chaszar materially affected the market structure of higher education in the postwar as well as the current era.

The 1960s

The decade of the 1960s divides into two equal parts, for universities and American society: from 1960 to 1964 the conservative preoccupation with the American way of life was replaced by a spirit of liberal reform. But after 1965 that spirit was increasingly confronted by radical challenges to fundamental features of the American experience. The election of John F. Kennedy in 1960 marked a symbolic and substantive commitment to reform. A conservative cold-warrior and calculating politician, Kennedy's New Frontier and his intellectual entourage promised a new openness to change, although it proved difficult to effect. Lyndon Johnson's promulgation of the Great Society in 1964 promised and delivered far more, an avalanche of reform legislation from 1964 to 1966.[40] On the most divisive issue of these years, civil rights, a consensus finally emerged that the treatment of African-Americans in the Jim Crow South was not only wrong but intolerable. Higher education shared in this mood of confident progress. *Time* placed Clark Kerr on a 1960 cover, celebrating the phenomenal expansion planned under the new California Master Plan and exhorting other state universities to rise to Cal's standard.[41]

Historian James Patterson has called 1965 the "hinge of the sixties"—the year that "transformed America." The chief triggers were the escalation of the war in Vietnam, which spawned the anti-war movement, and the urban insurrections of African Americans against social conditions that Great Society legislation could do little to alter. These events signaled the beginning of a far-reaching cultural revolution.[42] The final three chapters of this volume address issues conditioned by this ongoing transformation—the beginning of faculty unionization, challenges to authority at even the most conservative colleges, and the main thread of radicalization and rebellion at major universities.

Faculty unions and collective bargaining emerged unexpectedly at the end of the 1960s and accelerated into the 1970s. Timothy Cain's chapter explains the tentative beginnings of this movement in Illinois. When the City University of New York was organized in 1968, and the State University of New York the next year, the movement was in full swing. Scholarly analysis soon followed.[43] Legislation that allowed public employees to bargain collectively, like the Taylor Law in New York, opened the gates for unionization. Then, prevailing currents of anti-professionalism (anti-elitism) and egalitarianism predisposed faculty to union outlooks. Unions tended to be favored by faculty who were younger, untenured, left-of-center politically, and from the humanities and social sciences. Such faculty were legion "at the lower levels, in institutions where faculty independence, hence professional standing, is tenuous at best"; precisely those institutions where "the enormous expansion of higher education over the past decade [1963–1973] has occurred." Hence, the systems of former teachers colleges were first organized in SUNY, New Jersey, Pennsylvania, and eventually across the country. Where unionization was concerned, community colleges resembled the peak of the K-14 system, literally in Cain's cases of the City Colleges of Chicago and Bellville College. Outside of research universities, by the end of the century 89 percent of faculty at public institutions were unionized (1995).[44]

Faculty who chose to unionize would seem to bear little resemblance to those characterized by Christopher Jencks and David Riesman in the *Academic Revolution* (1968). The latter had risen through research and scholarship to dominate their universities and impose professional, meritocratic values.[45] Unionizing faculty populated those institutions that had supplied the places for mass higher education. They seemingly forsook competitive individual merit for collective security, especially at the end of the Postwar Era when retrenchment heightened anxieties over salaries, status, and job security. For them, collective bargaining largely delivered. In bargaining for parity in compensation, they achieved striking salary gains, especially for lower-paid echelons, made tenure readily attainable, and gave faculty a voice in management.

As Cain indicates, the initial differences between the three organizations was a prominent factor in early unionization. The National Education Association predominated in K-12 education, and was consequently favored by community colleges. The American Federation of Teachers was associated with trade unionism and considered more militant; and it tended to be either shunned or embraced for that reason. The AAUP had traditionally defended the values of the academic profession.[46] Long reluctant to become a sole representative or engage in collective bargaining, it was consequently preferred by those who disdained trade unions. However, tiny Bellville College changed that by first naming the AAUP as its exclusive bargaining agent, and then engaging in hard-nosed contract negotiations, including a pseudo-strike ("boycott"). In 1972, the AAUP overwhelmingly approved collective bargaining. Within a short time, it was apparent that there was no significant difference between the three organizations at the bargaining table.

The sector of higher education that Adam Laats addresses is little known in the mainstream of higher education literature. Perhaps one-half of all private colleges have some religious affiliation, but these relationships vary from nominal to all-encompassing. Most of the type of college Laats examines have affiliated with the Council for Christian Colleges and Universities (CCCU). They are accredited institutions offering arts and sciences curricula. Their distinguishing feature, however, is to "hire as full-time faculty members and administrators only persons who profess faith in Jesus Christ." This practice clearly separates them from the commitment to universalism and non-discrimination on the basis of religion that prevails elsewhere in American higher education. Laats describes the origins and fissures of this sector. Despite an antagonistic cultural atmosphere, these institutions upheld their principles in the 1960s, while other schools abandoned rules, requirements, and *in loco parentis* in the face of student protests. But since the 1970s, increasing numbers of parents and students have sought out faith-based institutions committed to providing moral and personal guidance, and these institutions have generally flourished. CCCU members have grown from 38 founding members in 1976 to 117, enrolling 450,000 students.[47]

Jencks and Riesman called such institutions "holdouts," and gave ample reason why the tides of the 1960s were running against them. They were at a comparative disadvantage on academic reputation, social distinction, and price; and thus remained dependent on "Protestant enclaves" that were themselves shrinking in industrial America.[48] Laats describes the extreme conservatism, particularly of fundamentalist colleges. Even under Wheaton's posture of enlightened evangelicalism, the older generation—the administration and alumni—harbored strong belief in authoritarian governance and enforced discipline. These attitudes shaped the draconian reactions to the free speech challenge. However, the racial issue touched matters of basic Christian doctrine that could not be dismissed. Wheaton was forced to confront its latent racist practices, even though a good part of its constituency would have preferred otherwise. Market forces within the Protestant enclave made reforms all the more difficult. In regarding them as laggards in the rush to modernity, Jencks and Riesman underestimated the faith-based colleges. For them, the same tumult of the 1960s that rocked other institutions was refracted through a lens of Christian doctrine. Rather than consignment to the dustbin of history, they ultimately emerged stronger for it.

The final chapter interprets the main current of campus rebellion led principally by Students for a Democratic Society (SDS). For this topic, it offers a definite chronology in contrast to amorphous definitions of the "1960s" noted by Laats. The origins of SDS in 1960 reflected the rising challenges to the conservative 1950s. From the Free Speech Movement in the fall of 1964 through 1967, the critique of American society and campus protests grew steeply more radical. Then, for the two years of the "1968 Era" rationality and order seemed to be suspended, beginning with the shutdown of Columbia University in April 1968, and culminating with the killings at Kent State and Jackson State in May 1970. By this juncture, radicals purveyed a dystopian inversion of the American way of life and actively sought to foment revolution. Although few in number, they received sympathy and support from far larger numbers of Americans, especially students, who were dismayed and frustrated with the war in Vietnam, the Cold War arms race, the persistence of racism, and/or restrictive bourgeois mores. They were opposed, wholly or in part, by the majority of Americans who elected Richard Nixon—twice. But no matter. The 1950s consensus on the American way of life was moribund. The cultural revolution that ensued changed a great deal in American society, but also marked a turning point for the colleges and universities that had endured the brunt of the student rebellion.

Thus, for the student rebellion and for the other developments described in this volume, 1970 marked the end of the Postwar Era in American higher education.[49] General education and core curricula were dead letter by 1970, done in less by student protest than by the academic revolution and the evaporation of any consensus over what knowledge an educated person ought to possess. Harvard dropped its watered-down requirements in 1966.[50] The old association of teachers colleges changed its identity to state colleges and universities in 1961, but in 1971 the Carnegie Commission on Higher Education dubbed most of these institutions as Comprehensive Colleges and Universities, offering professional and liberal arts curricula, including master's degrees.[51] Most had advanced halfway to university status, but progress would be rare after 1970. By this date the Carnegie Commission strongly urged the further expansion of the supply of urban higher education, stressing service and access, including more open-admission places and multiple campuses for ease of attendance.[52] ICSS shuttered its operations in 1965, but the baton was passed to the National Collegiate Honors Council. For the next decade, unlike the previous one, cultural headwinds were blowing against rather than with the movement, but general honors education had become institutionalized in American universities.[53] Faculty unions by 1970 had established the beachhead from which they would expand to dominate entire sectors of higher education. Evangelical colleges, judging from Wheaton's example, adapted to at least some aspects of the changing culture, particularly in racial matters. For contemporaries, developments in and around 1970 may have appeared bewildering and threatening, but in retrospect it is apparent that a far-reaching transformation of the American system of higher education had crystalized in the Postwar Era.

Notes

1 For the range of topics, Wilson Smith and Thomas Bender, eds., *American Higher Education Transformed, 1940–2005* (Baltimore: Johns Hopkins University Press, 2008); Roger L. Geiger, "Postwar American Higher Education: Documenting Recent History," *Perspectives on the History of Higher Education*, 27 (2008): 141–152; Roger L. Geiger, *Research and Relevant Knowledge American Research Universities Since World War II* (New Brunswick: Transaction, 2004 [1993]); Ellen Schrecker, *No Ivory Tower: McCarthyism and the Universities* (New York: Oxford University Press, 1986).

2 Bruce A. Kimball, *Orators and Philosophers: A History of the Idea of Liberal Education* (New York: Teachers College Press, 1986), 192–199; Roger L. Geiger, *the History of American Higher Education Since 1940* (in process). For a critique of contemporary

trends and defense of liberal education: Norman Forester, *The Future of the Liberal College* (New York: Arno Press, 1969 [1938]).
3 Earl J. McGrath issued a manifesto for general education in the first issue of the *Journal of General Education*: "The General Education Movement," I, 1 (October 1946): 3–8.
4 John D. Millett, *Financing Higher Education in the United States* (New York: Columbia University Press, 1952), 32.
5 *General Education in a Free Society: Report of the Harvard Committee* (Cambridge: Harvard University, 1945). Daniel Bell, *The Reforming of General Education: The Columbia Experience in Its National Setting* (New York: Columbia University Press, 1966), 38–50. From Bell's perspective, the Red Book combined the heritage emphasis of Columbia's Contemporary Civilization course and the intellectual processes of Chicago's general education in the Hutchins College. Bell notes that the Red Book contains no mention of graduate education.
6 President's Commission on Higher Education, *Higher Education for American Democracy* (New York: Harper & Brothers, 1947–1948), vol. I, *Establishing the Goals*, quotes pp. 49, 51–57; Ethan Schrum, "Establishing a Democratic Religion: Metaphysics and Democracy in the Debates over the President's Commission on Higher Education," *History of Education Quarterly*, 47, 3 (August 2007): 277–301, esp. 286–288. John Dewey was not named in the report.
7 President's Commission on Higher Education, *Establishing the Goals*, 32, 41.
8 John D. Millett, *Financing Higher Education in the United States* (New York: Columbia University Press, 1952); Commission on Financing Higher Education, *Nature and Needs of Higher Education* (New York: Columbia University Press, 1952).
9 Byron S. Hollinshead, *Who Should Go to College?* (New York: Columbia University Press, 1952). Hollinshead had been a member of the Harvard committee.
10 John D. Millett, *Financing Higher Education in the United States* (New York: Columbia University Press, 1952), 42–57; Commission on Financing Higher Education, *Nature and Needs*, 45–54, quote 45–46. Dael Wolfle, Director of the Commission on Human Resources and Advanced Training, reported findings in several publications: "America's Intellectual Resources," *NAASP Bulletin* 36, 183 (January 1952): 125–135. Wolfle endorsed the PC figure of 32 percent of youth intellectually qualified for college.
11 Commission on Financing Higher Education, *Nature and Needs*, 16 and *passim*; Millett, *Financing*, 11–19, 42–47; Richard Hofstadter and C. DeWitt Hardy, *The Development and Scope of Higher Education in the United States* (New York: Columbia University Press, 1952), 207–225 (a publication of the Commission on Financing Higher Education).
12 With an average Army General Classification Test (AGCT) score of 100 for the total population, high school graduates averaged 110; college entrants, 115; and college graduates, 121: Dael Wolfle, *America's Resources of Specialized Talent* (New York: Harper & Brothers, 1954), 146–162; Hollinshead, *Who Should Go to College?* 28–41.
13 Wolfle, *America's Resources*.
14 Hollinshead, *Who Should Go to College?* 79–84.
15 Public tuition ranged from 0 to $300, plus fees; private tuition from $300–$600; room and board from $500 to $900: Estimated from Mary Irwin, *American Colleges and Universities*, 6th edn (American Council on Education, 1952).
16 Walter Goldschmidt, "Social Class in America—A Critical Review," *American Anthropologist*, 52, 4 (October–December 1950): 483–498, quote 494.
17 Alan Brinkley, "The Illusion of Unity in Cold War Culture," in Peter J. Kuznick and James Gilbert, eds., *Rethinking Cold War Culture* (Washington, DC: Smithsonian Institution Press, 2001), 61–73, 66.
18 Caroline M. Hoxby has compared the number of freshman seats with the number of high school graduates. From 1955 to 1965 both figures roughly doubled; from 1965 to 1975 high school graduates increased by 18 percent (*c.*500) and freshman seats by

74 percent (c.1,000): "The Changing Selectivity of American Colleges," *Journal of Economic Perspectives* 23, 4 (Fall 2009): 95–118, 101.
19 Dongbin Kim and John L. Rury, "The Rise of the Commuter Student: Changing Patterns of College Attendance for Students Living at Home in the United States, 1960–1980," *Teachers College Record*, 113, 5 (2011): 1031–1066. This study documents the increase in commuter students from 1960 to 1980, when they comprised the largest category. It credits the availability of places (supply) and the expanding middle class, as well as demography, factors that were clearly operating in the 1950s.
20 US Department of Education, *Digest of Education Statistics, 1967*, 68.
21 Anthony O. Edmonds and E. Bruce Geelhoed, *Ball State University: An Interpretive History* (Bloomington: Indiana University Press, 2001), 148.
22 Collegiate activities were adopted by normal schools since early in the century, but had been suppressed in New York: Cynthia A. Ogren, *The American State Normal School: An Institution of Great Good* (New York: Palgrave Macmillan, 2005).
23 David R. Raichle, "Richard J. Hughes, Frederick M. Raubinger, and the Struggle for New Jersey Public Higher Education," *New Jersey History*, 114, 1–2 (Spring–Summer 1996): 19–47; Harold L. Hodgkinson, *Institutions in Transition: A Profile of Change in Higher Education* (New York: McGraw-Hill, 1971), 183–195.
24 Alden Dunham chose Brockport in 1968 to exemplify the rapid transformation of these institutions: *Colleges of the Forgotten Americans: A Profile of State Colleges and Regional Universities* (Berkeley: Carnegie Commission on Higher Education, 1969), 8–19. When President Brown arrived in 1965, he estimated that Brockport was a decade behind his former institution, Eastern Michigan University (p. 11).
25 Dunham, *Colleges of the Forgotten Americans*, 51–56; Carnegie Foundation for the Advancement of Teaching, *A Classification of Institutions of Higher Education* (Princeton: CFAT, 1971).
26 When the University of Massachusetts at Boston opened in 1965, the faculty typically devised a liberal arts curriculum for full-time students, one hardly appropriate for its lower-income clientele: Richard M. Freeland, *Academia's Golden Age: Universities in Massachusetts, 1945–1970* (New York: Oxford University Press, 1992), 327–335.
27 Merle E. Reed, *Educating the New South: Atlanta and the Rise of Georgia State University, 1913–1969* (Macon: Mercer University Press, 2009).
28 Roger L. Geiger, *The History of American Higher Education: Learning and Culture from the Founding to World War II* (Princeton: Princeton University Press, 2015), 440–441.
29 Fred W. Beuttler, "Envisioning an Urban University: President David Henry and the Chicago Circle Campus of the University of Illinois, 1955–1975," *History of Higher Education Annual*, 23 (2003–2004): 107–142, quote 119.
30 Roger L. Geiger, "Universities and the Land-Grant Mission Since 1930: Introduction," *Perspectives on the History of Higher Education*, 30 (2013): 277–283; Ethan Schrum, "Social Science over Agriculture: Reimagining the Land-Grant Mission at the University of California-Irvine in the 1960s," *Perspectives on the History of Higher Education*, 30 (2013): 311–334.
31 Robert J. Havighurst, *American Higher Education in the 1960s* (Columbus: Ohio State University Press, 1960), 32.
32 Patricia Albjerg Graham, *Schooling in America: How the Public Schools Meet the Nation's Changing Needs* (New York: Oxford University Press, 2005), 103–124; for the reaction against progressive education: Diane Ravitch, *Left Back: A Century of Battles over School Reform* (New York: Simon & Schuster, 2000), 322–365.
33 Paul Taubman and Terence Wales, *Mental Ability and Higher Educational Attainment in the 20th Century* (Berkeley: Carnegie Commission on Higher Education, 1972).
34 Elizabeth A. Duffy and Idana Goldberg, *Crafting a Class: College Admissions and Financial Aid, 1955–1994* (Princeton: Princeton University Press, 1998). Relatively

unselective at the beginning of this period, the selective sector was able to raise the academic qualifications of admitted students from 1950 to the late 1960s.
35 *The Superior Student*, 3, 9 (January 1961): 2–3; *The Superior Student*, 2, 6 (October 1959): 3; "Master Planner," *Time Magazine* (October 17, 1960). Although it favored general honors programs, the ICSS promoted all forms of honors and advised institutions to devise programs best suited to their needs; hence, the participation of large numbers of private colleges, although they were less likely to institute general honors for underclassmen.
36 Several public universities, including Texas and Michigan State, actively recruited National Merit finalist and semi-finalists using their honors colleges. In 1962, Michigan State enrolled the largest number of National Merit scholars using Honors College scholarship funds: Paul L. Dressel, *College to University: The Hannah Years at Michigan State, 1935–1969* (East Lansing: Michigan State University, 1987), 141–142.
37 Caroline M. Hoxby, "How the Changing Market Structure of U.S. Higher Education Explains College Tuition," NBER Working Paper 6323 (December 1997); "The Changing Selectivity of American Colleges," *Journal of Economic Perspectives* 23, 4 (Fall 2009): 95–118.
38 Hoxby, "Changing Market Structure," 32, 21.
39 Roger L. Geiger, "The Competition for High-Ability Students: Universities in a Key Marketplace," in Steven Brint, ed., *The Future of the City of Intellect: The Changing American University* (Stanford: Stanford University Press, 2002), 82–106.
40 G. Calvin Mackenzie and Robert Weisbrot, *The Liberal Hour: Washington and the Politics of Change in the 1960s* (New York: Penguin, 2008).
41 "Master Planner."
42 James T. Patterson, *The Eve of Destruction: How 1965 Transformed America* (New York: Basic Books, 2012); David Steigerwald, *The Sixties and the End of Modern America* (New York: St. Martin's, 1995).
43 Everett Carll Ladd, Jr. and Seymour Martin Lipset, *Professors, Unions, and American Higher Education* (Berkeley: Carnegie Commission on Higher Education, 1973); Robert K. Carr and Daniel K. Van Eyck, *Collective Bargaining Comes to the Campus* (Washington, DC: American Council on Education, 1973).
44 Gary Rhoades, *Managed Professionals: Unionized Faculty and Restructuring Academic Labor* (Albany: SUNY Press, 1998), 10.
45 Christopher Jencks and David Riesman, *The Academic Revolution* (Chicago: University of Chicago Press, 1968); the contrast is discussed in David Riesman, Joseph Gusfield, and Zelda Gamson, *Academic Values and Mass Higher Education* (Garden City: Doubleday, 1970), 9–10.
46 Philo A. Hutcheson, *A Professional Professoriate: Unionization, Bureaucratization, and the AAUP* (Nashville: Vanderbilt University Press, 2000).
47 www.cccu.org/; Samuel Schuman, *Seeing the Light: Religious Colleges in Twenty-First Century America* (Baltimore: Johns Hopkins University Press, 2010). Enrollments at CCCU institutions grew by 71 percent from 1996 to 2006.
48 Jencks and Riesman, *Academic Revolution*, 328–330.
49 Economist Robert J. Gordon has identified 1970 as the terminus of a special century of extraordinary growth in American living standards, and hence the beginning of important changes in American society. The end of the growth phase of higher education was one of these significant changes: *The Rise and Fall of American Growth: The U.S. Standard of Living Since the Civil War* (Princeton: Princeton University Press, 2016).
50 Roger L. Geiger, "Demography and Curriculum: The Humanities in American Higher Education from the 1950s through the 1980s," in David A. Hollinger, ed., *The Humanities and the Dynamics of Inclusion Since World War II* (Baltimore: Johns Hopkins University Press, 2006), 50–72.

51 By 1982 these institutions awarded 35 percent of all bachelor's degrees. Fred F. Harcleroad and Allan W. Ostar, *College and Universities for Change: America's Comprehensive Public State Colleges and Universities* (Washington, DC: AASCU Press, 1987). The American Association of State Colleges and Universities (AASCU), which represents most "Comprehensive" institutions, was formed in 1961, with 138 of 160 charter members formerly belonging to the Association of Teacher Education Institutions, which AASCU superseded.
52 Carnegie Commission on Higher Education, *The Campus and the City* (December 1972). David Henry was a member of the Carnegie Commission.
53 The concerns of the late 1960s had changed so completely that the encyclopedic Carnegie Commission failed to mention honors education.

2

THE SURPRISING HISTORY OF THE POST-WORLD WAR II STATE TEACHERS COLLEGE

W. Bruce Leslie and Kenneth P. O'Brien

Pioneering mass higher education was one of post-World War II America's greatest achievements. Widely envied and admired, it spread around much of the world by the end of the century. But one of its building blocks, the state teachers college, has largely remained in the historical shadows. "Perhaps no segment of American higher education has remained more obscure than its state colleges" as V. R. Cardozier has noted.[1] Although over 200 state teachers colleges existed across the country after World War II, they have attracted little attention since being abandoned after the Sputnik-induced demand for educational reform. Subsequently colleges ran away from the name and some even hid their history as they were transformed into publicly supported comprehensive colleges and regional universities.

However their story adds an essential piece to our understanding of the dynamics of post-World War II American higher education. Although a short-lived institution (the name was only in common usage from the 1920s into the 1960s), state teachers colleges educated about 10 percent of American students in the years after World War II.[2] Historians' understanding of postwar collegiate life has been primarily shaped by that of elite private colleges and universities and their public counterparts, the state research universities. However, a close examination of state teachers colleges will inform us why another segment of American youth chose higher education, what their educational and social experience was, and how it affected their lives. Our study provides a rare look at the collegiate ambitions and experiences of students who hailed largely from working and lower-middle class families, and found themselves in the state teachers colleges.

In the 1960s and 1970s these institutions morphed into the workhorses of mass higher education in most state systems, most as multipurpose state colleges and a few as regional universities.[3] Although they changed dramatically, in their time as state teachers colleges they played a role in the evolving experiment of mass higher education, a developmental stage that also left an indelible heritage on the institutions themselves. The arc of this history is well known, the development of normal schools that evolved into state teachers colleges and then metamorphosed into comprehensive regional state colleges and universities.[4] What's missing, however, is a clear understanding of the nature of state teachers colleges' student populations, campus cultures, curricula, and evolution into comprehensive colleges.

Toward that end, this chapter offers a case study of Brockport State Teachers College in western New York State. Built upon an unusually rich database for a state college, our study reconstructs the life in one of the institutions that morphed into building blocks for America's pioneering experiment in mass higher education. It also evaluates the dramatic post-Sputnik criticisms of state teachers colleges that contributed to their demise as single-purpose institutions and their historical invisibility. Finally, the chapter examines Brockport's transformation from a typical state teachers college into a surprisingly experimental comprehensive college.

The Case Study: Its Setting

Brockport State Teachers College, its official name from 1942 to 1959, was a teachers college until the mid-1960s, one of the 11 such New York colleges that formed the largest sector when the State University of New York was founded in 1948 (see Figure 2.1). Through the post-World War II decades, it remained an average-sized SUNY teachers college with a president who was a protégé of Herman Cooper, SUNY's guardian angel of state teachers colleges.[5] Like most of New York's teachers colleges, Brockport was located in an upstate village, in this case one on the Erie Canal, 20 miles west of Rochester, the home of Eastman Kodak and a number of other industrial firms. Given its history, we believe Brockport provides a reasonably representative case study for SUNY's state teachers colleges and many other state teachers colleges across the country.

The College had been established more than a century earlier as one of those audaciously optimistic ventures that combined local boosterism and denominationalism to found educational institutions in unpromising places. In the early nineteenth century, the village was a child of the Erie Canal. As its western terminus from 1823 until its completion in 1825, Brockport prospered as a boisterous canal boomtown, shipping agricultural goods from the Lake Ontario Plain and finished goods from several manufacturing enterprises. Town leaders proposed that uniquely American idea of founding a college to promote the town and create a more respectable atmosphere. The Baptists of western New York were looking to found an institution west of Colgate, and the match was made. Unfortunately, after opening its doors in 1835, it quickly shut them, a victim of the financial

FIGURE 2.1 State Teachers College Portico

Note
Finished in 1941, with a portico optimistically inscribed before official conversion from normal school to state teachers college, Hartwell Hall remains the campus' iconic building, though a later president had the name airbrushed out of publicity photos.

Panic of 1837. Local residents rallied, however, and re-opened the building as an academy in 1841, and it has operated continuously on the same location ever since, though not without several near-death experiences.

Stability was eventually attained thanks to the Horace Mann model of normal schools. Until the 1860s, except for the state-supported New York State Normal School in Albany, New York relied on local academies to train teachers, providing a small payment for each graduate.[6] Then supporters of the normal school model gained legislative approval to create one in Oswego in 1862 and a few years later, to add four more by competitive application. Brockport was one of the winners and the nearly bankrupt academy emerged as Brockport Normal School in 1867.[7]

Although the status and name continued for the next 75 years, the form and curriculum evolved. Initially the institution continued operating essentially as an academy under local control with a normal school attached. But after 1900 the New York State Board of Regents began exerting control, increasingly focusing on teacher training while reducing and eventually eliminating its provision of local schooling. With the reduction of local influence and the academy curriculum, the normal school was reduced to offering a narrow one- and two-year curricula designed to train teachers.

In the 1920s a third year was added and the curriculum broadened again. During the 1930s Brockport, like many normal schools across the country, began planning for state teacher college status, making the curriculum more academic and hiring faculty with stronger academic credentials. Gov. Herbert Lehman, who repeatedly vetoed the enabling legislation to protect downstate institutions, however, delayed converting upstate New York's normal schools into four-year baccalaureate institutions. By the time he finally signed the legislation in April 1942, the United States had entered World War II and meaningful implementation of the new status was shelved for the duration.[8]

Thus, renaming New York's "normal schools" as "state teachers colleges," with the right to award baccalaureate degrees, came later in the state than in many others. However, New York was more typical than the nomenclature suggested. A 1930 study found that only one-quarter of America's teachers had more than two years of higher education, a time when New York's normal schools required three years. While New York was not among the 11 states that required a college degree to teach in 1940, it joined 20 others in requiring a bachelor's degree by 1950.[9]

As the Board of Regents planned for the postwar world, it assigned a specialty to each of its state teachers colleges to supplement their principal task of training elementary school teachers. In addition to continuing to train elementary school teachers, Brockport and Cortland State Teachers College were each assigned the preparation of health and physical education teachers for all grade levels. Thus, Brockport emerged from the war years as a dramatically different institution, with a new name, baccalaureate status, curricular specialty, freshly minted building, and, underwritten by the GI Bill, an unexpected influx of students. Our story begins there.[10]

The Students: Who Attended and Why?

Relatively little is known about the socio-economic characteristics of students who entered state teachers colleges in the decades following the Great Depression. One of the few studies was George Kaluger's "Background of State Teachers' College Students" that used an extensive database of Pennsylvania students entering the state teachers colleges that had been collected in 1949 (3,300 were in that sample) and then compared it to previous datasets for 1929 and 1939 (which had an undisclosed number of respondents). Most simply summarized, Kaluger found that Pennsylvania's state teachers college students mirrored the larger population in several important instances: they came in similar proportions from rural, suburban, and urban areas and 90 percent were born in the state. His 1949 data showed that 13 percent of fathers were in the professions, 44 percent had managerial or proprietary positions, 44 percent held skilled, semi-skilled, or unskilled jobs, and only about 5 percent of students came from farm families. Across the decades, the proportion of students whose parents were in the professions and business increased. In terms of parental education, about half of parents had graduated from high school, with relatively few earning college degrees.[11]

How does Brockport compare? While there are some differences, the socioeconomic pattern is roughly similar. We base much of our case study on data accumulated from the alumni in 16 classes that graduated from 1948 through 1964. They stretch from the first postwar classes through the last year in which all students formally committed to enroll in a teacher-training curriculum. Our data was compiled over 14 years from questionnaires sent to classes nearing their 40th or 50th reunions. In total we received 700 responses from 365 women and 335 men, with return rates averaging 15–20 percent of the surviving graduates.[12] The quantitative data and qualitative narratives give us an invaluable insight into the relationship of an important segment of post-World War II higher education and postwar American society.

Particularly striking is the extent to which these students were educational pioneers in their families. Much like their Pennsylvania counterparts, just under half (49.8 percent) of their parents, 44.7 percent of fathers and 54.9 percent of mothers, had even graduated from high school. Not surprisingly the percentage is higher for the classes graduating in the 1960s than in the 1950s, but only marginally.[13] Thus, almost exactly half of the students were in the first generation of their family to graduate from high school. And only a small minority of the students came from homes with parents who had experienced higher education. The alumni reported that 19.2 percent of their fathers and 22.8 percent of their mothers had attended a normal school or college.[14]

Parental occupations reflected their educational background. Most commonly fathers worked in the skilled crafts, especially as machinists, and in such services as bus drivers, and police, fire, and sanitation workers. Together they invariably constituted 33–40 percent of the total. A smaller number were in clerical or sales occupations, or small business. Approximately 10 percent worked in semi-skilled and unskilled jobs and less than 10 percent came from farming families. Only about 20 percent of fathers held professional or managerial positions, somewhat lower than the Pennsylvania data, perhaps because our categories are not identical. Invariably mothers were listed as housewives or homemakers; about half were also listed with an occupation, usually in clerical or sales work. About 10 percent of the students had a parent who was a teacher, usually the mother. Thus most Brockport graduates came to college from working and lower-middle class families to whom higher education was new and teaching was not a family tradition. Graduation from Brockport State Teachers College represented dramatic psychic and considerable social and economic upward mobility.[15]

Many Brockport students were descended from the "new" (i.e., Eastern and Southern European) immigration of the late nineteenth and early twentieth century, while others were from families whose lineage no doubt went back many generations in America. Persistently the most common ancestral origins cited were Italian, German, and Irish, with moderate numbers from Great Britain and Eastern Europe. The number of African-Americans was small, though interestingly they occupied a surprising number of campus elected offices. Native Americans were rare and no one in our sample reported Asian ancestry (Table 2.1).

Of the 94 percent who reported having had a religious affiliation or identity during their college years, Protestants and Catholics were equally represented with 43+ percent each, and about 5 percent were Jewish.[16] Protestants were spread across the mainstream denominations, especially Methodist, Presbyterian, and Episcopalian. The Catholic Newman Club provided the most vibrant religious presence on campus for the surprisingly high number of Catholic students.[17] In 1947 and 1953 the Brockport contingent co-chaired the New York Federation of Newman Clubs. In 1963, with a dynamic priest who was one of the most popular figures on campus, it successfully acquired its own building.[18] College events often opened with Christian prayers and there were religiously based ceremonies, especially the Christmas Vespers. A baccalaureate service at one of the local Protestant churches was part of graduation activities. Anecdotal evidence from Jewish alumni suggests their acceptance and overall positive experience accompanied by some sense of cultural distance, especially at Christmas (Table 2.2).

Why did these youth choose to attend Brockport since most students came from homes where higher education was not part of family history? Perhaps as a consequence, only a small proportion mentioned parental or familial expectations as the reason for their decision. By far the most commonly mentioned incentive was to learn to teach, coach, and work with children. While the majority of students followed the General Education curriculum to become elementary school teachers, about a third enrolled in the Health and Physical Education program. For those hoping to turn their interest in athletics into a career, Brockport and Cortland State Teachers Colleges were the only options

TABLE 2.1 Ethnic Ancestry

	Number	*% of Those Specifying Ethnicity*
European, unspecified	87	17.1
Western European	271	53.2
Eastern European	46	9.0
Southern European	99.5	19.5
Native American	1.5	0.3
Africa	4	0.8
Asia	0	0.0

Notes
$N = 509$ who specified ethnic ancestry. 72 blanks are omitted.

TABLE 2.2 Religious Identity while in College

	Number	% of Those Who Responded
Christian, unspecified	5	0.9
Protestant	236	43.6
Catholic	234	43.3
Jewish	30	5.5
Orthodox	2	0.4
None/no religion	34	6.3

Notes
$N = 541$. 105 blank responses were omitted.

within SUNY. A smaller number of alumni said their main incentive had been a belief that college would lead to a better life than their parents had, or to satisfy a thirst for more learning, or to delay entering the workforce. Comments by alumni from the Class of 1953 such as "I always wanted to teach," "I wanted to be a teacher," and "So I could obtain a better job than my parents," were typical.

When asked why they chose Brockport State Teachers College two answers dominated; it was nearby and affordable. In the 1950s the College was predominantly a local and regional institution with over 40 percent of our sample coming from within its home county (Monroe) and nearly 80 percent from western New York while only about 15 percent came from "downstate" (i.e., New York City and suburbs) area and a mere 5 percent from central and northern New York.

In the early 1960s, the College's catchment region significantly diversified. The number from within Monroe County fell to about one-quarter and the number from western New York dropped from over three-quarters to less than two-thirds while the proportion of those from central, northern, and downstate jumped from one-fifth to over one-third (Table 2.3). Few came from outside New York State.

Presumably SUNY's rising reputation during the early Rockefeller years increased its desirability and created more statewide consciousness of its

TABLE 2.3 Geographic Origins of Brockport Students

Classes of	1950–1959 (%)	1960–1964 (%)
Monroe County	41.4	24.8
Western NY	37.5	38.2
Central and Northern NY	4.6	11.0
Downstate	15.4	26.0
Out-of-state	0.4	2.0

campuses. More concretely (pun intended), the construction of dormitories facilitated the attendance of residential students from beyond commuting distance. Like other SUNY colleges, Brockport had been prohibited from having housing students after a tragic fire at Fredonia in 1900. The ban was not lifted until after World War II and Brockport did not open its first permanent residence hall until 1950. Shrinking enrollments after the GI Bill enrollment bubble reduced the incentive to provide additional beds until the late 1950s when another spate of dormitory construction began.

Affordability was the other reason alumni most frequently cited for choosing Brockport. Some respondents mentioned having wanted to attend a private college but not doing so due to expense. Tuition could not have been lower! The quid pro quo for studying to become a teacher was no charge for tuition, which remained the case until the early 1960s. Local students could live at home; a number commuted by bus or car from Rochester, 20 miles to the east. Regional students could go home on the weekends after "basket boarding" during the week on food brought from home.

Others chose Brockport on the recommendation of high school teachers, siblings, relatives, and friends. The location in a village and the intimate atmosphere of a campus that did not reach 2,000 students until the 1960s attracted some. And while many were brought to the campus by its accessibility, a few recalled wanting to be away from home. This sometimes contradictory range of reasons for attending Brockport is captured in comments by Class of 1953 alumni: "No tuition and I loved the small town atmosphere," "Low cost & proximity to home – commuted," "It was the furthest from Brooklyn," "To play soccer," "I could commute daily by Greyhound bus from Rochester," "I had to stay close to home – parents ill," "Location – far enough to live there & still come home weekends," and "Small village – small enrollment – admissions people warm and friendly."

Thus, a confluence of factors brought students to Brockport. Our data supports the notion that state teachers colleges attracted primarily a local and regional student body though the range widened in the 1960s. It also confirms that most students were from families without prior experience of higher education or, in about half the cases, with parents who had not graduated from high school. Also typical of state colleges, affordability was critical for the high percentage of students from working class and lower-middle class families. Almost all students were of European ancestry, a high percentage of whom were Catholic.[19]

Student Life

The creation of a collegiate culture at Brockport after the war is a curious, even intriguing, development. The postwar state teachers college developed a very different social tone than the normal school, whose culture resembled an extension of high school. For example, in the 1930s the few athletic teams, usually basketball and baseball, competed with high schools and other normal schools and a very strict principal banned fraternities and sororities and enforced high school style discipline. The presence of the campus school with nearly as many younger pupils as there were students enrolled in the normal school further distinguished the atmosphere from that at colleges. Although Brockport officially became a college in 1942, the war effectively suspended the few social activities which seemed frivolous at a time of sacrifice and a warped gender ratio hindered traditional heterosexual socialization. All that remained was a social life that largely centered on supporting the war effort with Brockport students annually participating in the fall harvest and community drives for precious materials, such as kitchen fats. By V-E Day enrollment had shrunk to 300, including only five males. It was a culture that would not survive the war itself, but the wartime experience cast a large shadow over the campus in the next decade.

As at other colleges, veterans played a major role in reshaping the postwar campus.[20] Brockport's designation as one of SUNY's two colleges with a specialization in Health and Physical Education made it especially attractive to males who composed 98 percent of GI Bill recipients. As was true nationally, the number who took up the GI Bill's higher education provisions, with the resulting influx of veterans, was unforeseen at Brockport. The New York State Regents (which controlled New York's state teachers colleges until SUNY was founded in 1948) had predicted the campus would grow to 500 by 1950. Instead, classes for the spring 1946 term had to be delayed a week as enrollment soared past that figure and President Donald Tower pleaded with residents to open their homes to returning veterans. For the rest of the 1940s veterans composed about one-third of an enrollment that soon approached 1,000, peaking at 300 among 1,015 students for the 1948/9 academic year. It is worth noting that while veterans were an important component of the postwar college, even without them the enrollment still outstripped all wartime estimates of postwar growth.

Some of the impact of the enrollment rush was temporary. Housing over 1,000 students and 100 faculty and staff in a village of 4,000 called for special measures. Veterans' needs differed from previous students, especially as many were married and had children. War-surplus barracks, formerly housing American troops in training centers or Germans and Italians in prisoner-of-war camps, were moved to Brockport for married housing. Although their quarters look very modest in retrospect, responses to our questionnaires reveal remarkable nostalgia for their experience. A Class of 1953 alumni's enthusiastic response that "I absolutely *loved* living in the old Quonset hut dorms" was not uncommon.[21] In contrast, faculty memories of three Quonset huts brought from Newport Naval Base with little heat control and positioned next to railroad tracks to house the art, science, and social science departments, and that remained in use until 1968, were decidedly less nostalgic.

Although veterans' numbers soon decreased and Brockport returned to a more traditional age and smaller student body by the early 1950s, the veterans left a lasting imprint on the campus. Even though they were "mature" students, veterans at Brockport contributed to building a collegiate culture. A number were leaders in the burgeoning campus drama and music organizations and the Veteran's Club became an important presence on campus. Veterans pressed for the creation of a football team and composed a majority of the inaugural squad that first took the field in 1947 in uniforms handed down from service teams (see Figure 2.2). They also formed the majority of the remarkably successful early soccer teams and captained a number of other athletic teams. They left a campus that was much more "collegiate" in nature than the one they entered.

Intriguingly, despite the lack of collegiate experience in most families and the lack of collegiate traditions at Brockport, many students seem to have brought a definite sense of what college life should entail. With the arrival of veterans and postwar students, there was an immediate demand for the trappings of collegiate life. While some initiatives came from the administration, students campaigned for and participated in the panoply of activities commonly associated with collegiate life.

No clear evidence proves that students arrived with such images of collegiate life, but in retrospect, classic campus activities dominate the memories of many alumni, which is especially intriguing given the initial contemporary criticism of the GI Bill as wasteful and predictions that it held little interest for veterans.[22] One can hazard a supposition that the pervasive depictions of collegiate life in American popular culture, through intercollegiate athletics, movies, magazines, and styles, was absorbed by these students before they came to the campus. In the more popular movies of the pre- and early war years that were set on college campuses, such as *Knute Rockne, All-American*, *Let's Go Collegiate*, and *The Male Animal*, many of the plots revolved in one way or another around collegiate athletics. That emphasis and college athletics' prominence in sports pages may have counteracted the elite 1930s image found in magazines.[23] Additionally, veterans may have had collegiate images reinforced by fellow servicemen who had been to college before they faced the rigors of basic training. During the immediate postwar years, a number of films focused on campus life for veterans and their families, such as *Apartment for Peggy*.

Intercollegiate athletics were certainly at the top of the students' list and by 1948 football and soccer teams were playing collegiate schedules, encouraged by female cheerleaders and a marching band. To help launch football, students filled a giant piggy bank with coins and voluntarily taxed themselves $5 to support it and other teams. By 1949 the teams were competing with private and public colleges across New York and neighboring states. Football and soccer weekends became important social events, despite the former's initial decade of losing seasons.

The soccer team had more immediate success, becoming a national power and improbably sharing the 1955 national championship with Penn State.

FIGURE 2.2 Football, Soccer, and the Associated Social Life Dominated Autumnal Weekends

Brockport had the luxury of two popular fall sports and, unlike most colleges, the soccer crowds usually outnumbered those for football and it sometimes replaced football as the Homecoming game. Golf, cross-country, track, and swimming teams were soon added. Women's intercollegiate competition had gone out of fashion in the 1930s, but the Women's Athletic Association provided an extensive intramural program and sponsored "play days" with other teachers colleges.

Brockport adopted other collegiate traditions after the war as well. The first Homecoming was held in 1948, creating an annual, much anticipated, ritual. An energized Alumni Association began to focus its activities on that fall weekend. The event quickly expanded, beginning each year with a parade through the village featuring alumni and student floats and bands passing a reviewing stand on Main Street. Competition for Homecoming parade prizes became the object of secretive planning. After the football or soccer game the day ended with a formal dinner-dance and alumni awards.

Other organizations flourished. The campus newspaper, *The Stylus*, founded in 1914 as a monthly, became a weekly after the war. The editors soon decided that any self-respecting college needed a mascot and launched a campaign to secure one. Students nominated the badger, the bear, the beaver, and the golden eagle; the latter won the election. The feathery victor was given an image by a *Stylus* cartoonist who was also a football player; he nicknamed it Ellsworth, his coach's middle name. Ellsworth the Eagle roams the campus to this day, nearly seven decades later.

The late 1940s were fertile days for founding student associations. Musical, dramatic, religious, and academic organizations flourished. *The Saga* yearbook was considerably expanded, providing a well-produced and extensive record of student life. A Winter Carnival and formal dances provided social highlights, all within the strict behavioral rules of the era and with faculty participation. The opening of the first student union in 1950 provided a focus for daily student life with improved dining and recreational opportunities and space for dances.

And graduation became a memorable and nostalgia-inducing week-long event organized by the student government. The week typically began with a picnic at Lake Ontario, followed by informal parties and then a formal dance in Rochester. Finally, a baccalaureate service in a local church and graduation launched them into the wider world.

While a robust campus life and extracurriculum formed rapidly after World War II, residential accommodations did not keep pace. When the first veterans enrolled, they found a "campus" of a single permanent building housing not only all offices and classrooms, but a gymnasium, bowling alleys, swimming pool, a cafeteria, a library, and a dark walnut auditorium-cum-theater. The Quonset huts housing veterans and a badly constructed temporary women's dormitory provided only temporary refuge. The first permanent dormitories in a half-century were opened in 1950 for women only. Increasing the number of dormitory beds and providing them for men had to wait until the late 1950s when enrollments recovered after the dip following the World War II veterans' graduation. However, the surrounding village offered a comfortable home to many faculty, staff, and students—a classic small-town setting for a college community. Most students lived in the Village of Brockport and depended on it for recreation and shopping. Some complained about the lack of activity, but most had fond memories of walks along the Erie Canal, movies at The Strand, dining on the fast food of the day, and drinking and dancing at a local hotel. In turn, many villagers attended cultural and athletic events on campus.

Responses to our questionnaires, augmented by interviews and *Saga* yearbooks and student research papers, have suggested two interesting conclusions about women's roles at Brockport State Teachers College, with implications for their subsequent careers. Betty Friedan's *Feminine Mystique* popularized the idea that collegiate women in the 1950s were relatively passive, preoccupied with achieving a "ring by senior spring" while foregoing professional aspirations. That depiction is certainly not borne out by student life at Brockport. For instance, women made major contributions to the student publications, *The Stylus* newspaper and *Saga* yearbook, often making up the majority of the newspaper's editorial board and dominating the yearbook staff (see Figure 2.3). Many women were not only active in other campus organizations, but frequently assumed leadership roles.[24] The leadership of Kappa Delta Pi, an education honor society, was predominantly female, suggesting a strong career motivation.

The women's organizational participation and leadership roles are particularly striking as Brockport had an unusually high proportion of men for a teachers college specializing in elementary education due to its Health and Physical Education program. The 47.9 percent of our questionnaire respondents who were male reflected Brockport's high postwar enrollments of men, whereas males were typically between 33 and 40 percent of enrollments at most other SUNY teachers colleges. In short, women's roles as Brockport campus leaders were not due to a lack of male students!

If Friedan's depiction of elite women in private, often single-sex, colleges is accurate, the difference from Brockport may well lie in its students' class origins. Predominantly the children of lower-middle and working-class families, the women at Brockport enrolled for both the collegiate experience, and the reality that their collegiate experience provided entrée to a profession. Their willingness to seek leadership roles was an extension of their professional expectations, which, however modest by elite liberal arts collegiate standards, were real. Equally important (see Table 2.4), these women not only entered the teaching profession, but most sustained long careers in addition to marriage and motherhood.

Connorton, Terry, Moyer, Bridgeman, Disinger, Bugbee, Osband, Reed, Voisey

FIGURE 2.3 The 1951/1952 Editors of *The Stylus*

Although Brockport quickly assumed the trappings of a residential college with accompanying activities after World War II, there were significant social divides. Responses to our questionnaire, while revealing a rich cultural and social life for many, also exposed a significant minority who lived at a distance and worked or had family responsibilities, foreshadowing the later rise of the "mature student." Their comments often expressed regret at not having shared in the full collegiate experience. Between these extremes were students who participated in weekday campus life, but returned home on weekends. The range is revealed in comments from the Class of 1956 such as "I was concert master of the orchestra throughout college," "Loved going camping with the Rod & Gun Club," "I enjoyed the many clubs, especially the winter trips to Camp Totem," "I did not have time for any activities; I worked my way through college," and "Took 4:10 Greyhound every day & went to work in downtown Rochester."

In short, Brockport's student life did not fully replicate the elite liberal arts colleges, but it provided an inexpensive version for many and a glimpse for others. The alumni's fondness for their alma mater, their vivid memories of the social life a half-century earlier, and their testimony to its effect on their later lives reflect the type of collegiate experience that was becoming a rite of passage for increasing numbers of American youth.

Curriculum: The "Poor Man's" Liberal Arts College?

When Sputnik launched in October 1958 youth of all ages enjoyed the nightly ritual of watching it pass high in the sky overhead. But the beeping ball set off a moral panic in their parents' generation. Some attributed the embarrassment to the belief that the Soviets had snatched the better German scientists at the end of World War II. Democratic presidential hopefuls blamed Eisenhower. And almost everyone blamed the schools, which were suddenly on the frontline of the Cold War and found wanting. Students were exhorted to shape up physically and mentally and regaled with the importance of "keeping up" with little Ivans.

The teaching profession and teacher training were the critics' targets, with state teachers colleges among the leading suspects in the perceived national failure. Sputnik seemed to confirm a growing chorus of educational critics. Arthur Bestor's provocatively titled *Educational Wastelands* attacked the supposedly flabby progressivism of Life Adjustment education in 1953, and set the aggressive tone.[25] Then Admiral Hyman Rickover, the architect of America's nuclear submarine fleet, wrote the most influential post-Sputnik criticism. He attacked progressive education's supposedly pernicious effects and called for more rigor, especially in science and mathematics. He wanted to exorcise the ghost of John Dewey from American educational philosophy and practice.[26]

Rickover's charges landed on fertile ground and inspired other critics. The most enduring attack on teacher education was James Koerner's influential *The*

Miseducation of American Teachers, which savaged teacher education and especially teacher colleges.[27] "Faculty, students, curriculum – all come under his verbal lash" and he inspired decades of similar attacks.[28] His study led to claims that although states only required an average of 23 credits of education courses for students preparing to teach in elementary schools, colleges required an average of 35 credits in courses he considered sub-standard. His examination of 435 transcripts of students preparing for elementary education at 32 institutions found that their average requirement was 50 credits of pedagogical courses. Worse in his view, teachers college students averaged 55 credits in education as opposed to 37 in liberal arts colleges and 50 in universities.

His attack was so well documented that few challenged it, though some defended the quality and necessity of the education courses. His charge has been repeated for decades, especially the claim that future teachers spend about half their time on pedagogy courses.[29] Christopher Lucas' questioning "whether educationists for their part truly deserved the calumny heaped on them by their academic colleagues" raised a rare note of skepticism among later commentators.[30]

When the students ascended the steps into Brockport's new (and until 1950 only) building, they passed under a portico with "State Teachers College" etched overhead. That title accurately reflected the College's primary mission which, like that of nine of the other ten SUNY State Teachers Colleges, was to prepare elementary school teachers. The resulting certification later extended to the first two years of six-year high school (aka junior high school). Only in the designated specialties, like Health and Physical Education at Brockport, did certification extend to secondary school.[31]

Given the institution's name and the later post-Sputnik critiques, the first postwar catalogue surprisingly announced that Brockport aimed to provide "both a sound liberal education and a specialized professional education for young people carefully selected to become future teachers in the public schools."[32] In the mid-1950s the statement was slightly revised to state that Brockport's curriculum provided "a broad cultural program in arts and science, plus a professional sequence in education."[33]

Did such pronouncements reflect curricular reality? Seemingly so. The "General Elementary Education" curriculum offered returning veterans and other students a broad curriculum. Except during the "practicum" (i.e., "practice teaching"), students took a wide variety of "content" subjects. In each of the other seven semesters students took courses in English and social studies. They also had six semesters of science and mathematics, five semesters of "Liberal-Cultural Electives," and two each of art and music and health, and one in industrial arts. Alumni noted this curricular breadth in comments such as these from the Class of 1954 that what they valued most highly in the curriculum was having received "a good liberal arts education," and "a full liberal arts exposure, not just 'teacher training'." Another alum put the two together, commenting that the highlight of his Brockport education was both "practice teaching and courses in the Civil War and political science."

These future teachers only took one education course in each of those seven on-campus semesters. Freshmen first studied Child Development, followed by a year-and-a-half of Child and the Curriculum, a title echoing John Dewey's classic book, and finished with a senior Seminar in Elementary Education. Thus, only 36 of the 128 credits (28 percent) were in Education courses, which was considerably below the 55 credits (46 percent) that Koerner claimed to have found in his reading of state teachers colleges' transcripts. Brockport's 36 credits are even marginally lower than those he computed for liberal arts colleges.

These figures may exaggerate Brockport's liberal arts and sciences as nine credits of Industrial Arts and of Health Education were classified as "Liberal-Cultural" whereas Koerner categorized them as professional. But even fitting those courses into Koerner's categories, professional education courses constituted 32 percent of Brockport students' credit hours, far less than Koerner's 46 percent.

And Koerner's figures underestimate required academic courses at Brockport. While he claimed that teachers college elementary education students averaged only 25 credits (or 20 percent of 120 credits) of English, math and science, Brockport students were required to take 39 (or 30 percent of 128) and some no doubt usually took more as electives. In total, Koerner's figures would have predicted considerably more professional courses, and considerably fewer in the arts and sciences, at Brockport.[34]

When Sputnik launched, Brockport's General Elementary Curriculum was essentially the same as greeted veterans immediately after World War II. The number of required Education credits remained at 36. Somewhat more electives were permitted. It is possible that through electives in "Education, Psychology and Philosophy," "Health & Physical Education," and "Industrial Arts", some students may have approached the figures Koerner cited, but few are likely to have done so.[35] An examination of Brockport's elementary education program does not sustain Koerner's damaging charge, which has been repeated for decades, that teachers colleges devoted nearly half of their curricula to courses in pedagogy.

In addition to the dominant elementary education curriculum, about one-third of the students pursued Brockport's specialist program in Health and Physical Education. It prescribed a similarly broad program for the first two years as the elementary education curriculum though with more emphasis on science and with an added physical education skills course. The latter two years were more specialized and professional, with a preponderance of health and physical education courses.

The claim that Brockport offered "a sound liberal education" must be judged in terms of both breadth and depth. It certainly passed the breadth test. Writing in the same year as Koerner in a book that attracted less popular attention, former Harvard President James Bryant Conant reached a conclusion similar to ours, that "there simply is no reason for concluding that the so-called general education of elementary school teachers is better or worse than the general education of other college students."[36]

Clearly, the depth provided by an academic "major" was absent, a weakness noted by both students in the questionnaire and faculty interviews. Indeed the only recurrent curricular complaint expressed by our alumni respondents was the lack of curricular choice and depth. By the late 1950s, some faculty addressed the issue by creating an Honors Program, teaching extra courses without additional compensation to enrich both the education of their students and their own sense of fulfillment. They offered in-depth, inter-disciplinary, team-taught seminars with titles such as "The Greek Foundations of Western Culture," "Great Ideas and the American Experience," and "The Romantic Movement."[37] In a real sense, the Honors Program was the curricular analog of what we found with student life, the creation of a state teachers college that increasingly mirrored the traditional images of collegiate life. The Honors Program, which admittedly was kept small, presaged the changes that would come after the 1960 Heald Commission Report's call to transform SUNY's State Teachers Colleges into Colleges of Arts and Sciences with traditional baccalaureate degrees in a wide range of traditional liberal arts disciplines. A critical mass of faculty were ready and able to heed the call.

Life After College

The commitment to teaching and coaching that brought most students to Brockport State Teachers College was largely fulfilled after graduation. Over 95 percent began teaching and most alumni made it a lifetime career; men averaged over 32 years in education and women nearly 24 years. New York State got its money's worth!

The length of the women's careers undermines the common assumption that female graduates of teachers colleges taught for only a few years and then left the profession to raise a family, never to return. And their lengthy careers did not come at the cost of marriage and motherhood. Well over 95 percent of our female respondents married and nearly 95 percent had children, averaging almost three offspring. Most indicated that they left teaching to raise families, but the vast majority returned to the teaching profession and their careers, averaging 24 years, were only about eight years shorter than the male alumni. Most men also combined long careers in teaching with family life, with over 95 percent marrying and having children.[38] Many alumni seem to have "had it all."

TABLE 2.4 Years of Service in Education

Class	Did You Teach?		How Many Years Did You Teach?	
	Yes	No	Men	Women
1951	32	0	31.1	23.2
1952	49	2	32.7	21.8
1953	43	4	30.6	24.5
1954	28	0	33.3	24.9
1955	25	0	29.2	27.1
1956	26	1	30.5	28.5
1957	41	2	34.5	19.1
1958	37	0	33.9	22.4
1959	32	0	30.4	21.5
1960	32	1	33.9	22.7
1961	42	0	34.6	26.5
1962	30	1	31.3	17.0
1963	50	3	33.9	26.6
1964	41	1	31.4	29.2
	508 (97.1%)	15 (2.9%)	32.2	23.9

Notes
Fifteen blanks are omitted. Those who did not enter or stay in the education profession may have been less likely to answer the questionnaire, which could slightly bias the results. But clearly most alumni became teachers.

From State Teacher College to Comprehensive College

By the early 1960s Brockport—and SUNY's other teachers colleges—were on the brink of dramatic change, and it came relatively quickly. Newly elected Governor Nelson Rockefeller appointed the high-powered Heald Commission. Its November 1960 report laid the foundation for the immediate expansion of SUNY's size and mission, principally by recommending the creation of four university centers and that "the state colleges of education be converted into liberal arts, starting immediately." SUNY's Board of Trustees accepted the idea and its 1960 Master Plan proposed that each state teachers college would be converted into a "multi-purpose institution embracing liberal arts and sciences along with teacher education."[39] Planning for the curricular expansion at Brockport immediately ensued.

At Brockport, the planning relied on many of the same professors who had created and staffed the Honors Program. A campus-wide curriculum committee, chaired by Professor Wayne Dedman, began its deliberations in fall, 1961, and within two years, the proposal for a new liberal arts curriculum had been circulated, revised, and then finally, implemented. The initial plan called for what was then named the "Liberal Arts" program, with an expanded liberal arts faculty to teach it, that would accompany Brockport's traditional majors in General Elementary Education and Health and Physical Education. The Liberal Arts program, with majors in English, Mathematics, Natural Science, Social Science, Speech, and American Studies, was made available to juniors in 1963, with plans to extend it to freshmen in 1965.

In the meantime, Brockport had fully entered the world of preparing secondary school educators, adding certification programs in Mathematics and in General Science and Biology for the 1961/2 academic year. Three years later, Secondary Education in English and in Social Studies was added to the Education program. The new programs fit President Donald Tower's expectation that the teacher college tradition would continue, but he mistakenly predicted that no more than 10 percent of Brockport's students would choose the liberal arts curriculum rather than the certification programs in the near future.

By 1965 President Tower was gone, summarily dismissed by SUNY. In two decades under President Tower enrollment had soared from under 500 to over 2,500 and the campus had mushroomed from one building, adding a library, a science building, a gymnasium, dormitories, and a student union. But Tower was committed to the state teacher college model. The dynamic new SUNY Chancellor, Samuel Gould, who had worked in the burgeoning University of California system under Clark Kerr, had another vision. Tower was pushed into retirement and a very different kind of president was imposed on the college. President Albert W. Brown, who arrived after running Michigan Governor George Romney's Economic Opportunity Program, transformed Brockport into a fully liberal arts college and an engine of urban reform for the Rochester region. The year after Brown's arrival, teacher certification was removed from the list of majors and designated as a program that students could take in addition to an academic major. By 1970 more than two dozen traditional liberal arts majors vied for student enrollments while graduate programs proliferated.

The new majors were a genuine expansion of the curriculum, building in many instances on the past. For example, Brockport developed an extraordinary dance program, which was created by Professor Rose Strasser, originally hired as a member of the Physical Education program teaching dance and movement. The Physical Education and Health curriculum had necessitated a strong program in human biology, which now supported the addition of the secondary certification programs in mathematics and science.

That said, the Liberal Arts program of 1965 was quickly transformed into a 45-hour distributed general education program required of all students. No longer could Brockport students major in the college's traditional education programs, for after 1967 all Brockport students needed an "academic" major, with certification programs becoming the equivalent of either second majors or minors. While Brockport's insistence on the necessity of the academic major in a traditional field was almost unique in the state, it was a curricular pattern that would be recommended by almost every governing body looking at teacher education over the next 30 years.

Beyond curricular continuity, the new president, unlike many who faced similar circumstances, used existing administrators and faculty to fill the myriad new administrative positions, bringing no one in from the outside. The major assignments of these early years went to veteran Brockport faculty and administrators, all of whom were familiar to faculty and staff of the old Brockport.

A striking indicator of President Brown's impact on the pace and scope of change is to compare the "Academic Plan" of November 1965 with its successor, which had been presented to SUNY only eight months later. The document, which had been so carefully crafted before Brown's arrival, was reviewed, revised, and, like everything else at Brockport at this time, significantly expanded. First, there was the expansive vision of campus geography. The new plan requested the purchase of an additional 200 acres of land adjoining the campus to the west, thus ending the pattern of piecemeal purchases of private homes surrounding the campus that had generated enormous hostility between the college and town residents. Second, representative governance bodies were reformed, as the Faculty-Student Association was split into a Faculty Senate and a Student Government, each with its own constitution and by-laws.

The expansive nature of the changes introduced by President Brown were predicated on significant, and ultimately disruptive, projected enrollment growth. The college had been planning for more students, not just new majors. The enrollment in 1960 had been 1,954, with 1,454 full-time undergraduates. By fall, 1965, the college enrolled 2,500 full-time undergraduates, almost all of whom had begun their careers as Brockport freshmen. According to the "Ten-Year Academic Plan" of November 1965, which had been the result of a major planning process involving the entire college community, the undergraduate student body was expected to increase over the next half-decade to 3,550 full-time students, which is where it was expected to stabilize. This was a fairly typical projection among the SUNY colleges, with the exception that part of Brockport's growth was to be accomplished by increasing the number of transfer students, from fewer than 100 in 1965 to 260 by 1970.

The new administration modified the plan within six months, sending SUNY a far more ambitious proposal. The undergraduate student population that was to be stabilized at 3,750 students was now projected to grow much larger, much faster: 3,700 in 1968, 5,000 in 1970, and 7,500 by 1975. Again, much of the growth was to be through increased numbers of transfer students, a project favored by SUNY administrators who believed they were creating an integrated system of public education. According to the SUNY Master Plans of 1964 and 1968, the arts and sciences colleges had a special responsibility to provide seats for the increasing numbers of transfer students who were being produced at newly created and expanding community colleges. In this regard, Brockport would lead the SUNY system, actively recruiting community college

transfers from throughout the state. The original projection had been for 260 new transfers in 1970, but the new realities quickly swamped such numbers as the college enrolled 600 new transfers in 1967, 1,400 in 1970, and more than 2,000 the next year.

In 1967, the college created its projections for the 1968 Master Plan. The full-time enrollment estimates for 1975 were increased again, from 7,500 undergraduates to 10,500, with an additional 1,200 full-time graduate students expected. When the more than 8,000 part-time students, both undergraduate and graduate, were added to these figures, the official planning document in 1968 estimated that total enrollment would exceed 20,000 by 1975!

And to accompany this expected growth, even if the most ambitious levels were never realized, the campus had to add new buildings at a furious pace, hire hundreds of new faculty and staff, more than 100 in both 1970 and 1971, and recreate an administration that provided for expanded services at every turn. The composition of the faculty changed, with the flood of young teacher-scholars, most of whom arrived with doctorates in hand, resulting in the percentage of faculty with terminal degrees doubling between 1965 and 1975. Published scholarship became an essential element in tenure and promotion cases for the first time. To a greater extent than any other SUNY college, Brockport embraced a rapid expansion of the campus, fueling hopes—campus legends—that it was destined to become the fifth doctoral university center in the SUNY system. A campus self-delusion to be sure, but it underlay proposals, such as that of the Psychology faculty for three distinct Ph.D. programs, in the 1966 Revision to the Master Plan.

In another planning memo from the Assistant to the President for Planning in April 1967, marked "confidential," the true measure of the campus's aspirations can be found. This document, which was preliminary to the campus Master Plan of 1968, includes references to planned doctoral programs in Education (both Ph.D. and Ed.D.), Physical Education, Art History, Art Education, Theater, Spanish, French, Philosophy (supported by a department of 25), General Speech, Public Address, Speech and Hearing, Geology, Limnology, and Economics. State teachers college? Not any more. College of Liberal Arts and Sciences? Yes, but only as a way-station on the road to university-center status.

And Brockport's extraordinary trajectory was noticed. In the late 1960s Alden Dunham's *Colleges of the Forgotten Americans* portrayed Brockport as an institution on the move, evolving much more quickly than most former teachers colleges.

> If Kansas State Teachers College at Emporia is a locomotive still sitting at the station building up steam, Brockport has its throttle wide open and is speeding down the track. Like most Eastern teachers colleges, it ran way behind schedule, but in the past two or three years it has made up much of its lost time.[40]

Graduate education was certainly not neglected either. English was the first of the new M.A. programs, but others quickly followed, and the 1968 campus Master Plan names 32 additional master's programs planned for implementation in the next three years. The 870 graduate students (almost all part-time) in 1967 were projected to number almost 7,500 by 1975, with the expectation that 1,200 would be full-time! Our point is not that the planning for any of these programs proceeded very far, but rather, the fact that so many departments in the spring of 1967 saw doctoral programs in their near-term future (ten years) speaks volumes about faculty expectations for the college.

Across the country state teachers colleges changed their names with undue haste and embarrassing rapidity.[41] Although most states had sponsored state teachers colleges, they soon disappeared, at least in name, little lamented in the decade after Sputnik, hounded by exposés of their presumed academic failings. The state teachers college days became an embarrassing episode best forgotten. College marketing departments, including Brockport's, have airbrushed the name from pictures and at least one college sandblasted the offending title from a façade.[42] Even in more recent years the *New York Times* occasionally attacks colleges of education, long after their demise.[43]

Historians, perhaps reluctant to go down a road not taken, have written little about an institution that educated 10 percent of American college students in the 1950s. John Thelin's recent survey of American higher education makes no mention of them.[44] James Fraser's history of teacher preparation carefully examines their evolution from "normal schools" to "teachers colleges" but dismisses the latter's postwar role with the questionable chronological claim that "such single-purpose schools virtually disappeared from the American scene in the decade after World War II."[45]

The former SUNY State Teachers Colleges played a major role in meeting New York's ever growing demand for higher education. Albany, the one upstate college that trained secondary teachers in the traditional academic subjects, is now a research university enrolling over 15,000 students. The remaining ten University Colleges that taught elementary teachers and specialists such as physical education teachers enroll over 60,000 students and offer master's programs across the disciplines and professions. Together they account for 20 percent of SUNY's full-time equivalent enrollments and about half of its baccalaureate degrees.[46]

Conclusions

Although generalizations based on a single case study are always vulnerable, we venture some tentative conclusions. First, we contend that Brockport, and probably other state teachers colleges, were vehicles of upward psychic, economic, and social mobility that appealed especially to first-generation students in an immediate region. Half of the respondents were in the first generation in their family to graduate from high school. About 80 percent were in the first generation in their families to even attend college and thus potentially enter professional life.

Second, Brockport was particularly a vehicle of Catholic upward mobility. The Catholic hierarchy, headed in New York by Cardinal Spellman, fiercely opposed the creation of SUNY, and successfully limited its growth until the Rockefeller years. It accurately foresaw the challenge SUNY posed to the ideal of enrolling all Catholic students in colleges under the Church's auspices. A free alternative to Catholic colleges attracted many youth. SUNY's attraction may have been especially true for Italian-Americans whose ethnicity was the most commonly cited among our respondents. And it may be indicative that the Newman Society was the most vibrant religious organization on campus, one that eventually constructed its own building on the edge of the campus. We suspect that SUNY's role in promoting the upward mobility of the state's largely Catholic ethnic communities is one of its hidden stories.

Third, Brockport functioned as a "poor man's" liberal arts college. It not only provided a broad liberal arts education, at least in its breadth, but it also offered a collegiate student culture echoing that of private colleges and larger state universities. Enrolling about 10 percent of postwar students, the state teachers colleges made higher education familiar to, and an expectation of, many families, contributing to the attitudes that stimulated the mass higher education soon to follow. Teachers colleges made higher education familiar to numerous American families which had previously experienced it vicariously at best.

Higher education occupies a unique cultural space in America. State teachers colleges played at least a modest role in expanding the visibility of collegiate culture in the United States. Brockport provided a campus life much like that in liberal arts colleges for many. Other students, who lived at home or returned there for weekends, at least glimpsed it.

Fourth, our study challenges the image popularized in *The Feminine Mystique* of female student passivity and brief careers, if any, after graduation. It is certainly inaccurate for Brockport State Teachers College, where many women assumed leadership roles on campus and most pursued long teaching careers in succeeding decades of professional service.

Fifth, our evidence suggests that the state teachers colleges were unfairly scapegoated after Sputnik; they provided a broad (though not deep) liberal arts curriculum with about as many pedagogy courses as are typical in today's teacher training programs. The creation of an Honors Program suggests an intellectual vitality rarely credited to such institutions.

Finally, although we believe that Brockport was typical of most of the institutions that made transitions from normal schools to state teachers colleges, it was clearly atypical of those that morphed into state-supported comprehensive colleges in the 1960s and early 1970s. At the least, it was clearly atypical among the SUNY colleges. Hiring President Albert W. Brown made the critical difference. His vision was significantly grander and, in this case, size did matter. Discreetly imposed on the campus by a SUNY administration eager to absorb the rapidly growing demand for higher education in the Rochester area, Brown commanded Chancellor Samuel Gould's backing for his ambitious projects. Gould later named him as one of his best presidents.[47]

Thus, state teachers colleges may have morphed into liberal arts and sciences colleges and comprehensive colleges relatively easily. The base for a wider and more varied curriculum was already built and the campus life desired by growing numbers of youth was already in place. State teachers colleges may properly be seen as a significant building block of mass higher education as well as one of its future engines.

Daniel Webster famously commented that Dartmouth was "a small college. And yet, there are those who love it."[48] Although few historians or marketing departments love the state teachers college, virtually all of our alumni respondents remembered their small Brockport State Teachers College with enduring fondness and appreciation for the change it made possible in their lives.

Notes

1 V. R. Cardozier, "America's State Colleges," *Minerva*, Vol. 26, No. 4 (December 1988), 549–574. Retrieved from www. jstor.org/stable/41820812.
2 David F. Labaree, *The Trouble with Ed Schools* (New Haven: Yale University Press, 2004), 29.
3 Patricia J. Gumport, "Public Universities as Academic Workplaces," *Daedalus*, Vol. 126, No. 4. (Fall 1997), 116.
4 Allan C. Ornstein, "Past and Present Trends in Teacher Education," *American Secondary Education*, Vol. 11, No. 3 (Fall 1981).
5 The New York Board of Regents oversaw the state's 11 normal schools, which had been renamed "state teachers colleges" in 1942, and which joined the State University of New York (aka SUNY) as founding members in 1948. Controversially, the legislation creating SUNY removed the state teachers colleges from the control of the Regents with the creation of a separate Board of Trustees for the newly formed system. SUNY's creation had little effect on the colleges in its first decade and one-half. For simplicity, we anachronistically use "SUNY colleges" throughout the 1940s.
6 Walter Crosby Eells and Ernest V. Hollis, "Origin and Development of the Public College in the United States," *Journal of Negro Education*, Vol. 31, No. 3 (Summer 1962), 226.
7 Christine Ogren, *The American State Normal School* (New York: Palgrave Macmillan, 2005) provides a very insightful history of normal schools, with considerable attention to New York's.
8 Brockport's standard history, W. Wayne Dedman, *Cherishing This Heritage: The Centennial History of the State University College at Brockport, New York* (New York: Appleton-Century-Crofts, 1969), provides a finely textured account that deftly places the institution within its local context up to World War II. As the author modestly told us, his postwar chapters are less useful. It is available online at: http://digitalcommons.brockport.edu/cgi/viewcontent.cgi?article=1041&context=student_archpapers. For a shorter pictorial history emphasizing the period since World War II, see Mary Jo Gigliotti, W. Bruce Leslie, and Kenneth P. O'Brien, *State University of New York at Brockport* (Charleston: Arcadia Publishing, 2006).

9 James Fraser, *Preparing America's Teachers: A History* (New York: Teachers College Press, 2007), 179–189 offers an excellent review of changing institutional names and their connection to teacher training reality. California led the change, converting its normal schools into state teachers colleges by 1921. In 1935 "Teachers" was removed from their names and they began offering non-teacher training curricula, which were immediately popular. John Aubrey Douglass, *The California Idea and American Higher Education* (Stanford: Stanford University Press, 2000), 137–140, 155–157. Ogren, *American State Normal School*, 202.

10 For 20 years we have studied the history of SUNY's College at Brockport with particular emphasis upon the state teachers college decades (c.1945–1965). In addition to standard research in catalogues, student publications, and administrative records, we have compiled oral histories of alumni and faculty and collected 700 questionnaires from alumni from the Class of 1948 through the Class of 1964. We have also directed over 50 student research papers on the College's history. Thus, we draw upon unusually rich archival resources for a state teachers college. They are available in the Rose Archive in Drake Library at The College at Brockport.

11 George Kaluger, "Background of State Teachers' College Students," *The School Review*, Vol. 59, No. 9 (December 1951), 537–542.

12 The differences in the Pennsylvania and our datasets are obvious: the Pennsylvania data is self-reported information from students in the state colleges, while ours is self-reported data collected 40 or 50 years after graduation from a single college. Our questionnaires were sent to graduates about six months before their reunions asking for their memories as well as demographic information. The Class of 1950 was missed and the classes of 1954, 1959, 1962, 1962, and 1964 participated twice, ten years apart. For the latter classes, only the data from the 50th reunion is tabulated in the tables in the chapter. The classes of 1948 and 1949 were surveyed a few years after their 50th reunions. Thus, there is data from 16 classes with a total of 21 cohorts that ranged in size from 10 to 53. Class return rates ranged from 12 to 38 percent.

13 Of 1,336 parents, 665 parents had graduated from high school and 671 had not. More mothers were high school graduates in 13 classes, fathers in three, and in two they were the same.

14 With an $N=1,344$, 282 (21 percent) had experienced education beyond high school, 129 of 672 fathers and 153 of 672 mothers The mothers' higher high school graduation rate reflects long-standing national historical patterns, but their slightly higher participation in higher education contrasts with national proportions.

15 Occupation is notoriously difficult to measure with precision, but the consistency of the figures across the years was striking.

16 As 16 percent of respondents left the question blank, the number of those with no religious identity in their college years is probably undercounted. But the proportion of Protestants, Catholics, and Jews was strikingly consistent across the period.

17 The Catholic hierarchy in New York had fought the establishment of SUNY, a campaign that appears rational given the large number of Catholic students who came to SUNY.

18 John Kutolowski, "The Newman Movement at SUNY Brockport: A Half Century, 1940–1990," 1990, Rose College Archives, The College at Brockport. Available online at: http://digitalcommons.brockport.edu/cgi/viewcontent.cgi?article=1040&context=student_archpapers.

19 Our data helps explain the fervent opposition of the Catholic hierarchy to SUNY's creation in 1947.

20 See Thomas N. Bonner, "The Unintended Revolution," *Change*, Vol. 18, No. 5 (September–October 1986), 44–51 for a personal remembrance of the impact of the "GI Bill" on his generation of veterans; Keith W. Olsen, "The G.I. Bill and Higher Education: Success and Surprise," *American Quarterly*, Vol. 25, No. 5 (December

1973); and Lynette Sengel Taylor, "Invasion on the Homefront: The Veterans at Arkansas State Teachers College, 1945–1949," *Arkansas Historical Quarterly*, Vol. 47, No. 2 (Summer 1988). Our understanding of the impact of veterans on Brockport is informed by a paper by our student: Mark Sample, "GI Joe, or How I Stopped Worrying and Learned to Love the Bill: Veterans at Brockport Post-WWII," Rose College Archive, The College at Brockport.

21 Our discussion of student life has been informed by research papers now held in the Rose College Archives at The College at Brockport, written by our students Anthony Carpenter, Daniel Cody, Glen Cummings, Thom Jennings, Todd Klefehn, Colleen Hogan Myers, Jane Oakes, Beth Ramsperger, Mark Sample, and Joseph Yockel. Many of these papers and others are available online at: http://digitalcommons.brockport.edu/student_archpapers/33/.

22 Dan Clark, "'The Two Joes Meet – Joe College, Joe Veteran': College Education, and Postwar College Education," *History of Education Quarterly*, Vol. 38 (Summer 1998), 165–189. Clark insightfully shows the impact of the GI Bill on American perceptions of college life after veterans unexpectedly stormed college gates, but shares our inability to explain why so many entered an institution whose pre-war image in print media had been elite.

23 Ibid., 169–173.

24 Robin Bossard, "Women at Brockport in 1950s," Rose College Archives. Betty Friedan, *The Feminine Mystique* (New York: Dell, 1963), Ch. 7.

25 Arthur E. Bestor, *Educational Wastelands* (Urbana: University of Illinois Press, 1953).

26 H. G. Rickover, *Education and Freedom* (New York: Dutton & Co., 1959).

27 James Koerner, *The Miseducation of American Teachers* (Baltimore: Penguin, 1965), 118–139.

28 Labaree, *The Trouble with Ed Schools*, 4.

29 In 1981 a critic claimed that future teachers "are required by law to serve time, often as much as one half of their undergraduate program, in the classes of the teacher-trainers." Richard Mitchell, *The Graves of Academe* (Boston: Little Brown, 1981), 15. A decade later another critique, whose subtitle borrowed Koerner's title, claimed that colleges of education offered "three or four years of concentration on pedagogy to students barely out of high school, whose general education was slighted.... All of them knew more about how to teach than what to teach." Rita Kramer, *Ed School Follies: The Miseducation of America's Teachers* (New York: Free Press, 1991), 6–7.

30 Christopher Lucas, *Teacher Education in America: Reform Agendas for the Twenty-First Century* (New York: St. Martin's Press, 1997), 73. Lucas summarizes post-World War II critics, including Bestor's and Koerner's books and James Bryant Conant's *The Education of American Teachers* (New York: McGraw-Hill, 1963) on pp. 67–80. As Lucas points out, Conant's less dramatic and less widely read report was not as critical of teacher training curricula.

31 Nine SUNY State Teachers Colleges had similar curricula though different specialty programs: Buffalo, Cortland, Fredonia, Geneseo, New Paltz, Oneonta, Oswego, Plattsburgh, and Potsdam. In later years Buffalo was permitted to create some programs to train secondary teachers. The New York State College for Teachers at Albany was the exception, solely training secondary teachers.

32 Brockport State Teachers College, *Bulletin: General Catalogue Issue, 1946–47*, 1.

33 State University of New York, Teachers College at Brockport, *General Catalogue, 1954–1955–1956*, 23.

34 Brockport State Teachers College, *Bulletin: General Catalogue Issue, 1947–48*. Koerner, *Miseducation*, Ch. V.

35 State University of New York, Teachers College at Brockport, *General Catalogue, 1956/7–1958/9*, 34–47.

36 Conant, *Education*, 153.

37 Helen Helenbrook, "History of the Honors Program at SUNY Brockport," 1999, Rose Archive, The College at Brockport.
38 Combining genders, 97.3 percent of the 490 respondents who answered the question married and 94.9 percent of 486 respondents had children. There were only 11 blanks for the question on marriage and 15 on children.
39 Sidney Gelber, *Politics and Public Higher Education in New York State: Stony Brook – A Case Study* (New York: Peter Lang, 2001), 138 and 141. Ch. 11 gives an excellent account of the beginning of the transformation of SUNY in the Rockefeller years. See Christopher Jencks and David Riesman, *The Academic Revolution* (Chicago: University of Chicago Press, 1968), 231–236, for a national perspective on the conversion to multipurpose colleges and universities.
40 E. Alden Dunham, *Colleges of the Forgotten Americans* (Berkeley: Carnegie Commission on Higher Education, 1969), 8.
41 Christine A. Ogren, "Rethinking the 'Nontraditional' Student From a Historical Perspective: State Normal Schools in the Late Nineteenth and Early Twentieth Centuries," *The Journal of Higher Education*, Vol. 74, No. 6 (November–December 2003), argues that in the mid-century in the transition from normal schools to state teachers colleges, the colleges gave up their unique identity, including their tradition of serving non-traditional student populations.
42 Karen Hallman, "Normal School to State College: Transitions in the 20th Century," History of Education Society Annual Meeting, 2004.
43 For instance an editorial, "Rising Above the Gathering Storm," *New York Times* (January 24, 2006), opined that "Many education colleges have become diploma mills."
44 John Thelin, *A History of American Higher Education* (Baltimore: Johns Hopkins Press, 2004).
45 Fraser, *Preparing America's Teachers*, 186.
46 For a bibliography of histories of SUNY institutions see John B. Clark, W. Bruce Leslie, and Kenneth O'Brien, *SUNY at Sixty* (Albany: SUNY Press, 2010), 330–341. For brief histories of all 64 of SUNY's institutions see W. Bruce Leslie and Kenneth P. O'Brien, *Sixty-Four Campuses, One University: The Story of SUNY* (Albany: SUNY Press, 2017).
47 Martin Fausold, Interview with Samuel Gould, October 1, 1991. Martin Fausold Papers. M. E. Grenander Department of Special Collections and Archives, University at Albany, SUNY.
48 Richard Hofstadter and Wilson Smith, eds., *American Higher Education Documentary History* (Chicago: University of Chicago Press, 1961), Vol. I, 212.

3

"EDUCATION FOR CITIZENSHIP ... IS TOO IMPORTANT TO LEAVE TO CHANCE"

John Allen and the University of South Florida, 1956–1970

Charles Dorn

In 1957, just days following the launch of the first Soviet Sputnik satellite, local reporters pressed John S. Allen—president of the newly established University of South Florida (USF)—to explain why American higher education had failed to maintain US technological competitiveness. "It is clear we need more scientists and engineers," Allen responded, "but we do not need scientists and engineers who are politically naïve or economically illiterate." Allen went on to acknowledge that it was "a matter of national concern" that in the same year the United States graduated 22,000 students with bachelor of science degrees, the Soviet Union graduated 60,000 students with master's degrees in scientific fields. Yet, he observed, there was "one principal difference" between US and Soviet scientists. Theirs were "selected for training on the basis of political reliability," Allen claimed, "while ours are free to think for themselves and serve humanity in many ways." "In this connection," he continued,

> let us remember that atomic power cannot teach a Sunday school class, write a poem or compose a song. Scientists must be citizens in the fullest sense if their country is to perform its responsibilities to the world at large.[1]

Allen's observations on the importance of educating for citizenship reflected the priorities he would pursue at USF over the next 13 years. The first four-year public university "conceived, planned, and built in the United States in the 20th century," as Allen liked to boast, USF was intended to serve a "non-traditional," urban, commuter student population.[2] Rather than modeling this new metropolitan center of higher learning on America's flourishing research universities, however, Allen looked to the liberal arts college as an example of a teaching-oriented institution that embraced liberal education and was dedicated to fostering in students dispositions of civic-mindedness and a commitment to democratic citizenship.

Yet between his appointment in 1956 and retirement in 1970, Allen confronted a series of obstacles to his efforts to lead the fledgling institution in the direction of developing "citizens in the fullest sense." As he touted the importance of higher learning in preparing competent citizens, Cold War fears led the state-level, McCarthy-influenced Florida Legislative Investigating Committee to conduct what amounted to a witch-hunt on campus. As the Civil Rights Movement gained momentum in the United States, conservative critics lambasted USF's policy of racial and ethnic integration, while students of color and their allies accused the university of doing little to act affirmatively in the interests of students who were historically excluded from Florida's higher education institutions. As Allen promoted a civic-minded, liberal arts curriculum for undergraduates during their first two years of study, many students sought professional- and vocational-oriented training associated with lucrative, white-collar work.

Indeed, Allen's tenure as USF president brings into sharp relief the challenges and frequently conflicting demands that higher education administrators confronted during the decades following World War II as they sought to define and achieve the goals of general education for civic competence in the midst of political and social fragmentation. When conservative reactionaries such as Florida State Senator Charley Johns intruded on USF's autonomy, Allen forcefully defended the university's educational integrity. Yet, in an effort to mollify critics and sustain public and legislative support for the institution, he violated academic freedom and failed to proactively defend USF employees' right to privacy. Similarly, although Allen emphatically defended students' freedom of speech, he set strict limits on when and how that speech could be expressed. Moreover, his commitment to education for citizenship existed in marked tension with the educational objectives with which many students arrived to campus. Hoping to better themselves occupationally and financially, students were often motivated by vocational ambition rather than civic concerns. Accordingly, although Allen sustained a liberal arts curriculum at the university during his tenure, following his retirement USF joined flagship public universities nationally in reorienting academic programs toward professional and occupational training while seeking to become major research universities.

The literature on post-World War II US higher education that informs this study tends to follow one of two strands. The first, which is anchored in institutional history, characterizes the period between the end of World War II and 1970 as a "golden age" epitomized by expansion and growth.[3] Higher education participation rose 227 percent during these years, so that by 1970 over one-third of Americans between the ages of 18 and 24 enrolled in a college or university. Public institutions such as USF met much of this demand. In 1970, three-quarters of America's higher education student population attended public colleges and universities, with about one-fourth of the total number enrolling in two-year colleges.[4] And although veterans' benefits such as the GI Bill led to a significant increase in male enrollments immediately following the war (and, consequently, a decline in women's proportional representation), in absolute numbers women's participation in higher education during the early 1950s surpassed women's prewar enrollment peak by over 50,000 students. Indeed, more women are estimated to have received bachelor's degrees in 1952 than at any prior time in US history.[5]

Golden age portrayals also emphasize the tremendous growth of federal investment in higher education, especially in the area of sponsored research. Prior to World War II, few colleges and universities received significant federal research support. In 1940, private industry accounted for almost 70 percent of total expenditures for research and development, with the federal government accounting for only 20 percent.[6] Wartime technological advances resulting from university-based research, in particular the atom bomb, led policy-makers to urge dramatically increased financial investments in basic research, especially in mathematics and the sciences.[7] In addition, the rise of the Cold War and the launch of the Soviet Sputnik satellites catalyzed federal spending.[8] Within two decades of the end of World War II, federal investments in university research skyrocketed almost 900 percent.[9]

The second strand presented in the literature offers a very different portrayal of the post-World War II era. Anchored primarily in social history, it is characterized by strife, conflict, and consternation. Battles between students and college and university administrators over a range of issues, including freedom of expression, racial and ethnic minority student access and treatment, the status of women, and opposition to war, frequently form the core of these studies.[10] Moreover, overrepresentation in the historiography of higher education administrators such as Clark Kerr, whose response to the Free Speech Movement at the University of California, Berkeley, is frequently cited as an example of inept leadership during this period, impairs a thorough understanding of the intricate institutional dynamics in which higher education administrators operated during these years.

Seeking neither to defend nor rebuke John Allen's leadership, this study uses his tenure as president of a newly established public university to demonstrate the complex social, political, and economic conditions under which administrators set policy and leveraged their authority to shape higher education in the decades following World War II.[11] Rather than perpetuating a simple dichotomy of higher education as experiencing a golden age or confronting social transformation, this chapter illuminates some of the relationships between the two. Using Allen's administration as a case study, it examines a university president who tried to pick his way carefully across the minefields of expansion by maintaining public support for his institution; acting in what he understood to be the best interests of higher education; and satisfying the demands of students, faculty, and staff. Given that these three priorities often conflicted, administrators such as Allen frequently struggled to respond constructively to long-standing dilemmas in American higher education.

The Sunbelt University

In 1954, state legislators representing Florida's Hillsborough County, which included the Tampa metropolitan area, sought to capitalize on a recently released report encouraging the expansion of higher education opportunities throughout the state.[12] As with "Higher Education for Democracy," the national report issued in 1947 by US President Harry S. Truman's Commission on Higher Education, "Higher Education and Florida's Future" urged dramatically increased access to colleges and universities for the state's residents.[13] Predicting that Florida's rapidly rising population would lead higher education enrollments to skyrocket from 36,000 to over 132,000 students by 1970 (a number the report significantly underestimated; actual figures exceeded 240,000), it called on the legislature to establish at least one public, degree-granting institution and 18 new community colleges throughout the state.[14] Yet it was economic concerns that primarily drove the proposed expansion. Describing Florida as one of the fastest growing states in the nation, a promotional bulletin provided to state legislators noted that limited access to higher education institutions led to the state being ranked 36th in the nation in the number of students enrolled in a college or university. "Florida cannot expect to continue its remarkable rate of economic growth," the bulletin read, "unless it provides higher education facilities comparable to its neighboring states with which it competes for population, industry and investment capital."[15]

Growth in and around the Tampa Bay area was indeed extraordinary, with the metropolitan region's population growing from approximately 209,000 residents to over a million and a half between 1940 and 1980.[16] By 1970, Tampa Bay had become the third largest metropolitan area in the South, a transformation that resulted from a confluence of factors.[17] First, the area had multiple population centers. Thriving Cuban, Italian, and Spanish communities, for instance, comprised Tampa's "Latin" quarter known as Ybor City (economically, the area was a center of US cigar production).[18] The region also had vibrant African-American and Bahamian communities and was home to a variety of social and civic organizations, including the Knights of Pythias, the Prince Hall Masons, the Young Women's Christian Association, and the City Federation of Colored Women's Clubs.[19]

Second, as part of mobilizing for national defense in the years leading up to World War II, the federal government constructed MacDill Air Field at the lower end of the interbay peninsula, converted Drew Field municipal airport to military use, and established the 2,000-acre Hillsborough Army Air Field in northeast Tampa as a training base. At the height of the war, the Army Air Corps stationed over 40,000 soldiers at the three installations, many who later returned and made the area home.[20] Third, defense industries sprung up throughout the region, luring thousands of Americans still reeling from effects of the Great Depression to relatively well-paying jobs. At their height, the Tampa shipyards, for instance, constructed by industrialist Matthew McCloskey in 1942 to build ships for the US Maritime Commission, employed 16,000 civilians and maintained a weekly payroll of $750,000.[21] Finally, the City of St. Petersburg, located directly across the bay, amplified these developments, growing even faster in population than Tampa-proper throughout the 1940s.[22]

Still, the Tampa Bay region's growth was not unusual. Part of the emerging Sunbelt, which stretched from coast to coast along the southern part of the United States, Tampa's experience was shared by metropolitan areas such as Los Angeles, Phoenix, and Dallas. Historians have published dozens of studies examining the Sunbelt, its origins, significance, and, perhaps most importantly, whether the term describes an identifiable region with a shared political, economic, and social culture or a "state of mind" characterized by "an evolving brand of modern conservatism."[23] Amidst scholarly disagreement, most historians nevertheless contend that economic development stimulated by federal subsidies and tied to industrial growth in the areas of national security, defense contracts, military expansion, and technology catalyzed the Sunbelt's rise. This growth, according to Sean Cunningham, was "concurrently fueled by and cyclically reflected in" the expansion of postindustrial sectors of the economy, such as real estate, tourism, retail, and especially higher education.[24]

Although Florida's population had been on the rise for decades, following World War II the state experienced what historian Gary Mormino has described the "Big Bang."[25] In 1950, approximately 2.7 million people called the state home. Twenty years later, that number had reached over 6.7 million. "No other state matched Florida's velocity," Mormino writes, "and only California attracted more new residents during the 1950s" (Florida would continue its remarkable growth with a six-fold population increase between 1950 and 2000, a rate two times that of California's).[26] As members of the state's Council for the Study of Higher Education observed, however, educational provision failed to keep up with the dramatic expansion. In 1954, nine accredited private colleges and universities, three state universities, and five two-year junior or community colleges enrolled a total of only 36,000 students across Florida.[27] Moreover, segregation characterized these institutions, severely limiting educational opportunities for racial and ethnic minorities, particularly African-Americans.

The Council acknowledged that Florida's greatest areas of population growth were remote from the established public universities: the University of Florida in Gainesville, Florida State University in Tallahassee, and the historically Black Florida Agricultural and Mechanical University, also in Tallahassee. To compensate, they proposed building commuter institutions in high growth regions, permitting the state to save on the cost of dormitory construction, while students (who they expected would live at home) would save on the cost of room and board. Accordingly, Florida's Board of Control, the body that held authority over the state's public higher education institutions, took initial steps to establish a new university in the Tampa Bay area. After much wrangling over whether to locate the new institution in the City of Tampa or St. Petersburg, the Board chose a 1,694-acre tract near the northeast edge of Tampa.[28]

The Board's plan for the university thoroughly reflected the characteristics of a rising Sunbelt metropolis. Rather than building the institution in the city center, it was located in an area of anticipated growth, about nine miles from Tampa's central business district, on a barren site near the former Hillsborough Army Air Field (which the federal government turned over to Hillsborough County following the end of World War II). An industrial park was constructed nearby that, when combined with the new university, was expected to promote regional commercial and residential development as well as tourism (August Busch would open his brewery and beer garden in the vicinity just three years later).[29] Funds from the 1956 Federal Highway Act supported building roads and highways that dramatically increased access to the unincorporated area, while the conversion of Drew Field (which had also been decommissioned following the war) into an international airport further expanded access into and out of the region.[30] It was in that expanding metropolitan locale that Allen and his staff began the process of building a new four-year state university "from the ground up."[31]

The "New Vocationalism"

One of Allen's primary tasks in establishing USF involved hiring talented faculty willing to take a risk on a new institution. In doing so, his prime concern was that new hires emphasize teaching over all other responsibilities. As College of Liberal Arts Dean Russell M. Cooper later recalled, Allen instructed deans to select faculty members based primarily on "evidence of active, provocative engagement with students in the process of learning." Under Allen's leadership, Cooper concluded, "The most important criterion for advancement in faculty rank and salary was effective teaching."[32] Accordingly, when Allen addressed the university's charter faculty in September 1960, he identified teaching as the university's central function, noting that professors' duties were "teaching, advising and research"—in that order.[33] In his capacity as chairman of the institution's "Role and Scope Committee," USF's director of institutional research, Lewis B. Mayhew, affirmed Allen's emphasis on instruction when he drafted the university's mission statement. "Since the University is to be essentially an undergraduate institution," he wrote, "and since undergraduate students pose particular instructional problems, the importance of teaching and learning will be stressed. During its formative years graduate research will not be central but teaching will be all-important."[34]

Just months before USF opened in May 1960, Mayhew reported on a survey that his office had conducted of high school seniors attending schools in the surrounding region. The results confirmed much of what state legislators had anticipated when they established the university. Of the 607 prospective applicants, most had parents who had not attended college, while the parents of a substantial minority (235) had not graduated from high school. In addition, a majority of the students planned on living at home and commuting to the university, while many intended to enroll part-time and work part-time to finance their studies.[35]

The survey, however, also revealed a tension between students' educational objectives and Allen's institutional ones. Prior to arriving at USF, Allen served as a faculty member at the University of Minnesota and Colgate University, directed the New York State Board of Regents Division of Higher Education, and held the positions of vice president and acting president of the University of Florida in Gainesville. Having received his bachelor's degree in mathematics from Indiana's Earlham College, a Quaker-affiliated liberal arts institution, however, it was his undergraduate liberal arts experience that most informed Allen's goals for USF. Accordingly, Mayhew noted the problem that the survey results posed for Allen. Of the reasons students gave for wanting to attend college, the greatest number (228 males and 146 females) indicated "prepare for work," while far fewer (71 males and 56 females) noted "become generally educated." Of the specific occupations in which young men expressed an interest, well-paying fields such as business, engineering, and "pre-professional" were the leading choices, whereas young women ranked education (school teaching) and pre-professional as their preferences.[36] This data, Mayhew advised Allen, "presents evidence which is of considerable significance to the faculty of the University of South Florida." "The institution has been organized to give major emphasis to the Liberal Arts and Sciences," he continued.

> This institutional orientation needs to be reconciled with the overwhelming vocational concern of the first freshman class. This is not to say that these two are irreconcilable or antithetical. It does place the burden of motivation on the faculty. Students will need to be shown the explicit relevance of courses in the Liberal Arts for their personal aspirations.[37]

Allen's commitment to the liberal arts reflected his belief that USF should maintain as its primary concern the education of competent citizens, while also providing students with opportunities to prepare for future vocations. In an address to the university's first faculty, Allen observed,

> We believe that education for a person's civic responsibilities, education for personal responsibilities and education for family responsibilities, i.e., education for citizenship—if you will give a very broad definition to the

term "citizenship"—is too important to leave to chance. We are all citizens, members of families, and members of community groups. We must *all* understand human behavior, government, international relations, science, mathematics, philosophy, literature and fine arts.[38]

These comments were not simply rhetorical. One of USF's early marketing brochures, entitled "The University of South Florida: An Invitation to Learn," urged students *not* to attend the university if what they wanted was simply to "prepare for a job." "Consider a technical or trade school," it advised.[39] Similarly, the university's first catalogue urged students to "think twice" about enrolling if their primary objective was to achieve social status through a university degree. "[W]hile a college experience may be important to some persons for its supposed values of social prestige," the catalogue pronounced,

> this should not be the determining factor in deciding to go to college. There are many other ways to achieve such values and college is not designed as a place to spend four pleasant socializing years—and a good bit of Dad's bank account—waiting to grow up.[40]

As Mayhew's survey indicated, however, many students had other ideas.

By the time USF opened, the United States had become, as historian Lizabeth Cohen deftly documents, a consumer's republic.[41] Consequently, many Americans began viewing higher education as a commodity to be purchased solely for the credential it provided. In the minds of many, a university degree had become a ticket to the good life—a passport to the American Dream—practically guaranteeing the wealth necessary to fully participate in America's expanding consumer culture and achieve elevated social status.[42] As W. Norton Grubb and Marvin Lazerson write of higher education during this period, many students enrolled in colleges and universities, not to acquire "useful knowledge" or even practical skills, but solely because of "the possibilities for individual gain."[43]

Hoping to counter students' "overwhelming vocational concern," as Mayhew described it, Allen led the development of an undergraduate curriculum that during its first two years included coursework taken primarily in a College of Basic Studies. The College offered seven full-year courses in the following areas: Functional English (writing, reading, speaking, listening); Functional Foreign Language (French, German, Russian, or Spanish); Human Behavior—Effective Living and Thinking (psychology, anthropology, sociology, logic); The American Idea—America and the World (history, government, geography, economics, sociology, and anthropology); Natural Science (a choice of biological science—botany, physiology, zoology—or physical science—astronomy, chemistry, geology, physics); Mathematics (algebra, geometry, trigonometry, calculus, statistics); and the Humanities (philosophy, literature, religion, intellectual history, drama, painting, sculpture, music).[44] During their first two years, all undergraduate students took Functional English and five out of the six remaining courses. Faculty offered honors sections of each of the courses to students with more rigorous academic preparations.[45]

During the junior and senior years, students pursued a major in one of the university's three additional colleges—Liberal Arts, Business Administration, and Education. Although many students, especially those intending to pursue graduate and professional study in law, medicine or engineering, enrolled in the College of the Liberal Arts, the colleges of Business Administration and Education offered professionally oriented coursework. Even in these colleges, however, the curriculum tended toward liberal studies. USF's first catalogue, for example, described the College of Business Administration as serving a "specialized function" in preparing students for "responsible positions in business and industry," while also characterizing the program as "broadly conceived to provide a sound, fundamental education in the field rather than to train narrowly for specific jobs." "These broad foundations," it read, "serve as well for the longer future when new responsibilities come to those who are prepared to receive them in a day when change is the rule we must live by."[46]

With USF's institutional priorities established, academic program in place, and opening scheduled for September 26, 1960, the Registrar's Office began processing applications from a range of students, male and female, young and old. The first student to enroll reflected the student demographic the institution anticipated serving. Twenty-two-year-old Barbara Campbell graduated from a local high school, married, and had three children, ages three months, two years, and four years. At her mother's and husband's urging, she decided to apply to USF to study elementary education. Upon Campbell's admission to the university, the *Campus Edition of the Tampa Daily Times* (which served as the campus newspaper until students established their own in 1966) illustrated the community's awareness of the non-traditional students USF intended to enroll, noting, "Had it been planned, there could not possibly be a better, more suited person to be the number one student at USF than Barbara Campbell."[47] Along with Campbell, the university admitted 1,996 students between the ages of 16 and 68 who paid a modest $180 per year in tuition.[48]

Within a year, USF enrollments surged to 2,698 students (1,590 men and 1,108 women).[49] Almost all commuters, they nevertheless began establishing a student culture on the three-building campus, which, despite landscapers' efforts in planting 500 trees, experienced frequent sandstorms.[50] Allen, in an effort to maintain what he called an "accent on learning," insisted that USF neither participate in intercollegiate athletic competitions nor form a football team.[51] Students responded by establishing intramural sports clubs as well as a host of other extracurricular activities.[52]

Yet throughout this period, many undergraduate students at USF and on campuses throughout the nation enrolled for reasons that did not reflect Allen's accent on learning. In 1974, *The Chronicle of Higher Education* reported on a "new vocationalism" in higher education, which it identified as "the most notable trend" among college and university students.[53] Although undergraduates earlier in the century had pursued higher education as a means of professional preparation, the paper reported, students were now "very, very worried" about being gainfully employed immediately following graduation. Consequently, they were "abandoning theoretical, abstract, and purely academic fields" for those that led directly to lucrative jobs. One survey the article cited, for instance, revealed that the number of students who planned to "start making it" upon graduating had increased by over 10 percent in just one year. In contrast, the students who indicated that they planned to "work for political or social change" had dropped to less than 1 percent.[54] Similarly, a Carnegie Foundation report indicated that undergraduates majoring in the "professions," a category in which the Foundation included vocational and occupational programs, increased from 38 to 58 percent between 1969 and 1976.[55]

One explanation for the rise of the new vocationalism among students nationally was enrollment growth at public urban universities. As J. Martin Klotsche, Chancellor of the University of Wisconsin, Milwaukee, observed in 1966, "The fact that large numbers of urban students work while attending the university causes them to be job-oriented to their course of study."[56] Klotsche had direct experience with students' interest in occupational training. His branch campus was established in 1956—the same year as USF—and like USF served a non-traditional, urban student population. Within a decade of the Milwaukee campus' opening, Klotsche noted, the institution began responding to students' anxieties over future careers by offering an educational program that "overstressed" occupational concerns, resulting in a disproportionate number of students enrolling in programs such as engineering, commerce, and pharmacy.[57]

As both Klotsche and the prospective USF student survey that Lewis Mayhew conducted in early 1960 suggested, the new vocationalism had been years in the making, with higher education institutions responding to it for almost as long. During the 1960s, for instance, John Allen met increasing demands for occupational training by implementing a Cooperative Education Program to provide students with work experience. "Students today are frequently heard to demand that their education be made more 'relevant'," he announced by way of describing the program.

> I believe that the Cooperative Education Program is one of the most effective answers we have developed to this demand for relevance. A Co-op student alternates a term in college with a term on a job in business, industry, science or government where he learns to apply his knowledge and theories to practical matters.[58]

USF placed students with national agencies such as the US Food and Drug Administration, US Weather Bureau, and Smithsonian Institution as well as with regional offices and corporations including Florida Power Corporation, General Telephone Co., and Pratt & Whitney, allowing Allen to maintain the integrity of the university's liberal arts-oriented academic program while responding to student demands for relevance.[59] In contrast with the many students who sought well-paying jobs, however, cooperative education served relatively few. Consequently, as had occurred at the University of Wisconsin, Milwaukee, USF eventually revised its curriculum to stress students' vocational and professional interests.

Following Allen's departure, USF's second president eliminated the College of Basic Studies, revised the academic program to emphasize vocational and professional offerings (including, again as at Milwaukee, engineering, nursing, mass communication, marketing, and international business), and supported establishing branch campuses that offered a greater variety of pre-professional, technical, and occupational coursework.[60] Combined with a rapidly increasing commitment to sponsored research, USF slowly transformed into a research university. As Russell M. Cooper would later write of this period, "After 1971 the University's emphasis upon integrated general, liberal, and professional education dissipated.... The Vision of a teaching-learning community was obscured by departmental fragmentation and the priority on research and publication."[61]

The Johns Committee

A decade earlier, just as USF was establishing itself as Florida's newest higher education institution, the university's academic program, employees, and students, came under scrutiny by anti-communist reactionaries. During the Cold War, conservatives such as US Senator Joseph McCarthy took advantage of Americans' growing fears of Soviet influence to accuse federal employees and members of the armed forces, as well as Americans working in public institutions, of communist infiltration, espionage, and subversion. Although McCarthy was ultimately discredited for his sensationalist politics and odious investigative tactics, bodies such as the US House Un-American Activities Committee continued to level allegations of disloyalty and subversive activity against Americans well into the 1960s, often violating the civil liberties of those it accused. Such violations also transpired at the state level, including in Florida, where State Senator Charley Johns led the Florida Legislative Investigating Committee (FLIC, or Johns Committee, as it was more popularly known) in charging employees of state governments and agencies, especially public schools, colleges, and universities, of suspected communist activity.[62]

As with the McCarthy-led Senate Permanent Subcommittee on Investigations before it, the Johns Committee also adopted exposing "sexually deviant" government employees—a euphemism for homosexuality—as central to its work. Moreover, Johns claimed that the Committee had the authority to detect and report on "morally suspect" guest speakers, lecturers, and curricular materials on college and university campuses.[63] Accordingly, in November 1961, a little more than a year after USF opened to students, Johns informed Allen that under his authority as chairman of the FLIC he would lead an investigation into the presence of "practicing homosexuals" on the USF campus.[64]

Allen heard no more from the Johns Committee until May 1962, when he learned that its members had already begun working out of Tampa's Hawaiian Village Motel, secretly interrogating students about "alleged wrongdoing" at the university without an institutional representative present. Insisting that USF had nothing to hide and demanding that the investigation be transparent, Allen compelled the committee to continue its inquiry in a room on campus in the presence of a board of control observer and a university employee who tape-recorded all proceedings. The committee initially agreed and participated in the open process for two weeks beginning in May before reverting to holding secret hearings off campus with no observers present.[65]

This was not the first time conservatives sought to impinge on Allen's authority. Months earlier, Allen had intervened in a faculty decision to invite sociologist and labor organizer Jerome Davis to address students in the American Idea course. Davis had previously failed to receive tenure as a faculty member at Yale Divinity School, his supporters argued, because of his liberal political beliefs. After a local newspaper condemned USF administrators for permitting Davis to speak on campus, Allen revoked the invitation. The USF chapter of the American Association of University Professors (AAUP) reacted almost immediately, accusing Allen of violating academic freedom. Asserting the importance of free inquiry in faculty members' roles as researchers and teachers, and identifying academic freedom as an essential element in colleges' and universities' capacity to contribute to the public welfare, the AAUP declared:

> Institutions of higher education are conducted for the common good and not to further the interests of either the individual teacher or the institution as a whole. The common good depends upon the free search for truth and its free expression.... We regard the cancellation of Jerome Davis's lecture to "The American Idea" classes to be a violation of the basic principle of academic freedom and we respectfully request the reconsideration and clarification of the classroom rights and responsibilities of the teacher at the University of South Florida.[66]

Simultaneously, however, Allen received a raft of letters expressing support for his decision. "Because there will be so many organized efforts on the part of outright Communists to attack you for refusing to allow a person of such obvious disloyalty as Jerome Davis on this campus," wrote Sarasota resident Margaret Jefferson, "I am hurrying to offer you my gratitude for your honest, good sense. Believe me thousands of parents feel as I do."[67]

No evidence links the Johns Committee investigation to Allen's decision to revoke Davis' invitation. Rather, Allen claimed that he made the decision several weeks prior to learning that the Committee had begun its investigation.[68] Just one month later, however, and well after the committee's investigation was underway, Allen again revoked an invitation to a controversial scholar to speak on campus. Earlier that year, Dean Russell M. Cooper had offered Vanderbilt University Professor Emeritus of International Relations Denna Frank Fleming a one-year, half-time appointment at USF. Fleming, a revisionist historian whose book on the origins of the Cold War portrayed Stalin in a sympathetic light, accepted the appointment and traveled to Florida in March to meet with his future colleagues in the Departments of History and Political Science. Yet in late June, Allen decided against nominating Fleming for the USF position to the Board of Control. Allen then revoked the invitation, claiming that because the Board had never confirmed the appointment, the university never officially hired Fleming.[69]

Fleming responded in September by requesting that the AAUP investigate Allen's actions. The organization agreed, this time sending representatives to visit the USF campus the following March. Determining that the university had, indeed, violated Fleming's rights "under accepted practices of due process," the AAUP report concluded, "the investigation has revealed unsatisfactory conditions of academic freedom at the University of South Florida."[70] Consequently, the AAUP censured USF, a designation that remained in place for the next six years.

In May 1962, the USF student government issued a statement condemning the Johns Committee's investigation. Declaring it "an unnecessary infringement of academic freedom" and "a manifest feature of totalitarian government," student representatives described the probe as "stimulated by a handful of disgruntled people" and "disruptive to the entire academic situation."[71] Four days later, students similarly but satirically registered their opposition to the committee when, in the campus newspaper, they "welcomed" its members to USF, writing:

> We didn't know they were so interested in our welfare. What we admire most about these people is their vocabulary. Communist, homosexual, pornography; communist, homosexual, pornography. There is rhythm, beat and emotional impact in that chant. It will serve as the perfect background music for any play they wish to direct on campus during the next few weeks. We do hope it won't be the "The Crucible."[72]

Other students registered their resentment by posting signs around campus declaring, "I AM NOT A COMMUNIST," "I AM NOT A HOMOSEXUAL," "I AM NOT A HETEROSEXUAL." Yet others satirically advertised a "short course in book burning."[73]

Soon after, the investigation became a witch-hunt. As numerous scholars have shown, the Johns Committee consistently violated Americans' civil liberties in its effort to purge public schools, colleges, and universities of employees and students it deemed subversive, often with nothing more than hearsay as evidence.[74] For their part, Allen and other USF administrators vigorously protested the methods the committee employed in its probe. They did not, however, question the legitimacy of the committee's efforts to identify and dismiss gay men and women. In July 1962, just three months after Johns launched the USF investigation, Allen established University Policy Statement No. 45, which gave him authority to fire any non-tenured faculty member and suspend any tenured faculty member for "behavior involving moral turpitude."[75] Before the investigation ended, Allen used the policy to dismiss two USF employees "for conduct connected with a psychological disorder," another euphemism for homosexuality.[76]

Although Johns had assured Allen that he would receive a copy of the committee's final report prior to its publication, Allen returned from his August vacation to learn that Johns had pre-emptively released the committee's findings to the press.[77] Among the charges leveled at the university, committee members denounced USF faculty who criticized Allen for canceling the Jerome Davis lecture as well as those who questioned "the validity of orthodox religious belief" in their teaching and research. The report also singled out Allen for asserting that it would be permissible for a known communist to speak on campus "under certain circumstances." Regarding the university's liberal arts-oriented curriculum, the committee contended, "Much of the required and recommended reading material, though not obscene under the legal definition, contains course [sic], profane, vile and vulgar language." Concerning homosexuals on the faculty, however, committee members failed to uncover a "campus of evil," as one informant had characterized USF.[78] Instead, the committee found "this problem not to be of great magnitude at the University of South Florida at the present time."[79]

The release of the Johns Committee report engulfed USF in controversy. Allen fired the first volley in what became a months-long battle over the legitimacy of the committee's findings when he declared:

> The Johns Committee has generated an endless flow of unfair and harmful publicity. It has probed beyond its legislative mandate into the University's curriculum, its choice of assigned reading material, the religious and political beliefs of its faculty, the professional judgment of its administrators, and even into the private lives of its staff, seeking to build the most one-sided and damaging case it could against the institution.[80]

The American Association of University Women joined Allen in condemning the committee's work. "The Legislative Investigating Committee," a spokeswoman declared, violated academic freedom, to the considerable harm of the universities and colleges of Florida; and it wasted public monies in doing so. Its efforts at censorship were a limiting of the citizens' right to higher education, based on free inquiry within responsible and professional standards.[81]

Editorial pages, too, impugned the committee's probe. The editorial board of the *Daytona Beach Evening Times*, wrote:

> Now, the committee ... has issued a strong indictment of a new and promising institution of higher learning. We would say this committee is not fulfilling any burning desire to save the country. On the contrary, it would force it into a narrow mold; into a vacuum of ignorance and prejudice where it would be a helpless target of its enemies.[82]

Similarly, the *Sarasota Herald Tribune* editorial page claimed:

> a careful perusal of the report reveals that it is only a catalogue of unsubstantiated allegations by critics of one phase or another of university activity. Far from being a balanced evaluation of favorable and unfavorable findings, it is a prosecuting attorney's brief, and a rather flimsy one at that.[83]

The *St. Petersburg Times* also lambasted the Johns Committee, albeit in a more concise fashion. "To say that the Johns Legislative Committee investigating the University of South Florida, like the mountain, labored and brought forth a mouse would be to give it too much credit."[84] Finally, the *Washington Post* brought national attention to the committee's investigation in an editorial entitled "Campus Cops." "The University of South Florida," it read,

> has recently undergone one of those hazings at the hands of a state legislative investigating committee which were so lamentably fashionable about a decade ago.... The investigating committee under the championship of State Sen. Charley Johns seems to take the attitude that *all* learning is a dangerous thing.... Education is a profession which cannot be subjected to this kind of reckless interference by self-appointed campus cops. The best that can be hoped for from this Florida incident is that it may serve as an object lesson to other legislatures in how NOT to handle a university.[85]

Over the next several months, Allen continued to publicly defend the university while the Florida Board of Control issued a report that both exonerated USF and took issue with the Johns Committee's usurpation of the Board's authority over the state's educational institutions.[86] Nevertheless, throughout the episode, Allen and the Board's members remained sensitive to the broader political context in which they operated. In the fall of 1962, as controversy over the committee's report raged, Allen suspended Assistant Professor of English Sheldon N. Grebstein, whom committee members had singled out for requiring a course reading that contained language its members deemed vulgar.[87] Allen struggled to justify the suspension, in no small part because of the charge's dubious nature. In the essay "The Know-Nothing Bohemians," which Grebstein assigned his students, author and commentator Norman Podhoretz conducted a blistering critique of the writings of beat poets such as Jack Kerouac and Allen Ginsberg by quoting directly from their work, which included some profanity.[88] Grebstein disputed both the charge and his suspension, requesting that the AAUP again investigate USF for violating academic freedom. Allen, undoubtedly aware of the tenuousness of his action, appointed a faculty advisory committee to investigate the matter.[89] When the committee recommended Grebstein's immediate reinstatement, Allen quickly acted on the recommendation, but not without mollifying reactionaries by censuring Grebstein for poor judgment.[90]

In April 1963, John Allen addressed the state legislature, clearly and methodically correcting inaccuracies, remedying false claims, and rectifying misstatements in the Johns Committee report. Yet Allen's defense, according to historian Stacy Braukman, also affirmed the belief that scholars deemed to have communist affiliations (such as Jerome Davis) should not be permitted to lecture on campus and that faculty and students with "homosexual tendencies" should receive psychiatric treatment and withdraw from the university. He also reassured legislators that the Podhoretz article previously included on Sheldon Grebstein's syllabus had been eliminated from the curriculum.[91] "In spite of Allen's defense of his university," Braukman concludes,

> replete with statistics about faculty PhD rates and impressive student achievements, and his warnings that the FLIC would do irreparable damage to the state's academic reputation and economic potential, it was clear that he had been backed into a corner by conservatives, implicitly conceding to the forces who urged government monitoring of the moral standards and practices of publicly funded universities.[92]

Civil Rights

Few major public educational institutions in Florida escaped the Johns Committee's scrutiny. USF provided the committee with a likely target, however, because of the conflict between the university's integrationist policies and the committee's association of communist activity with efforts to desegregate public education. Prior to USF's establishment, Florida had three public universities: the all-White universities of Florida and Florida State and the historically Black Florida Agricultural and Mechanical University. As Larry Johnson, Deirdre

Cobb-Roberts, and Barbara Shircliffe have demonstrated, state officials, and especially the Board of Control, provided "enlarged, but still not equal" higher education opportunities to African-Americans and other minorities in the wake of the Supreme Court's *Brown v. Board of Education* ruling.[93] Board members, for example, supported by Florida State Supreme Court rulings, attempted to prohibit Virgil D. Hawkins, a Black man, from enrolling in the University of Florida Law School even after the US Supreme Court ruled in Hawkins's favor in 1956.[94] It took nine years, from 1949 when Hawkins initially filed his suit until 1958, for the first African-American to gain access to the law school.[95]

Yet, USF was a relative exception to the state's extreme practices of racial exclusion. When established, the university was open to women and men, Whites and racial and ethnic minorities. Although the institution did not at first actively recruit students of color, it admitted Ernest Boger, the university's first African-American student, just one year after opening. Boger later recalled that he "participated fully in all the college activities," served as a student assistant in the psychology and music departments, and lived on campus during his junior year. He remembered experiencing relatively few instances of "ugliness" as a consequence of his race. "We did have a different, progressive environment here at South Florida," Boger observed, "and I've always been very proud of that."[96] Indeed, before construction began on USF's first building, state officials considered converting a private but foundering institution, the University of Tampa (UT), into the new state university. Following the *Brown* decision in 1954, however, UT trustees rejected state overtures because they believed that White students would flock to their private, segregated institution rather than attend the public, integrated USF.[97]

Even so, by 1968 African-Americans comprised only 2 percent of USF's 12,500 students.[98] As they did throughout the United States at predominantly White institutions as well as historically Black colleges and universities, student activists at USF responded to the status quo by agitating for change.[99] Forming "One-to-One," an organization that sought to educate Whites "about the nature of the black struggle in America," students rallied for increased access to higher education for racial and ethnic minorities while seeking to engage the university community in "working more closely with residents of the inner-city for the betterment of the total society." Consequently, members claimed that One-to-One had "the implied, yet imperative objective of mounting a massive, concerted, and calculated war on poverty, ignorance, discrimination, racism, bigotry, and oppression, since they are all interrelated and involved in the dynamics of the current crisis."[100] Over the next several years, One-to-One members participated in "Get-Out-The-Vote" campaigns sponsored by the NAACP (National Association for the Advancement of Colored People) and SCLC (Southern Christian Leadership Conference), volunteered with a variety of Tampa social service organizations, hosted panels on racial oppression in American society, and published a newsletter that promoted Black Power. "The Civil Rights Movement is dead," declared one such issue, "destroyed by the position of its own short-sightedness, naivete, and miscomprehension. Now is the age of the human rights and Black Power, distinguished by its unmistakable turnabout in mood, direction, and leadership—Black Leadership."[101]

Allen responded to student activism as well as pressure resulting from federal legislation (especially the 1964 Civil Rights Act) by leading USF administrators in developing an affirmative action program to recruit and support "disadvantaged" students, a euphemism for students of color (particularly African-Americans).[102] In a program proposal to the faculty, Dean of Women Margaret E. Fisher and College of Basic Studies Dean Edwin P. Martin claimed:

> The history of the Negro student population, has been discouraging to those of us who feel strongly that education is the Negro's major access to eventual full membership in society.... Clearly, the absence of discrimination, although necessary, is sufficient neither to attract potential Negro graduates nor to promote their success on the campus.

The program, which the USF faculty senate approved after only 55 minutes of debate, included: faculty member visits to regional high schools to recruit and interview African-American candidates, admitting candidates in good standing regardless of their test scores and high school record, allowing recruited students to remain at USF for two years regardless of their academic performance, providing housing, financial assistance, remedial counseling and other support services, and developing a targeted advising program that paired students with faculty members who served as "sponsors" throughout the entire time the students remained undergraduates.[103] "Let me emphasize that you alone are the judge of whether these students will be admitted and continued in the university," Martin wrote to participating faculty after USF officially launched the program.

> None of them is admissible according to routine procedure, but we are, in effect, betting that some of them can become successful students because of the help you will give them during a transition period between high school and college.[104]

Beginning with 20 students, the university's program for disadvantaged undergraduates quickly expanded, partly because it benefitted from Upward Bound, a federally subsidized program that USF established on campus in 1965. Upward Bound supported talented low-income students, mostly racial and ethnic minorities, in succeeding in high school and preparing for college. Of the 90 students who completed USF's Upward Bound program as high school seniors in 1968, the university admitted 80.[105] Consequently, Allen felt confident enough in USF's efforts to recruit and support students of color that he included a section in his 1969 State of the University address to faculty and staff on the institution's commitment to diversity. "For the past several months," Allen reported,

> we have had a group of black students acting as advisors to our Director of Admissions. Their particular duty has been to seek out additional black students who have the potential to succeed at the University of South Florida, but who may or may not yet have shown or developed their full potential.

Allen then announced progress in USF's efforts to establish an Afro-American Studies program. "[W]e have been fortunate," he described,

> in securing three highly qualified black professors to teach courses in our Afro-American studies program which begins this Fall. Using core courses in Afro-American studies, on the same basis as our baccalaureate programs in Latin American and American Studies, we have proposed to the Board of Regents that we be allowed to offer a bachelor's degree in Afro-American Studies.[106]

Finally, Allen reminded his audience that the university had adopted an affirmative action plan "to insure equal opportunity for all persons, regardless of race, religion, sex, or national origin." "The plan," he emphasized, "applies to students, faculty, administration and staff alike."[107]

Although Allen undoubtedly portrayed USF efforts on behalf of racial and ethnic minorities in the most positive light possible, evidence indicates that the university was, in fact, ahead of Florida's other public higher education institutions on issues of civil rights and affirmative action. When US Office for Civil Rights Regional Director Paul M. Rilling wrote to Florida Board of Regents Chancellor Robert B. Mautz in February 1970 to report on college and university compliance reviews recently conducted throughout the state, he asserted that "nearly all of the institutions reviewed" had failed to discharge their "affirmative duty to adopt measures necessary to overcome the effects of past segregation." USF provided the exception. "The University of South Florida," Rilling observed,

> has established an affirmative action program which indicates that it has set goals and is making progress toward these goals in adding minority faculty members and students. Such actions on the part of other universities would suggest that they would be moving in a desirable direction toward providing equal educational opportunities for all students in the State of Florida.[108]

In an effort to further increase enrollment of students of color, Allen hired former Harlem Globetrotter Troy Collier in 1971 to serve as assistant to the vice president for student affairs. Tasked with reaching out to minority communities and encouraging students of color to apply to the university, Collier explained the disproportionately low enrollment of African-American students partly as a result of mistrust between members of the Black community and the predominantly White university. "Our main problem," Collier claimed,

> is to get everyone informed with the real facts—and to get those facts believed. Minority group people need to have confidence that we are doing everything we can to help and that they are really wanted and have at least a few friends.[109]

Over the next three years, Collier led an aggressive recruiting program that expanded the number of African-American students on campus from approximately 200 to over 1,000, with total minority enrollment rising to just over 1,700. The growth, Collier noted, placed USF within its 1974–1975 equal opportunity goals. However, a decade's worth of rising enrollments led USF's student body to climb to 21,000. Consequently, minority enrollment rose to a mere 8 percent of the total. "We are about 50 per cent of where we should be," Collier concluded. "We need large increases."[110]

Combined with congressional passage of the 1965 Higher Education Act, which established the first major federal student financial aid program, affirmative action efforts such as those at USF increased access to higher education for impoverished minority youth. Nevertheless, between 1960 and 1980, the large majority of students at USF—as well as those at most large urban public institutions nationally—were non-traditional mostly to the extent that they lived at home and commuted to campus. As Dongbin Kim and John L. Rury have demonstrated, although students aged 19 and 20 residing with parents and commuting became the largest category of beginning college and university students during this period, these students were primarily from solidly middle-class backgrounds.[111] Another decade would pass before urban public universities such as USF began enrolling a significant proportion of poor students and students of color.

Conclusion

As on many college and university campuses throughout the 1960s and early 1970s, USF students who engaged in civil rights activism came to link their commitment to racial justice with the growing movement to end the war in Vietnam. Initially, campus-based antiwar organizations were small and frequently berated. In late 1966, a group calling itself "Students for Peace and Freedom" formed for the purpose of working toward the end of hostilities in

Southeast Asia. When the organization's spokesmen announced during a radio address that the group's 15 members would, if necessary, resort to public demonstrations, listeners called in to denounce them.[112] The following year, when approximately 30 students organized a rally against the war and dropped balloons with peace signs from the second story of the University Center, first-floor onlookers reportedly stomped on them. While one student displayed a sign that declared, "Fight Poverty, Not People," another carried one that asked, "Who preserved your right to be here?"[113]

Over time, as the war escalated, greater numbers of students became involved in the antiwar movement. When the National Mobilization Committee to End the War in Vietnam (established by a coalition of activists in 1967 to launch nationwide antiwar protests) reorganized in 1969 as the New Mobilization Committee to End the War in Vietnam, USF students joined in the organization's support for a national Vietnam War moratorium on October 15 of that year.[114] Students hosted speakers, organized panel discussions, sponsored a "peace-rock" concert, and held an all-night vigil. Of USF's over 15,000 students, the student newspaper, *The Oracle*, estimated that approximately 2,000 took part in the event.[115]

Responding to the moratorium, John Allen demanded that student protests be conducted "in an orderly fashion."[116] Indeed, Allen's response to antiwar activism during the late 1960s reflected the approach he had taken to university governance throughout this tenure; he paradoxically maintained public support for the university by defending its character as an institution of higher education while seeking to regulate student, faculty, and staff activity. Acknowledging students' right to protest, Allen nevertheless denied a student petition to form a chapter of Students for a Democratic Society because of the disruption, he claimed, the organization created at other institutions. When students announced that they would challenge the decision by holding a rally outside of Allen's office, the president issued a policy statement taking a "hard line" against violent protest and promising to use off-campus police forces to restore order when necessary.[117]

In addition to growing confrontations with students, Allen became increasingly embroiled in disputes with faculty members who opposed America's involvement in Vietnam and sought to leverage the university's influence in ending the war. Consequently, the 62-year-old Allen announced in November 1969 that he was considering "retirement prior to the mandatory age."[118] Five months later, Allen came into open conflict with the University Senate when he refused to endorse the institution's first constitution. Although Allen had proposed that a committee comprised of faculty, staff, and students draft a governing document for USF, he was unsatisfied with the resulting draft, which he claimed reorganized the university rather than simply encoded already existing policies.[119] Allen's rejection of the draft catalyzed faculty and student dissatisfaction. "The Senate is on a collision course with the President," Associate

Professor William Taft warned in April 1970, "waving a red flag in front of him."[120] Just weeks later, the collision occurred. In an open letter to the student newspaper, Allen asserted that the committee had failed to successfully complete the charge he had assigned. Rather than a constitution, Allen now advocated a set of "by-laws" that, he claimed, might someday be used as the basis for a university constitution.[121]

Although Allen never admitted publicly that increasing antagonism between himself and faculty and students was the primary reason for his decision to retire, he nevertheless resigned several weeks later.[122] In hindsight, Allen's timing preserved his legacy. Assuming USF's presidency during higher education's golden age, Allen led an institution that in its first year of operation had a $2.4 million budget, ten buildings, 341 employees, and fewer than 2,000 students. By the time of Allen's departure, USF's budget had grown to $38.4 million and the university encompassed 73 buildings, over 1,700 employees, and almost 18,000 students.[123] Moreover, Allen's resignation spared him what was clearly a growing conflict with members of the faculty as well as the provocations associated with heightened student protests. As on many college and university campuses, the killings at Kent State University in May 1970 mobilized USF students and inspired more radical activism. Less than a year following Allen's resignation, an unidentified assailant threw a Molotov cocktail through the window of a campus building that had been recently rededicated the "John and Gracie Allen Administration Building."[124]

Many of the challenges that Allen confronted during his tenure resulted directly from the time and place in which he served as president. An entirely new higher education institution rather than a branch of an existing university, USF was beholden to neither tradition nor precedent. This context provided significant opportunity as well as risk. The university's commitment to nontraditional students, for instance, especially its relatively open access to students of color, made it a site of educational aspiration as well as a target of reactionary activism in a state with a history of deeply embedded racism. In addition, although USF's location in the nation's Sunbelt practically assured rapid institutional growth, such swift expansion made the university's focus on educating for citizenship—its "accent on learning," as Allen called it—difficult to sustain over time.

On the other hand, Allen underwent experiences that were hardly unique to USF. Many higher education administrators in the decades following World War II, especially leaders of public institutions, were compelled to manage dramatic institutional change while simultaneously navigating profound societal transformation. They answered calls to make traditional liberal education more "relevant," navigated fierce political conflicts during a time of heightened Cold War anxieties, and grappled with demands that their institutions become more accessible and culturally tolerant. Whether Allen was more successful than his contemporaries in meeting these challenges is difficult to know. What is certain, however, is that higher education's golden age intersected with profound political, economic, and social forces to produce a remarkably tumultuous era in American life. Characterized by growth as well as discord, expansion as well as confrontation, this period tested the skills of even the most adept administrators, ultimately demanding a quality of leadership rare in the history of American higher education.

Notes

1. Andrew Huse, *USF Chronology* (Tampa: Florida Studies Center, 2002), 16. *Tampa Daily Times*, November 3, 1957.
2. John S. Allen, "The University of South Florida," in *New Universities in the Modern World*, ed. Murray G. Ross (New York: St. Martin's Press, 1966), 153. Although states founded many higher education institutions between 1900 and 1956, USF was the twentieth-century's first public, four-year university that was neither established as a branch of an existing university nor the product of the transformation of a former institution (such as a teachers college).
3. See, for instance, Arthur M. Cohen, *The Shaping of American Higher Education: Emergence and Growth of the Contemporary System* (San Francisco: Jossey-Bass, 1998); Marvin Lazerson, "The Disappointments of Success: Higher Education after World War II," *Annals of the American Academy of Political and Social Science* 559 (1998); John R. Thelin, *A History of American Higher Education* (Baltimore: The Johns Hopkins University Press, 2004), especially chapter 7.
4. Thomas D. Snyder, ed., *120 Years of American Education: A Statistical Portrait* (Washington, DC: U.S. Department of Education National Center for Education Statistics, 1993), 66, 78.
5. Linda Eisenmann, *Higher Education for Women in Postwar America, 1945–1965* (Baltimore: The Johns Hopkins University Press, 2006); Charles Dorn, "'War Conditions Made It Impossible ...': Historical Statistics and Women's Higher Education Enrollments, 1940–1952." *Studies in the Humanities* 36, no. 2 (2009), 108–115.
6. Richard C. Atkinson and William A. Blanpied, "Research Universities: Core of the US Science and Technology System," *Technology in Society* 30 (2008), 34.
7. One the best known of these policy-makers was Vannevar Bush, former Dean of Engineering at the Massachusetts Institute of Technology, president of the Carnegie Institution of Washington, and author of the influential 1945 report, "Science: The Endless Frontier," whom President Franklin Roosevelt appointed head of the Office of Scientific Research and Development, precursor to the National Science Foundation. See G. Pascal Zachary, *Endless Frontier: Vannevar Bush, Engineer of the American Century* (New York: Free Press, 1997).
8. For a detailed analysis of federal research support during this period, see Roger L. Geiger, *Research and Relevant Knowledge: American Research Universities since World War II* (New York: Oxford University Press, 1993), chapter 6.
9. Atkinson and Blanpied, "Research Universities," 36; Kristjan T. Sigurdson, "Clark Kerr's Multiversity and Technology Transfer in the Modern American Research University," *College Quarterly* 16, no. 2 (2013), www.collegequarterly.ca/2013-vol.16-num02-spring/sigurdson.html.
10. See, for instance, Stefan M. Bradley, *Harlem vs. Columbia University: Black Student Power in the Late 1960s* (Champaign: University of Illinois Press, 2009); Joy Ann Williamson, *Radicalizing the Ebony Tower: Black Colleges and the Black Freedom Struggle in Mississippi* (New York: Teachers College Press, 2008); Laura Kalman, *Yale Law*

School and the Sixties: Revolt and Reverberations (Chapel Hill: University of North Carolina Press, 2005); Kenneth J. Heineman, *Campus Wars: The Peace Movement at American State Universities in the Vietnam Era* (New York City: New York University Press, 1994); Todd Gitlin, *The Sixties: Years of Hope, Days of Rage* (London: Bantam, 1993).

11 Allen, "The University of South Florida," 153.
12 Mark I. Greenberg, Andrew T. Huse, and Marilyn Keltz Stephens, *University of South Florida: The First Fifty Years, 1956–2006* (Tampa: University of South Florida, 2006), 6.
13 On the Truman Commission, see the special issue, "History of Access to American Higher Education Commemorating the Sixtieth Anniversary of 'Higher Education for Democracy: The Report of the President's Commission on Higher Education'," *History of Education Quarterly* 47, no. 3 (2007).
14 Russell M. Cooper, "Anatomy of a University: A Case Study in American Higher Education," 3–4. Folder: Anatomy of a University, Box 105, The Papers of Dean Russell M. Cooper, University Archives, Special Collections, University of South Florida.
15 "15 Statements of Fact on Florida's Higher Education Needs." Folder: House Bill No. 1007—June 18, 1955, Box 1, The Papers of John S. Allen, University Archives, Special Collections, University of South Florida.
16 On the history of the Tampa Bay region, see Karl H. Grismer, *Tampa: A History of the City of Tampa and the Tampa Bay Region of Florida* (St. Petersburg: St. Petersburg Printing Company, 1950); Nancy A. Hewitt, *Southern Discomfort: Women's Activism in Tampa, Florida, 1880s–1920s* (Urbana: University of Illinois Press, 2001); Robert P. Ingalls, *Urban Vigilantes in the New South: Tampa, 1882–1936* (Knoxville: University of Tennessee Press, 1988); Nancy A. Hewitt, "Economic Crisis and Political Mobilization: Reshaping Cultures of Resistance in Tampa's Communities of Color, 1929–1939," in *Women's Labor in the Global Economy: Speaking in Multiple Voices*, ed. Sharon Harley (New Brunswick: Rutgers University Press, 2007); and Steven F. Lawson, "From Sit-in to Race Riot: Businessmen, Blacks, and the Pursuit of Moderation in Tampa, 1960–1967," in *Southern Businessmen and Desegregation*, ed. Elizabeth Jacoway and David R. Colburn (Baton Rouge: Louisiana State University Press, 1982), among others.
17 Gary R. Mormino, *Land of Sunshine, State of Dreams: A Social History of Modern Florida* (Gainesville: University of Florida Press, 2005), 19; Richard M. Bernard and Bradley R. Rice, "Introduction," in *Sunbelt Cities: Politics and Growth since World War II*, ed. Richard M. Bernard and Bradley R. Rice (Austin: University of Texas Press, 1983), 8.
18 Gary R. Mormino and Goerge E. Pozzetta, *The Immigrant World of Ybor City: Italians and Their Latin Neighbors in Tampa, 1885–1985* (Urbana: University of Illinois Press, 1990).
19 Elna C. Green, "Relief from Relief: The Tampa Sewing-Room Strike of 1937 and the Right to Welfare," *The Journal of American History* 95, no. 4 (2009), 1016; Walter T. Howard and Virginia M. Howard, "Family, Religion, and Education: A Profile of American-American Life in Tampa, Florida, 1900–1930," *The Journal of Negro History* 79, no. 1 (1994).
20 Grismer, *Tampa*, 280–281.
21 Gary R. Mormino, "Tampa: From Hell Hole to the Good Life," in *Sunbelt Cities: Politics and Growth since World War II*, ed. Richard M. Bernard and Bradley R. Rice (Austin: University of Texas Press, 1983), 141.
22 Robert Kerstein, *Politics and Growth in Twentieth-Century Tampa* (Gainesville: University Press of Florida, 2001), 108.
23 Sean P. Cunningham, *American Politics in the Postwar Sunbelt: Conservative Growth in a Battleground Region* (New York: Cambridge University Press, 2014), 11.

24 Ibid., 17.
25 Mormino, *Land of Sunshine, State of Dreams*, 12.
26 Ibid., 12–13.
27 Russell M. Cooper and Margaret B. Fisher, *The Vision of a Contemporary University: A Case Study of Expansion and Development in American Higher Education, 1950–1975* (Tampa: University of South Florida, 1982), 3.
28 Ibid., 3–5.
29 Ibid., 5; Mormino, *Land of Sunshine, State of Dreams*, 108–109.
30 Cunningham, *American Politics in the Postwar Sunbelt*, 38.
31 Allen, "The University of South Florida," 153.
32 Cooper and Fisher, *The Vision of a Contemporary University*, 21.
33 "Address to Charter Faculty, University of South Florida, September 6, 1960." Folder: Allen, President John S., Personal Speeches, Box 1, The Papers of John S. Allen, University Archives, Special Collections, University of South Florida.
34 "Role and Scope of the University of South Florida by Lewis B. Mayhew." Folder: USF Role and Scope Committee, Lewis B. Mayhew, B2/F6, Box 2, The Papers of John S. Allen, University Archives, Special Collections, University of South Florida.
35 "Office of Institutional Research, University of South Florida, May 15, 1960," 2–4. Folder: Educational Program, B1/F32, Box 1, The Papers of John S. Allen, University Archives, Special Collections, University of South Florida.
36 "Office of Institutional Research, University of South Florida, May 15, 1960," 3–4. Folder: Educational Program, B1/F32, Box 1, The Papers of John S. Allen, University Archives, Special Collections, University of South Florida.
37 "Office of Institutional Research, University of South Florida, May 15, 1960," 3. Folder: Educational Program, B1/F32, Box 1, The Papers of John S. Allen, University Archives, Special Collections, University of South Florida.
38 "Address to Charter Faculty, University of South Florida, September 6, 1960," 7–8. Folder: Dr. John S. Allen Personal, Box 1, The Papers of John S. Allen, University Archives, Special Collections, University of South Florida.
39 "The University of South Florida: An Invitation to Learn." Folder: Groundbreaking, B1/F7, Box 1, The Papers of John S. Allen, University Archives, Special Collections, University of South Florida.
40 *Accent on Learning*, vol. 1, no. 1 (publication of the University of South Florida, Tampa, Florida, 1959), 32.
41 Lizabeth Cohen, *A Consumer's Republic: The Politics of Mass Consumption in Postwar America* (New York: Knopf, 2003).
42 See, for instance, Marvin Lazerson, *Higher Education and the American Dream: Success and Its Discontents* (New York: Central European University Press, 2010).
43 W. Norton Grubb and Marvin Lazerson, *The Education Gospel: The Economic Power of Schooling* (Cambridge, MA: Harvard University Press, 2004), 65.
44 *Accent on Learning*, 69–79.
45 "Planning a New State University by John S. Allen," 24. Folder: John S. Allen, Personal & Speeches, B1/F6, Box 1, The Papers of John S. Allen, University Archives, Special Collections, University of South Florida.
46 *Accent on Learning*, 62.
47 Huse, *USF Chronology*, 25. *Tampa Times University of South Florida Campus Edition*, February 4, 1963.
48 Huse, *USF Chronology*, 24. *The Tampa Times*, September 26, 1960.
49 "Report of Grade Point Averages Fall Term 1961." Folder: Annual Reports 1961–1962, B3/F13, Box 3, The Papers of John S. Allen, University Archives, Special Collections, University of South Florida.
50 Huse, *USF Chronology*, 24. *The Tampa Times*, September 26, 1960.

"Education for Citizenship" 75

51 In this regard, USF under Allen's administration was a significant exception to the national trend, especially at state colleges. See, for instance, Marc A. Van Overbeke, "'Out of the Quietness, a Clamor: "We Want Football!"' The California State College, Educational Opportunity, and Athletics," *History of Education Quarterly* 53, no. 4 (2013).
52 Greenberg et al., *University of South Florida*, 38–40.
53 Malcolm G. Scully, "Student Focus on Practicality Hits Humanities," *The Chronicle of Higher Education* 8, no. 18 (1974), 1.
54 Ibid., 1.
55 Verne A. Stadtman, "Happenings on the Way to the 1980s," in *Higher Education in American Society*, ed. Philip G. Altbach and Robert O. Berdahl (Buffalo: Prometheus Books, 1981), 105–106.
56 J. Martin Klotsche, *The Urban University and the Future of Our Cities* (New York: Harper & Row, 1966), 93–94.
57 Ibid., 93–94.
58 "State of the University. An Address to the Faculty and Staff of the University of South Florida by John S. Allen, President. September 26, 1969," 19–21. Folder: Dr. John S. Allen Personal, Box 1, The Papers of John S. Allen, University Archives, Special Collections, University of South Florida.
59 Irma Rubin, "A Foot in the Door and More: Co-Op Program Is a Triple Winner," *USF Magazine*, January 1983, 12–13.
60 USF established its St. Petersburg campus in 1965, Fort Meyers in 1974, and Sarasota-Manatee in 1975. Greenberg et al., *University of South Florida*, 55–58, 128–130, 126–131.
61 Cooper and Fisher, *The Vision of a Contemporary University*, 78–80.
62 For a complete account, see Stacy Braukman, *Communists and Perverts under the Palms: The Johns Committee in Florida, 1956–1965* (Gainesville: University Press of Florida, 2012). For events at the University of South Florida, see chapter five.
63 Dan Bertwell, "'A Veritable Refuge for Practicing Homosexuals': The Johns Committee and the University of South Florida," *The Florida Historical Quarterly* 83, no. 4 (2005), 412.
64 "Letter from Charley Johns to Dr. John S. Allen," dated November 9, 1961. Folder 13: Johns Committee Investigation, 1962: Comments from the Public Concerning, Box 4, The Papers of John S. Allen, University Archives, Special Collections, University of South Florida. On earlier "gay purges" at colleges and universities, see Margaret A. Nash and Jennifer A. R. Silverman, "'An Indelible Mark': Gay Purges in Higher Education in the 1940s," *History of Education Quarterly* 55, no. 4 (2015).
65 "Chronology of events leading to the Johns Committee investigation." Folder: Johns Committee Investigation, 1962, B4/F14, Box 4, The Papers of John S. Allen, University Archives, Special Collections, University of South Florida.
66 "Inter-Office Memorandum, dated March 2, 1962. From: USF Chapter, AAUP, To: President Allen, Subject: Academic Freedom. Signed by Donald R. Harkness, President, USF Chapter, AAUP." Folder: American-Assn. of University Professors USF Chapter, B4/F2, 1961–1962, Box 4, The Papers of John S. Allen, University Archives, Special Collections, University of South Florida.
67 "Letter dated March 1962 from Margaret Jefferson (of Sarasota) to President Allen." Folder: Comments and Criticisms of USF Program, 1961, B4/F4, Box 4, The Papers of John S. Allen, University Archives, Special Collections, University of South Florida.
68 "Address to the State Legislature, April 24, 1963, by John Allen," 2–3. Folder: F26, President Allen's Address to the State Legislature 4/24/63, Box 739, American Association of University Women, University Archives, Special Collections, University of South Florida.

69 "Letter dated December 17, 1962, from John S. Allen to Winston W. Ehrman, American Association of University Professors." Folder: National Association of University Professors, National—and local USF Chapter, B3/F15, Box 3, The Papers of John S. Allen, University Archives, Special Collections, University of South Florida.
70 C. William Heywood and Robert M. Wallace, "Academic Freedom and Tenure: The University of South Florida," *AAUP Bulletin* 50, no. 1 (1964), 56.
71 "We, the Executive Council, dated May 24, 1962." Folder: Johns Committee Investigation 1962, B4/F13, Box 4, The Papers of John S. Allen, University Archives, Special Collections, University of South Florida.
72 Huse, *USF Chronology*, 39. *Tampa Times University of South Florida Campus Edition*, May 28, 1962.
73 Karen Graves, *And They Were Wonderful Teachers: Florida's Purge of Gay and Lesbian Teachers* (Urbana: University of Illinois Press, 2009), 59.
74 See, for instance, ibid.; Bertwell, "'A Veritable Refuge for Practicing Homosexuals'"; James A. Schnur, "Closet Crusaders: The Johns Committee and Homophobia, 1956–1965," in *Carryin' on in the Lesbian and Gay South*, ed. John Howard (New York: New York University Press, 1997); Steven F. Lawson, "The Florida Legislative Investigation Committee and the Constitutional Readjustment of Race Relations, 1956–1963," in *An Uncertain Tradition: Constitutionalism and the History of the South*, ed. Kermit L. Hall and Jr. James W. Ely (Athens: University of Georgia Press, 1989); Bonnie Stark, "Mccarthyism in Florida: Charley Johns and the Florida Legislative Investigation Committee, July, 1956 to July, 1968" (Master's Thesis, University of South Florida, 1985).
75 Bertwell, "'A Veritable Refuge for Practicing Homosexuals'," 420.
76 Ibid., 421.
77 "Statement in response to the Committee Report, dated August 27, 1962." Folder: Johns Committee Investigation 1962, B4/F14, Box 4, The Papers of John S. Allen, University Archives, Special Collections, University of South Florida.
78 Bertwell, "'A Veritable Refuge for Practicing Homosexuals'," 416.
79 "Report from Florida Legislative Investigating Committee to the State Board of Control and State Board of Education. Investigation of University of South Florida, dated August 24, 1962." Folder: Johns Committee Investigation 1962, B4/F14, Box 4, The Papers of John S. Allen, University Archives, Special Collections, University of South Florida.
80 "Statement in response to the Committee Report, dated August 27, 1962." Folder: Johns Committee Investigation 1962, B4/F14, Box 4, The Papers of John S. Allen, University Archives, Special Collections, University of South Florida.
81 "Report and Resolution, Tampa Area AAUW Study of Academic Freedom and of Legislative Investigation of Florida Universities." Folder: National Association of University Professors, National—and local USF Chapter, B3/F15, Box 3, The Papers of John S. Allen, University Archives, Special Collections, University of South Florida.
82 *Daytona Beach Evening Times*, August 28, 1962.
83 *Sarasota Herald Tribune*, August 29, 1962.
84 *St. Petersburg Times*, August 27, 1962, 10-A.
85 *Washington Post*, September 24, 1962, A12.
86 "Report of the Special Committee of the Board of Control, dated September 14, 1962." Folder: Johns Committee Investigation 1962, B4/F14, Box 4, The Papers of John S. Allen, University Archives, Special Collections, University of South Florida.
87 Greenberg et al., *University of South Florida*, 72.
88 Norman Podhoretz, "The Know-Nothing Bohemians," *Partisan Review* 25, no. 2 (1958).

89 "Report to the President of the University of South Florida by the President's Faculty Advisory Committee on the Suspension of Dr. Sheldon Grebstein" dated November 9, 1962. Folder: F12, Grebstein Case, 1962, Report to the Faculty Committee, Box 739, American Association of University Women, University Archives, Special Collections, University of South Florida.
90 "Letter dated November 2, 1962, from William P. Fidler, General Secretary of the American Association of University Professors, to John S. Allen." Folder: National Association of University Professors, National—and local USF Chapter, B3/F15, Box 3, The Papers of John S. Allen, University Archives, Special Collections, University of South Florida.
91 Braukman, *Communists and Perverts under the Palms*, 163.
92 Ibid., 163.
93 Larry Johnson, Deirdre Cobb-Roberts, and Barbara Shircliffe, "African Americans and the Struggle for Opportunity in Florida Public Higher Education, 1947–1977," *History of Education Quarterly* 47, no. 3 (2007), 329.
94 *Florida ex rel. Hawkins v. Board of Control*, 350 U.S. 413 (1956).
95 Johnson et al., "African Americans and the Struggle for Opportunity," 345.
96 Interview with Ernest Boger, USF Florida Studies Center, Oral History Program, USF 50th History Anniversary Project, Interviewer: Andrew Huse, Date of Interview: December 2, 2003, Location: Tampa.
97 Huse, *USF Chronology*, 2.
98 "White, Negro Undergraduates at Colleges Enrolling 500 or More, As Compiled from Reports to U.S. Office for Civil Rights," *Chronicle of Higher Education*, April 22, 1968. At the time, USF enrolled 11,571 White students and 225 Black students.
99 On Black college and university student activism, see Ibram H. Rogers, *The Black Campus Movement: Black Students and the Racial Reconstitution of Higher Education, 1965–1972* (New York: Palgrave Macmillan, 2012). On Southern student activism, specifically, see Robert Cohen and David J. Snyder, eds., *Rebellion in Black and White: Southern Student Activism in the 1960s* (Baltimore: Johns Hopkins University Press, 2013), among others.
100 Otha L. Favors, "The Idea of One-to-One," *One-to-One Group Newsletter*, vol. 2, no. 2, October 30, 1968. Folder: One-to-One, Box 124, The Papers of Student Affairs, University Archives, Special Collections, University of South Florida.
101 "Black Power," *One-to-One Group Newsletter*, vol. 2, no. 4, November 27, 1968. Folder: One-to-One, Box 124, The Papers of Student Affairs, University Archives, Special Collections, University of South Florida.
102 On the development of such programs throughout the United States and especially in the South, see, for instance, Julie A. Reuben, "Merit, Mission, and Minority Students: A History of Debates over Special Admissions Programs," in *A Faithful Mirror: Reflections on the College Board and Education in America*, ed. Michael Johanek (New York: College Board Press, 2001).
103 "U.S. Senate OK's Bill for Negro Education," *The Oracle*, vol. 3, no. 1, July 3, 1968, 1.
104 "Memo to participating faculty dated August 12, 1868, from Dean Edwin P. Martin." Folder: USF Programs: Disadvantaged Students, B105/F41, Box 105, Papers of Dean Russell M. Cooper, University Archives, Special Collections, University of South Florida.
105 "State of the University. An Address to the Faculty and Staff of the University of South Florida by John S. Allen, President. September 26, 1969," 19–21. Folder: Dr. John S. Allen Personal, Box 1, The Papers of John S. Allen, University Archives, Special Collections, University of South Florida.
106 Ibid.
107 Ibid., 22.

108 "Letter from U.S. Office for Civil Rights, Regional Civil Rights Director, Paul M. Rilling to Florida Board of Regents Chancellor Robert B. Mautz, dated February 26, 1970." Folder: USF Programs: Disadvantaged Students, B105/F41, Box 105, Papers of Dean Russell M. Cooper, University Archives, Special Collections, University of South Florida.
109 Quoted in Greenberg et al., *University of South Florida*, 119.
110 *The Tampa Times*, November 15, 1974, 8-A.
111 Dongbin Kim and John L. Rury, "The Rise of the Commuter Student: Changing Patterns of College Attendance for Students Living at Home in the United States, 1960–1980," *Teachers College Record* 113, no. 5 (2011), 1058.
112 Huse, *USF Chronology*, 25. *The Oracle*, October 19, 1966.
113 Huse, *USF Chronology*, 25. *The Oracle*, October 18, 1966.
114 Huse, *USF Chronology*, 25. *The Oracle*, October 2, 1969.
115 Huse, *USF Chronology*, 25. *The Oracle*, October 22, 1969.
116 Huse, *USF Chronology*, 25. *The Oracle*, October 15, 1969.
117 Huse, *USF Chronology*, 25. *The Oracle*, June 26, 1968.
118 Huse, *USF Chronology*, 25. *The Oracle*, November 12, 1969.
119 Huse, *USF Chronology*, 25. *The Oracle*, May 13, 1970.
120 Huse, *USF Chronology*, 25. *The Oracle*, April 22, 1970.
121 Huse, *USF Chronology*, 25. *The Oracle*, May 13, 1970.
122 Greenberg et al., *University of South Florida*, 79.
123 Ibid., 79.
124 Huse, *USF Chronology*, 25. *The Oracle*, April 7, 1971.

4

THE REINVENTION OF HONORS PROGRAMS IN AMERICAN HIGHER EDUCATION, 1955–1965[1]

Julianna K. Chaszar

Honors education is flourishing in American colleges and universities. The National Collegiate Honors Council, the umbrella organization for these programs, experienced a doubling of attendance at its annual conferences in the last quarter century to over 2,000. Honors colleges, which entail a larger investment and more intensive programs, have grown from 23 to 140.[2] And in 2013, major public institutions felt a need to create a loose organization for Honors in Research Universities. This burgeoning interest seems linked, most likely, with the rising competition for high achieving students throughout American higher education, but especially among institutions in the selective sector. Honors designations are anything but new, having existed in various forms since the nineteenth century. However, the current programs focused on incoming students were devised and popularized in the 1950s.

A century ago inspiration came from emulation of the honors degrees of Oxford and Cambridge, awarded to students who pursued individualized courses of study and underwent comprehensive examinations. In the 1920s Oxbridge honors were given an American interpretation by Frank Aydelotte, who established independent honors studies for upperclassmen at Swarthmore College. This approach was widely imitated in a variety of formats, but with sparse participation. All these honors programs were restricted to juniors and/or seniors, and offered in one or more departments.

In the 1950s, honors studies were reinvented at public universities to provide more challenging courses to selected groups of entering "superior students." Honors programs for freshmen and sophomores, with appropriate work for juniors and seniors, became the American system of honors education. This development, the subject of this chapter, was spearheaded by Joseph Cohen, a philosophy professor at the University of Colorado, and the organization he founded to promote the honors movement, the Inter-University Committee on the Superior Student (ICSS).

From Oxbridge to Swarthmore: Honors before World War II

The authority on honors education in the first several decades of the century was Frank Aydelotte, president of Swarthmore College (1921–1939). Aydelotte traced honors work as then understood to about the turn of the century. Although Harvard had instituted what it called final honors in the nineteenth century, President Charles Eliot declared that system a failure in 1903:

> The system of Final Honors at graduation, which was instituted by the Faculty in 1867–68 ... has never been successful. Final Honors have never been sought by any significant portion of the graduating class, and have never really affected, in any large measure, the scholarship of the College.... Final Honors were intended, first, to promote a reasonable degree of specialization by departments, and secondly, to promote scholarship by large subjects as distinguished from success in single courses.[3]

Eliot's successor, Abbott Lawrence Lowell, resurrected honors as the means to strengthen learning: "There is in the College today too much teaching and too little studying," and "Every serious man with health and ability should be encouraged to take honors in some subject." Lowell admired the traditions at Oxford and Cambridge that brought a "union of learning with the fine art of living" and applied this approach to boost student learning at Harvard.[4] In 1914–1915, the Division of History, Government, and Economics introduced a general examination as a condition of graduation for all of its students and a new tutorial system to help students prepare for their exams. The other Divisions of the College followed suit within the next few years, and a student's results on courses, examinations, plus an additional honors thesis became the basis for awarding honors degrees.[5]

A few years after the introduction of general exams at Harvard, Swarthmore College under its new president, Frank Aydelotte, instituted a more sweeping reform that gave new meaning to an honors system. A Rhodes Scholar himself and founding editor of *The American Oxonian*,[6] Aydelotte sought to counteract an "academic lockstep" in American undergraduate education—the course and credit requirements aimed at the median student, leaving highly talented and motivated students unchallenged. To Aydelotte, honors societies and the practice of awarding honors at graduation based on grade average simply rewarded students for docility, rather than cultivating independence and creativity. Like other supporters of liberal culture, he condemned the fragmentation of disciplinary learning and an elective system that allowed students to take unrelated courses. Finally, he deplored Swarthmore's collegiate culture of Greek life and athletics, which had overshadowed academic life throughout American higher education.[7]

Aydelotte sought to strengthen the educational mission of the college by incorporating an honors model similar to the system he experienced at Oxford 16 years earlier.[8] Since 1830, Oxford had recognized the reality of differing levels of academic commitment among students by making it possible to prepare for either "pass" or "honors" examinations. The latter, known as reading for honors, carried the expectation of intensive independent work in preparation for demanding comprehensive examinations by external examiners. Members of the faculty were assigned as tutors to guide their students in preparing for the exams. Aydelotte felt the pass course at Oxford was probably less demanding than a B.A. program in an accredited American college or university, but the standards for the honors degree surpassed the requirements of the best American colleges in both quantity and quality.[9]

When considering the Swarthmore presidency, Aydelotte had obtained the support of the faculty for an experiment in upper-division, independent study leading to an honors degree. In 1921–1922 faculty committees began developing honors courses. The Oxford honors curriculum, *Literae Humaniores* (known as Greats), was their model, and each course was a cooperative effort between two or three related departments, allowing for concentration on a field without narrow specialization in one department. The faculty chose seminars over individual tutorials as the method of instruction; they also decided to abolish the course and hour system for honors students, make class attendance voluntary, and use comprehensive written and oral examinations with outside examiners to evaluate the students' achievements. The two courses prepared in time for the fall 1922 term were in English literature and the social sciences.[10] Honors work evolved into a major feature of Swarthmore College, growing from 11 students in 1923 to 146 in 1939. Participation grew to just over 40 percent of upperclassmen by the early 1930s and was still at that level in the 1960s. Aydelotte had, in Burton Clark's words, transformed the "organizational saga" of the college away from its prior emphasis on social activities and football, and Swarthmore became synonymous with honors education.[11] Convinced of the need to nurture talented undergraduates beyond his own institution, Aydelotte became an advocate for honors programs throughout American higher education.

In the 1920s a widespread concern for improving student learning produced a variety of initiatives and innovations. The National Research Council's Division of Educational Relations commissioned a 1921 survey aimed at "the discovery and special encouragement of upper-class students especially capable of development into research workers."[12] The division appointed a special committee, including Aydelotte, to report on existing types of honors programs throughout the country. The study revealed that honors options existed in the bulletins of 93 colleges and universities: 75 institutions offered honors work in addition to their regular requirements for graduation, while 18 institutions allowed honors work to supersede the regular requirements. The overwhelming majority of institutions in the first category, and all institutions in the second, were privately controlled.[13] The vitality of these programs was questionable, and enrollments were quite small even at institutions having active programs. Only those at Swarthmore, Harvard, and the University of Toronto involved a significant portion of the student body in honors-level work.[14] Honors programs were a principal focus for a series of conferences over the next three years (1925–1928), led by the Association of American Colleges and including other major higher education associations. However, momentum waned in the late 1920s as the Division of Educational Relations withdrew from gifted student issues, deciding that the topic extended beyond the scope of the National Research Council's mission.[15]

In the arena of undergraduate education, honors programs were just one of many contemporary innovations. Throughout the 1920s and early 1930s, college administrators and faculty implemented a variety of experimental programs, and publications issued by institutions and national organizations chronicled these initiatives. One account, *Changes and Experiments in Liberal Arts Education* (1932), identified experiments and innovations at 128 institutions.[16] In an address to the Association of American Colleges in 1935, Aydelotte praised the experiments that had taken place in the previous decade. The increasing use of tutorials and comprehensive exams, organizational changes in the university structure, and the availability of honors options seemed to him "nothing less than a revolution in our academic methods, destined to produce a permanent improvement in our college and university work."[17]

Aydelotte's 1944 study of honors programs, *Breaking the Academic Lock-Step*, optimistically summarized the interwar honors movement and called for further progress. Some institutions had introduced comprehensive examinations to supplement the existing, "fragmentary" courses. The tutorial system had been adopted more widely, and Harvard, Yale, Claremont, and a few others, had emulated the organization of Oxbridge-style residential colleges. Finally, Aydelotte observed that nearly three-quarters of institutions approved by the American Association of Universities distinguished between honors and regular students, or at least provided the option of doing honors work. (Whether students were taking the challenge was another matter.) "So strong is the impulse throughout the country to break the tyranny of the rigid course and hour system," he wrote in 1944, "that it affects many institutions which have so far been unwilling to provide any special facilities for their better students."[18]

Despite Aydelotte's enthusiasm, the honors movement by 1940 was wide, but not deep. These programs usually involved upper-division students, engaged them in independent study or laboratory work in their major subject, and culminated in some combination of a thesis and written or oral examinations. The departmental honors programs established in the interwar period were fragile. By one characterization: "These programs, inadequately financed, subsidized by eager professors who for short periods of time were willing to assume extra burdens of instruction, were scarcely legislated before they became moribund."[19] This was the case for the 20-some state universities that listed honors programs. Their difficulty, according to Aydelotte, stemmed from "the presence of a considerable body of students whose ability to do university work is distinctly below the average." He found that most of their programs were "strictly departmentalized" and had many weaknesses.[20] Nor did Aydelotte think it would be possible in the near term to include freshman and sophomores in honors work. Although he approved of "sectioning elementary classes on the basis of ability," he noted the difficulty of identifying high ability in entering students. Moreover, he associated honors with independent study, which was scarcely possible for students "largely occupied with work of a secondary-school character."[21] Hence, all prewar honors programs regarded the first two years of college as a time for demonstrating fitness for honors work.

Reflecting on the characteristics of prewar honors education, Joseph Cohen felt that Swarthmore's program had been significant, but limited in effect. Aydelotte and the Swarthmore faculty made an important contribution with their development of seminars, colloquia, and the idea of divisional honors. Despite wide publicity and Aydelotte's interest in improving undergraduate education beyond Swarthmore, the model's adoption elsewhere was curtailed by what Cohen described as "the inescapably elitist nature of his British model, the restriction to the upper division, and the atypicality of Swarthmore itself." In particular, "public institutions did not have the conditions that would enable such programs to thrive on their campuses."[22]

Joseph Cohen and Honors for the Superior Student

Conditions in the 1940s were not conducive to the honors movement, and in fact led to the abandonment of many upper-division programs with few students.[23] The war first depopulated campuses before converting them to wartime projects; and peace brought a deluge of veterans under the GI Bill, as eager to complete their studies as the colleges were eager to see them depart. The dialogue surrounding higher education fixated on issues of access and questions of general or liberal education. The President's Commission on Higher Education (1947–1948) raised a controversy by claiming that nearly half of an age cohort was qualified for college work. Subsequent investigations revealed that a large proportion of potentially superior students were not even attending college. Educationally, a consensus emerged by the early 1950s that all lower-division students should receive a common foundation of liberal education. Most colleges and universities reformulated their curricula in these years to approximate this goal.[24]

Higher education was further unsettled by the Korean War and the pall of McCarthyism. However, attention soon turned to the challenge of improving the quality of American education. Richard Hofstadter voiced a growing concern as early as 1952:

> mass education, if it has done nothing else, has caused American higher education to lose sight of the superior student with genuine intellectual concerns and has tended to pitch the level of its work too close to the lowest common denominator.[25]

The Fund for the Advancement of Education, an early Ford Foundation initiative, created the Advanced Placement Program in 1952 (transferred to the College Entrance Examination Board in 1955). It allowed students to take college-level courses at their high schools—usually in the 12th grade—and subsequently "test out" of introductory courses in their freshman year of college. The National Merit Scholarship Examination was created in 1955 and awarded its first scholarships the following year. Concern for high ability students was increasingly evident when in 1957 the Soviet launch of Sputnik gave it the urgency of a national crisis.[26]

Following the Sputnik launches, the reform tendencies of the previous decade—including the nascent honors movement—intensified. Excellence became the "watchword for education," as demonstrated by numerous publications: *The Pursuit of Excellence* (Rockefeller Brothers, 1958), Jacques Barzun's "The Place and the Price of Excellence" (1959), *Recognition of Excellence* (Edgar Stern Family Fund, 1960), *Encouraging the Excellent* (Fund for the Advancement of Education, 1960), and John Gardner's *Excellence: Can We Be Equal and Excellent Too?* (1961).[27] Discussions about excellence in education assumed an urgent tone. A report published in 1959 by the Fund for the Advancement of Education declared: "At this time in history, it is not overstatement to say that our very survival depends on excellence in higher education."[28] Joseph Cohen's long preoccupation with honors education at the University of Colorado was energized by swelling recognition of a critical need to develop America's talent.

Cohen was drawn to honors education both out of anger with an educational system that allowed students to waste years on routine and superficial education, and interest in the philosophical question of how true intellectuals could be produced, particularly in a democratic society. Additionally, he believed it was possible to improve higher education for all students, using honors programs as "a nucleus of quality," which would influence the rest of the institution "to work to make as many students as possible into first-rate products."[29]

Cohen's involvement with honors had begun in 1928 as a young instructor, shortly after he arrived at the University of Colorado from the University of Toronto. He joined a committee charged with revising a system that awarded honors at graduation based on course grades. After reviewing college catalogs and Aydelotte's 1925 report, *Honors Courses in American Colleges and Universities*,

> we persuaded ourselves at Colorado to inaugurate an honors program which once and for all would abandon the grade as the sole criterion for award of honors and would embrace a concern for honors achievement in general as well as departmental studies.

The committee and its supporters had to overcome opposition from "devoted grade addicts" and from departments that resisted giving up any control to an honors council. Cohen recalled:

> We won that fight in 1930 first with juniors and seniors; but, as time passed, the inner logic of experience gradually dictated the need to fight for the extension of the program, semester by semester, until we were beginning with entering freshmen. With hindsight, I would say that the basic good fortune of our program was that its proponents on the faculty—an ever-increasing number—had the wits not to let it die out.[30]

The program thus included general (lower division) and departmental (upper division) honors, and it aimed to cultivate an honors outlook rather than a concern for grades. Budgetary support increased gradually, although even a partial reduction in the teaching load for honors faculty was resisted. A part-time director of honors was appointed in 1940, Professor E. F. D'Arms, who led the program until he accepted a wartime government post. Cohen became director in 1943. The honors faculty were able to maintain the program through the war years by offering a series of "World Crisis Courses," and in 1946 the university established the Division of General Education, developed in cooperation with the Honors Council, that strengthened the general honors program.

In 1947, Cohen visited Columbia and observed the Colloquium on Important Books, and shortly after that Colorado created an experimental honors colloquium for seniors. The colloquium (or seminar) format, after some practice and improvement, proved to be so popular among the students that a junior colloquium was added, and the students pressed the Honors Council to extend this technique to the existing general honors theme groups, which were criticized for their resemblance to regular classes. The Council members "found ourselves doing all we could by exhortation and pleading with the honors faculty to follow the [colloquium] method. It was no easy task."[31] Cohen felt that the program weathered difficult times due to the Honors Council's willingness to make such adjustments. The University of Colorado's pioneering program of general honors and its ability to sustain its program over the years provided a valuable case study for other public institutions that were contemplating new or revised honors programs.

By the early 1950s, Cohen could look to longer-term issues. He conducted a survey of 110 institutions that revealed about half of them had no honors course or honors degrees based only on the calculation of final grade average. About 40 institutions went beyond grade average to offer some honors courses, but the overwhelming majority of those programs were departmental with "almost no attempt to cope with the problem of inter-departmental and interdivisional criteria for honors work." Only about 20 institutions had honors programs that clearly extended beyond the departmental approach.[32]

Cohen hoped to expand his investigation to a scope that would benefit the many institutions that, by their own admission, were frustrated with the poor quality of their honors programs or complete lack of honors education. At the urging of Glenwood Walker of the Graduate Record Examination, who had visited the university, Cohen wrote to the Fund for the Advancement of Education in 1952 to propose a continuation of his survey for an additional semester or two, followed by the preparation of a report that would document successful practices among institutions.[33] The Colorado's honors program was already being scrutinized by faculty and administrators at other institutions. In response to their requests, he wanted to provide information not only about the program he oversaw, but also compile descriptions of successful activities taking place elsewhere and possibly formulate models that different types of institutions might follow. Cohen listed three kinds of institutions he was most interested in visiting. First were those with strong programs for high-achieving students. These included Harvard's general education program inspired by the Redbook; Columbia's colloquia and contemporary civilization courses; the survey courses in Chicago's "Hutchins College"; and Wesleyan's Russell House.[34] A second list named colleges with "strong established departmental programs": including Swarthmore, Amherst, Brown, Harvard, and Oregon. The third list comprised selected institutions where the colleges of liberal arts were revising their honors programs: Cornell, Michigan, Ohio State, Indiana, Illinois, Minnesota, University of Southern California, Kansas, and Montana State.[35] Cohen's three lists testify to the widespread efforts to upgrade undergraduate education, especially for superior students, but also to the fragmentary nature of these efforts, the absence of any cross-institutional collaboration.

Although his project was not funded, Cohen continued to observe the evolution of honors programs throughout the country, which heightened his desire to provide assistance and encouragement for developing programs. In 1952 Cohen also wrote to Edward D'Arms, the former Colorado director of honors who now served as an Associate Director of the Rockefeller Foundation's Humanities Division, suggesting that the foundation help promote non-departmental honors programs at universities.[36]

In 1956, Cohen again contacted D'Arms, sending reports on Colorado's honors program from the past three years and informing him of developments since his tenure there.[37] D'Arms then wrote a memorandum to the officers of the Foundation recommending financial support to the program, noting that among state universities, Colorado had the longest and most impressive history of honors education. "There is continual groping for new ways in which to extend Honors work and to encourage capable students to enter it." However, the university administration "has never given proper recognition of support to the accomplishments of the Honors systems there." Cohen's efforts and voluntary contributions of time by faculty members had made the honors program successful. The surge in enrollments that could be expected at state universities made it especially important to encourage those institutions to pay attention to the intellectual development of their best students. A small sum of money could help strengthen Colorado's program and provide a model for other state institutions to follow.[38]

In response to D'Arms' memo, John Marshall, associate director of the Rockefeller Foundation's Division of Humanities, commented: "Perhaps even more important than direct assistance to the U. of Col. is a means of planting this important activity in a number of key places over the country." He suggested that D'Arms revisit the issue to identify "how RF aid might be most productive."[39]

D'Arms visited the Boulder campus for several days in late February 1956. He spoke with President Ward Darley, Vice President W. F. Dyde, Dean Jacob Van Ek of the College of Arts and Sciences, and Joseph Cohen. They agreed that the honors program at Colorado needed greater financial support to maintain its high standards during the impending enrollment boom, and that other institutions could benefit by becoming familiar with the Colorado program. Cohen frequently received requests for information on honors at Colorado, and in some cases institutions invited him to visit their campuses. While directing the Colorado program, teaching courses, and responding to requests for information, Cohen had no time to write up the lessons from 25 years of experience with honors education at Colorado.[40]

In May 1956, the Rockefeller Foundation awarded the University of Colorado a grant of $28,000 to expand its honors program, stipulating that UC help other institutions develop their programs. Accordingly, the grant included funds for travel by the program director, the organization of a national conference on honors education, and a program for visiting interns. The Foundation grant focused on the university's role in terms of the effects on overall quality of education. The impending increase in students would require greater numbers of faculty, despite a "growing scarcity of fully qualified teaching personnel," and this could lead to the "risk of serious decline in the quality of higher education." The Foundation saw in Colorado a means to counter that grim prospect:

> Among state universities, the University of Colorado is making a conspicuous effort to offset the decline through an honors program which recognizes the potentialities of superior students and which provides for the

faculty incentives in teaching that often are lacking when instruction involves large numbers of students. If this program at the University of Colorado has the significance the officers attach to it, its success might well lead to similar efforts in other state universities.[41]

Cohen used the Rockefeller grant to travel widely spreading the gospel of honors education and to organize a conference on honors, scheduled for June 1957.

In early December 1956 Cohen visited Ohio State, Indiana, Michigan, and Illinois. A second trip later that month covered UCLA (with representatives of UC Riverside and UC Santa Barbara in attendance), Oregon, UC-Berkeley, UC-Davis, Washington, and Montana State. A typical visit involved meetings between institutional representatives and Cohen regarding the institution's honors efforts and the program at Colorado.[42] The meetings allowed Cohen to assess where institutions were on the road to developing honors programs and identify issues that needed attention. This information-gathering also helped him prepare for the 1957 conference. He reported to D'Arms, "this travel is more important than I anticipated."[43]

The next set of site visits took Cohen to Texas, Oklahoma, Oklahoma A & M, Arkansas, Missouri, Kansas, and Kansas State. He met with an average of 30 or more people at each institution. Cohen observed:

> My experiences during my travels have given me a tremendous respect for the new spirit I detect everywhere in responsible administrative people, to say nothing of the faculties. An atmosphere of far greater maturity seems to have invaded our culture for all the denegration [sic] of many Angst-ridden elites, and for all the other-direction obsessionists. Am I being a naïve optimist again?[44]

By this time, honors education existed at some public institutions but was not widespread. According to a February 1956 internal memo that Edward D'Arms prepared for his Rockefeller Foundation colleagues, upon reviewing catalogs from a number of public institutions he found "nothing comparable to the Honors System at the University of Colorado." Most institutions with honors provisions were upholding the long-standing focus on departmental work in the upper-division years. The catalogs made no references to senior colloquia, use of the Graduate Record Examination, or a mandatory combination of general and departmental honors exams except at Colorado. The closest approximations he found were the programs at City College of New York and at the University of Oregon.[45]

Cohen discovered great interest and enthusiasm on his visits, with many institutions preparing to revise or introduce honors provisions. Some of these initiatives began before the Inter-University Committee on the Superior

Student took form: e.g., Michigan State University's new honors program was approved in 1956 after more than a year of study, and Ohio State University and the University Washington had reported progress with their honors plans.[46] A committee of University of North Carolina faculty began in fall 1953 to discuss what could be done for talented freshmen, and in 1954 successfully conducted an experimental general honors program with 25 students.[47] After visiting universities in the Southwest in early 1957, Cohen commented: "It is curious, the way land-grant colleges are turning to the liberal arts everywhere, and in this connection seem to be bent on honors programs."[48]

In May 1957, D'Arms advised Cohen that the Rockefeller Foundation's Division of Humanities was unlikely to provide further support, and he suggested that representatives of the Carnegie Corporation of New York be invited to the June conference.[49] Cohen visited the Corporation's headquarters in April and made a favorable impression on Frederick Jackson, Program Officer, and Robert Wert, Executive Associate at the Carnegie Corporation. Wert found Cohen to be "a walking encyclopedia and apparently an extraordinarily able missionary on behalf of honors work." A follow-up letter from Cohen received an encouraging reply from Jackson.[50]

One month prior to the June meeting, Cohen wrote again to the Corporation and invited Wert and Jackson to attend the meeting and witness the enthusiasm of its participants. Cohen was optimistic about the future.

> Personally I am confident that what has already transpired promises very rich developments and that the time is peculiarly ripe for these to be accelerated and expanded.... The trend will fit in with at least three new developments, the Merit Scholarship Corporation, the Advanced Placement Tests, and the expanded Woodrow Wilson program. I think that our conference is something of a pioneering affair and that it will have genuine results. My direct visits to universities ... make me feel confident that we are here dealing with no passing fashion ... I am personally prepared to devote much time in the next year or two to increasing the momentum of this trend.[51]

On June 24–28, 1957, 48 deans and faculty members from 30 colleges and universities met at Libby Hall on the University of Colorado campus. In preparation for the conference, Cohen had written a form letter describing the conference as "organized around the problems of the superior student and of possible honors programs in state universities."[52] A list of possible topics for the conference included the rationale for honors programs, with specific reference to "fundamental theoretical justifications and implications" and the problems of large universities. Administrative issues for discussion included budget, organization, personnel, counseling, and publicity. The obstacles of "faculty conservatism, inertia, and departmentalism" were also listed on the preliminary agenda, along with pedagogical and procedural questions: the effect of the course credit system on honors, types of honors work, and the extent of separation between honors and regular programs.[53]

The conference on the Superior Student produced a ten-page statement explaining why state universities needed honors programs, how such programs could be started and maintained, and how to garner national attention for honors education.[54] The attendees formulated several basic principles for honors education, including: starting programs in the freshman year if possible; accommodating the goals of liberal education as well as those of specific departments; ensuring that honors faculty and non-honors students would benefit from honors programs; and removing obstacles to "earlier, faster and more intensive studies" for gifted students. The conference also produced 11 specific suggestions for building a successful honors program. The first of these, however, noted that no single solution would apply to all institutions; rather, adjustments should be made according to local circumstances—"the problems and practicalities of each campus." The remaining points briefly addressed: faculty involvement, integration with the overall goals of the college, adequate structural and budgetary conditions, the selection of honors students, special facilities, counseling, program evaluation, liaison with high schools, and publicizing programs within and outside the institution.[55]

The June meeting was "the first step toward a systematic analysis of the need for new approaches to challenging the superior student."[56] It was felt that the expected, rapid increase in enrollments at state universities would endanger the quality of education. The appropriate institutional response would be to preserve and improve quality despite that increase. Programs for gifted students would promote academic excellence and would benefit not only their academic communities, but also prepare future college teachers and national leaders.[57]

Cohen was pleased with the proceedings, as evident in his report on the conference to D'Arms, who was unable to attend:

> The level of interest and discussion was high and sustained throughout the week—very little of mere deanish talk.... The variety of approaches within the membership of the conference was a genuine gain.... All the sessions seemed decidedly relevant and the problems were explored at every level. Though the state universities, big and small, remained the central theme, the land grant college and the high school received good initial attention.... The inclusion of private institutions ... enriched and deepened the approach.[58]

Although honors work had existed in some form since the late nineteenth century, the "relatively weak and ineffective form in which the honors idea has usually been put into practice" led Cohen and his colleagues to aspire to something better. Some programs in the past existed only on paper and others were confined to a tiny proportion of students or departments and lacked resources other than the commitment of a few faculty members who kept the honors idea alive. "When the honors scene of the last century is surveyed in terms of quality instead of number of programs, the need for a new effort is apparent."[59] A committee dedicated to honors education could encourage the needed changes, and the success of the conference boded well for the acceptance of such a body.

Carnegie Corporation Support and the Creation of the Inter-University Committee on the Superior Student (ICSS)

The June 1957 meeting was the beginning of the Inter-University Committee on the Superior Student (ICSS) as an organization, although it was first called the Conference on the Superior Student in the State Universities. The plan of action included the creation of a clearinghouse for information on honors education, additional conferences, promotion of greater cooperation between high schools, colleges, and graduate schools, and more research on high talent and ability.[60] In practice, the ICSS focused on the first two of these activities.

Frederick Jackson had attended the June meeting and became the main contact at the Carnegie Corporation. His notes from Boulder touched on several key aspects, including the uniqueness of the conference, the enthusiasm of its participants, the potential for a long-term significance, and the lack of foundation support for honors education. Jackson then contacted the Rockefeller Foundation to verify the likely discontinuation of its financial support "in this general area." John Marshall confirmed for him that "any further support of this sort of thinking was in the 'public domain'."[61]

In mid-October, Carnegie awarded the University of Colorado $2,000 for a meeting of the steering committee in Boulder on October 26, 1957, the purpose of which was to identify the various means through which the group could promote honors education. The 11-member committee included one representative from each of the following universities: Ohio State, Iowa State, Cornell, Minnesota, Texas, Michigan, California, Kansas, and New Mexico. Cohen and Walter Weir represented the University of Colorado. Each of these institutions had maintained or experimented with honors programs since at least the 1940s, some a decade or two longer. Cornell (1951), Minnesota (1950), and Ohio State (1955) were the exceptions.

Frederick Jackson urged the committee to consider activities that could be accomplished with minimal or no outside funds, in addition to those activities that would require substantial funding. Jackson also conveyed Carnegie's reluctance to support a permanent or semi-permanent organization, and suggested exploring existing organizations as potential homes for the committee's activities. The Corporation would "look sympathetically" on funding requests from the committee or individual institutions, but made no promises.[62]

The steering committee synthesized its discussions in an 11-page report to the Carnegie Corporation. The report reflected a refinement of ideas and recommendations from the June conference as well as deliberations that directly addressed Jackson's suggestions. The steering committee reiterated the need for a central clearinghouse of information on honors education, citing "snowballing requests" for summaries of the June conference and for general literature on honors programs. It noted, "the unofficial information service in operation at the University of Colorado has begun to strain its facilities seriously."[63]

The committee recommended that these activities be converted into an "Inter-University Committee on the Superior Student (ICSS)," and that its chief function be the operation of a formal information service.[64] Its activities would include the publication of a newsletter. A second role would be to organize regional conferences, beginning with the South and Northeast. The June conference recommended a national conference on honors education for professional schools, as well as "all-state" conferences. The steering committee also envisioned increasing the presence of honors education by writing articles for publications and recommending speakers for national and regional meetings of administrators and academic professional associations. Finally, the committee outlined a two- to three-week internship program at Boulder that would allow honors administrators from other institutions to visit instructors and observe the operation of Colorado's honors program.[65]

Despite indications by the Carnegie Corporation that it was reluctant to support a separate organization, the ICSS steering committee made a strong case for organizational independence in the short term. Negotiations to join a possible sponsor would delay work that was already in demand and to some extent already being accomplished informally. Finding an appropriate home for the ICSS was also problematic, given that existing agencies had neither experience in honors nor could be expected to provide sufficient emphasis. The steering committee argued that its "singleness of purpose enables it to concentrate its energies on this goal in a way not possible for existing established national organizations, most of which have multiple aims." The limited constituencies of national associations were a further deterrent. Administrators—the chief members of the national groups—certainly needed to be involved in planning and operating an effective honors program, but the cooperation of teaching faculty was essential: "At the heart of all promotional effort for honors programs there must be a direct appeal to creative faculty minds." Although the ICSS planned to work closely with national organizations, its status as an independent group would allow it to focus attention on faculty involvement.[66]

The steering committee continued to aim the activities of the ICSS primarily at large, publicly supported institutions. Such institutions faced problems that differed from those of small liberal arts colleges and required different approaches—a fact that "was clearly brought out at the June conference." The committee estimated that the ICSS and its information service needed three years of financial support, after which time they would become self-sufficient or close down if their mission to serve as "catalytic agents" had been fulfilled. The committee originally estimated it would need $170,000 for its proposed three-year program.[67]

Cohen submitted the formal grant proposal in late November 1957, and in it the committee requested a more modest budget of $149,500 for three years. In early December, a handwritten note to Cohen from Jackson's home address cautioned: "Don't count on anything, Joe, for there are many snags a proposal can hit as it goes over the rapids."[68] Nevertheless, in January 1958 the Corporation awarded a grant of $125,000 for a two-and-a-half year period to the University of Colorado for support of the ICSS.[69]

The University of Colorado at Boulder became the permanent headquarters for the new organization, with Cohen as director. The significant role he played in gathering supporters for the ICSS, his past experience as director of the honors program at Colorado, and his active promotion of honors education in general, all made him the obvious choice. Howard Quint, an assistant professor of journalism, replaced Weir and became the full-time managing editor for the newsletter.[70]

During the 1950s, the University of Colorado underwent a period of expanding enrollments, facilities, and programs in both teaching and research, and the institution attained a leading position in its region. Nevertheless, in 1957 it was still struggling to keep pace as "enrollments continued to climb and construction continued to lag behind constantly rising demand. The goal of excellence, pursued until then with little fanfare, remained an elusive dream."[71] The renewed focus on honors education enabled the university to address at least one of its concerns: how to promote high standards even as its classrooms overflowed with students. Honors courses permitted at least part of the student body and professoriate to strive toward excellence. The strengthening of the university's long-standing honors program and its backing of the ICSS may be viewed as a facet of the university's new policy of increased visibility and leadership. One historian of the university observed that the institution had changed from a state of seclusion into "an arena for conflicting interests, subject to a sense of urgency for solving contemporary problems."[72]

The ICSS's practical needs—funding and a physical home—were satisfied for the time being. Within a few months the organization was running at full force. It announced two broad goals in the first issue of its newsletter, *The Superior Student* (April 1958): to promote the sharing of information and production of new ideas and techniques, and "to stimulate nationwide discussion of the fundamental honors questions."[73] The organization would develop a strategy that combined personal contacts and printed materials to address its goals.

The honors movement that Cohen expanded into the ICSS was distinctive in two respects: it was originally focused on major public universities and it emphasized *general honors* for freshman and sophomores. These institutions were experiencing rapid growth in a heterogeneous student population, and thus had immediate concerns about the quality of their education. And, in keeping with earlier concerns about providing a common core of liberal education, they wished to enhance the educational experience of their most able students, especially in such courses. Once in operation, ICSS became far more eclectic, essentially welcoming any and all forms of interest in the honors movement, but its main focus remained the major state universities. The ICSS did not propose that a single solution would work at all institutions; instead, it provided general recommendations and encouraged institutions to do as much as possible according to their local circumstances. The first formulation of guidelines for a successful honors program occurred at the June 1957 conference in Boulder. The 11 points, entitled "Building an Honors Program," appeared in the inaugural issue of the ICSS newsletter the following spring (Appendix A).

The main characteristics of honors education in the 1920s and 1930s, according to Cohen, had been an interest primarily in recognizing and training future scholars (i.e., specialists), with honors work, thus focusing on the major field of study, and emphasized "the student's intellective, analytical, critical, and research prowess, not on his creative, intuitive, or symbolic powers."[74] In contrast, the ICSS adopted a broader definition of honors education that encouraged lower division honors work in general education in addition to upper division and departmental honors. It also took a less restrictive view of talent and talent recognition.

The ICSS continued to work on its guidelines after the initial formulation in 1957. In April 1959, Cohen presented a list of 13 points at the Eastern Invitational Conference, referring to it as "an inventory of some of the very specific procedures which on analysis I find being most advocated throughout the country." Although the list resembled the 11 points from 1957, it was more specific and added several new ideas, including, programs in (pre)professional areas; various formats for honors work (sections, seminars, colloquia, independent study); limiting the size of seminars to 5–20 students; selecting top faculty who are supportive of the program; and using honors students as research assistants or student advisors to the general student body. Cohen's reference to the new list as an inventory of procedures "being most advocated throughout the country" and its modification during conferences highlights the consensual evolution of the guidelines. Cohen felt some of the guidelines were solid while others were still being debated.

The steering committee's report to the Carnegie Corporation following its meeting in October 1957 had refined the concept of sharing information among institutions. "Concrete and up-to-date" information on the practical aspects of implementing honors programs was not readily available, according to the steering committee's report. To supply the "specific information that universities attempting to cope with the problems of honors desire and need,"[75] the ICSS launched *The Superior Student* in April 1958. As of August that year, the monthly publication circulated to roughly 3,000 recipients. The ICSS office reported receiving new requests at a rate of about a dozen per week during the summer of 1958.[76] The newsletter went primarily to tax-supported, four-year institutions, although the mailing list included some private institutions. It was addressed to presidents and deans of liberal arts, interested faculty members, college libraries, and chairmen of honors committees.[77]

Regional conferences were another significant part of the ICSS agenda. The steering committee, following the recommendation of the general conference in June 1957, designated the South and Northeast as the two regions that should have conferences early on, in order to achieve "national coverage." The June meeting participants had suggested that a conference on honors in professional schools be organized as well. The steering committee refined the idea to focus on land-grant institutions, since many of them were in a transitional stage of becoming "large universities with ever stronger colleges of arts and sciences."[78] Finally, the committee suggested that the ICSS encourage "all-state conferences" by both public and private institutions within a region, the organization and financing of which would fall to the participating institutions.[79]

The first regional conference took place in November 1958 in Louisville, Kentucky.[80] Earlier that year, Cohen made two rounds of visits to Southern institutions—25 in all—finding an "alertness everywhere" to the needs of high-ability students.[81] Representatives of 36 Southern colleges and universities attended the Louisville conference; the list included every state university in the South except the University of South Carolina. Several education associations also sent participants, some of whom were included in the program: Alvin Eurich of the Fund for the Advancement of Education gave the opening address; Charles Bish of the National Education Association, Frederick Jackson of the Carnegie Corporation, and Ned Bryan of the North Central Association of Colleges and Secondary Schools were panelists.[82]

Prior to the Eastern conference in June 1959 Cohen again prepared with visits to institutions in the region, meeting with faculty and administrators at about 30 Northeastern and Midwestern institutions.[83] Of the institutions Cohen visited in spring 1959, only eight did not send a representative to the conference at Ann Arbor, which attracted attendees from 37 colleges and universities representing a total enrollment of over 600,000 students.[84] In 1960, the ICSS continued its series of major meetings with a conference on gifted Black students (co-organized with Southern University) in Baton Rouge, and the Western Invitational Conference held at Berkeley (see Appendix B).

The ICSS helped organize the Baton Rouge conference at the request of Felton Clark, President of Southern University. In a letter to Frederick Jackson seeking financial support from the Carnegie Corporation, Clark explained that he hoped to focus attention on the encouragement of talent through honors programs while compensating for "deterring cultural factors" that impeded the identification and development of talent among Black youth. The conference participants came primarily from historically Black colleges in the Southeast and Southwest.[85]

The keynote speaker, John Hope Franklin, identified several difficulties that Black youth faced in the educational systems of the 1950s. Physical facilities in the South were improving, he noted, but this could be seen as a relatively easy way for authorities to create the appearance of improvements for Black communities without addressing the quality of educational programs. The task of identifying academically gifted students for honors work presented particular obstacles related to the suitability of standardized tests, developed with typical White high school students in mind, and the need for remediation, particularly in reading, even for many of those students who showed academic promise. Furthermore, the tension endured by talented Black youth in a White-dominated society was enough to endanger their academic progress. Franklin felt that in the course of regular classroom lessons about American values and institutions, questions about one's place in a society that was purported to be democratic and free could distract students from their field of study as they sought answers or, worse yet, could traumatize them.[86] Participants in the conference discussed the need to counter these challenges, through special programs to identify talented Black students and nurture them to the best of the institution's ability, even if it fell short of ideal standards. The Baton Rouge conference provided momentum and inspiration for that group of institutions, and several of them subsequently presented plans to their faculty for development or initial approval.[87]

In general, the success of the ICSS regional conferences varied. Institutions with honors programs in the formative stage would have found the content of the conferences useful as a means to consider options and anticipate obstacles. Institutions with established programs benefited less. Michigan State honors director Stanley Idzerda was dissatisfied with both the national conference at Boulder in 1957 and the Eastern Regional Conference at Ann Arbor. The agendas included too much about starting programs and not enough about how they should evolve once established, as was the case with MSU's program. Ohio State University (OSU) conveyed a similar sentiment that the regional conferences were unhelpful because of "the diversity of curricula, student personnel, and general educational aims among the colleges and universities represented." It felt that a conference of large state universities—perhaps a Big 11 group similar to other Big 11 committees—would have served OSU's needs better.[88]

The site visits were an effective spur to developments at a number of campuses. Cohen received letters stating the benefit of his consultations. The director of freshman honors at the University of Tennessee, Knoxville, for example, wrote that several members of the faculty were in favor of honors education for some time, but "the decision to begin this program was stimulated by your visit here in the spring of 1958."[89] The University of Georgia likewise reported that Cohen's visit in summer, 1958, along with the Southern

Regional Conference, had "definitely influenced" its move toward starting an honors program.[90] Frederick Jackson received similar remarks at the Carnegie Corporation. He wrote to the ICSS:

> I get a good deal of evidence that the work of the Inter-University Committee is paying off quite handsomely. People from universities, especially in the South, come in and tell us how much Joe's visits meant in stimulating them to develop a program on their particular campuses.[91]

By summer, 1959, Cohen's demanding travel schedule was increasingly a matter for concern. The Executive Committee discussed a division of labor among committee members in order to lessen the strain on Cohen. They also discussed a reorganization of the Executive Committee to make it more nationally representative.[92] These issues presaged organizational change, even as the honors movement gained momentum. In September 1959, Cohen reported on the status of honors education throughout the country. He noted that the following public institutions had strong programs or were "fully engaged" with honors education: Colorado, Howard, Illinois, Indiana, Iowa, Kansas, Kansas State, Michigan, Michigan State, Mississippi, New Mexico, North Carolina, North Carolina State, South Dakota, Texas, Wichita, and Wisconsin. Many others were in the process of working out new programs and had sent representatives to an ICSS regional conference or hosted a visit by the ICSS. Two institutions, Illinois and Wisconsin, had approved full honors programs, starting in the freshman year and extending to the upper divisions, which Cohen described as "a most important development for the country as a whole."[93]

Extending and Ending the ICSS, 1959–1965

July and August 1959 were "transitional months" for the organization, marked by staff changes, the preparation of Eastern Conference report, and the evaluation of past activities. Questions about the organization's future remained unresolved. In his September 1959 report to the Carnegie Corporation, Cohen proposed sending a letter to the 20 or more individuals who were most closely associated with the ICSS, asking them to share their opinions about past work and what future activities, if any, the organization should pursue.[94] Jackson advised Cohen to send the letter of inquiry to the Carnegie Corporation to resolve the question of the organization's financial future well before the upcoming regional conference in Berkeley, set for April 1960.[95]

The bulk of responses to Cohen's letter indicated a consensus in favor of prolonging the ICSS for at least another year or two with some shifting of its focus, as well as continuing the publication of its popular newsletter. The newsletter, declared one dean, had clearly benefited his campus, and he received "many favorable and grateful comments" from faculty on the mailing list.

"In higher education in the absence of such a periodical, there is simply no way of finding out just what is going on elsewhere except to travel extensively."[96] Jackson summed up the situation after meeting with Cohen in November 1959: "There is also considerable feeling that the center of emphasis of the ICSS program should change from how to organize, operate and finance an honors program to what the academic content of honors programs are and should be." The high demand for institutional visits by Cohen or other representatives of ICSS and the effectiveness of past visits warranted the continuation of that activity. Jackson opposed the expansion of the ICSS that Cohen had requested and recommended limiting any grant renewal to a period of one year. He advocated a shift in emphasis from public to private institutions, which were traditionally the benefactors of foundation patronage. The transition during 1960–1961 would entail finding a new director from the private sector. Jackson hinted at this change to Cohen and believed that "he has taken it rather well."[97] Jackson also argued for reducing Cohen's travel schedule so that Cohen would have time to begin writing "the kind of a report on Honors work, or book if you will, that he talks about and which I think he could undoubtedly do and do quite well."[98]

In his recommendation and overview of the grant proposal for the Corporation's Board, Jackson praised the effectiveness of the ICSS, noting, "that dollar for dollar probably more has been accomplished through this grant than through any he has handled." Institutional visits would be reduced, and travel would be divided more among Executive Committee members. Future conferences would be smaller and focus on specific problems rather than discussing how to set up an honors program.[99] The Carnegie Corporation ultimately agreed to provide a second grant of $140,000 allowing the ICSS to operate until July 31, 1962. The ICSS staff would continue to arrange conferences and site visits for the time being but curtail activities during 1961–1962, in accordance with the original plan of not creating a permanent organization.[100]

The renewal of its Carnegie Corporation grant in spring 1960 brought new areas into the portfolio of ICSS activities. The proceedings of the Western Invitational Conference in April 1960 reflected a shift in the organization's focus to more advanced issues, including research on honors education and the promotion of honors programs in professional fields. These topics proved resistant to the ICSS mode of cooperative, guided coordination. Both professional and graduate education had little interest in honors approaches, which would have disrupted established practices. Evaluation of honors programs occurred in individual schools, but a research program on the effects of honors programs was beyond the capability of ICSS or the wishes of its patron.[101] At the same time, the staff continued to monitor the development of new programs, provided assistance to institutions that requested it, and participated in regional and national conferences.

By fall 1961, the ICSS mailing list comprised 9,000 names. Staff and Executive Committee members had visited 230 institutions since the organization's inception.[102] The major ICSS event in 1961 was an invitational Conference of Honors Directors, held on June 20–23, 1961, in Boulder, with participants from 22 state colleges. Part of the agenda was devoted to issues that honors administrators were facing as their programs were implemented and matured, including faculty participation, goals of honors programs, selection and retention, departmental and interdepartmental content and organization, all-university honors programs, and women in honors education.

After 1960, a growing unease arose toward the contradiction between traditional roles for women as homemakers or as members of the workforce with limited career opportunities and the academic attainments of women in higher education. The postwar trend of early marriages created the impression that talented female students were more interested in finding a husband than in intellectual pursuits.[103] ICSS broached this subject with an article in *The Superior Student* by Margaret Mead, the eminent anthropologist and member of the ICSS Executive Committee for several years. She observed that talented females used to have at least a few years of freedom after college to pursue their academic and professional interests. Social norms had shifted in favor of earlier marriage, eliminating the intermission that women had before establishing a family.[104] This situation made the timing and format of education for women even more important in discussions about curtailing loss of female talent during and after college. Mead and others argued that women were discouraged from female ways of using language and ordering information. This assertion was not widely accepted, but it promoted the examination of how female students approached their academic work and raised awareness of the extent to which college studies were a male-dominated activity with few female role models.[105]

In 1961, the National Opinion Research Center conducted a survey of graduating college seniors and found that women, even those in honors programs, "tended to be more conventional, conforming, and cautious than their male counterparts; though better grade-getters, women honors students felt less adequate in their field than the male honors students." Sixty-five percent of the women had no vocational or psychological guidance during college.[106] At the ICSS Conference of Honors Directors, it was noted that three times as many men were attending graduate school although women outscored men on academic measures. The participants raised questions about the adequacy of current counseling for women, whether sex-segregated or unsegregated classrooms were better, and whether "we seek to turn superior women into superior men."[107]

The ICSS confronted these issues again in a 1964 conference on women in honors education. By this date, recognition had grown that "there is in fact a problem—that talented women in the United States are, in a real sense, the victims of social definitions that are becoming archaic."[108] The conference took place at Columbia University on May 20–23, 1964, organized in cooperation with the US Office of Education. Counseling was emphasized as an important facet of services for honors women, in order to make them aware of the different educational patterns they might face, encourage creativity and rigorous course selections, plan their educations around their other commitments, and help them "live with the frustration which accompanies being the member of a minority."[109]

By this date, however, the ICSS was already behind the curve of advancing feminine sensibilities. Notes filed by two female members of the Carnegie Corporation staff who attended the conference indicate that the discussions were not productive beyond exposing honors directors to some of the issues that women students faced. Florence Anderson concluded that "although most of them were in the position of running honors programs, many had a shockingly unrealistic image of the girls they were dealing with." Her colleague, Margaret Mahoney, noted that talented female students and professionals were all but missing from the conference roster.[110]

The ICSS staff and Executive Committee continued to assess whether the organization's life should be extended, and if so, how to go about funding its operations. The Carnegie Corporation was unwilling to continue its funding, and in discussions during spring 1960, the Executive Committee had anticipated curtailing activities in 1961–1962 in preparation for the conclusion of the Carnegie grant in July 1962. However, when that time came the Executive Committee decided the organization should carry on. In 1962, after polling newsletter recipients to find out if they would be willing to pay a membership fee, the staff found that many institutions were interested enough to bear some cost. As of October that year, 160 institutions had joined and others were still considering membership. The membership list included 73 state, 35 independent, non-denominational, and 52 denominational institutions (26 Protestant, 26 Catholic). Income from membership fees, determined according to institutional size and ranging from $5 to $400, amounted to $25,225.[111]

Membership fees alone could not sustain the organization, so the ICSS staff pursued other forms of support as well. One successful proposal won a National Science Foundation (NSF) grant of $89,100 for one year, to be used for "an extended study of the impact of Honors programs on the improvement of both learning and teaching in the sciences, social sciences and allied professional fields."[112] Although the NSF funds were devoted to a specific project, the grant helped the ICSS through its first year without Carnegie funds.

Cohen had visited the Rockefeller Foundation in December 1961 and, although no additional Rockefeller funds were forthcoming, he came away with valuable advice for approaching a number of family and corporate foundations, asking each to consider a grant of $10,000 to $25,000 per year for three years, beginning in July 1962. The strategy succeeded in finding the means to operate for three more years, up to mid-1965 when the ICSS closed its offices. Supporters included the Edgar Stern Family Fund (contributing $10,000 per year for the last two years), United States Steel Foundation, Fund for the Advancement of Education, NSF, Laurel Foundation, Pittsburgh Forgings

Company Foundation, and US Office of Education, in addition to 338 institutional memberships.[113]

When the Executive Committee met in Boulder on February 23–24, 1963, it decided that the ICSS "could be safely and definitely terminated as of June 30, 1965." Its activities would include continuing the clearinghouse function and newsletter publication, with six issues per year, assisting with publications related to the NSF sponsored projects, and publishing a book on honors education with Carnegie Corporation assistance. Campus visits would continue, as well as the encouragement of regional institutes and conferences. The ICSS would also carry on its collaboration with national agencies concerned with improving the quality of higher education and encouraging the development of evaluation techniques to measure the results and impacts of honors education. A possible extension of support from the NSF, as well as the funding from the US Office of Education, would be pursued, and the committee expected that existing national agencies would take over the main functions of the ICSS.[114]

By 1963, Cohen was no longer able to maintain his frenetic pace. Frederick Jackson suggested that he resign from the directorship in the summer and begin work on the long-delayed book on honors education. Cohen's resignation went into effect on September 15, 1963. The ICSS had set aside $9,600 from its previous Carnegie Corporation grant and the Corporation augmented that sum with $12,500 to help cover Cohen's salary while he prepared the anticipated book summarizing the honors movement.[115] Dr. Philip I. Mitterling replaced Cohen as Director and Editor-in-Chief and continued in that role until the ICSS officially ended its operations in 1965. Mitterling was closely involved in honors education at Thiel College, where he served as Dean and Professor of History until his move to Colorado.[116] Mitterling's appointment reflected the shift in attention to private higher education, in keeping with the Carnegie Corporation's wishes.

With the ongoing development of honors programs in mind, the ICSS worked on several publications aimed at sharing the experiences of the honors movement with institutions needing guidance or inspiration. Foremost among these was the volume Cohen managed to edit, *The Superior Student in American Higher Education* (1966). A second projected publication would have served as a practical manual "detailing and evaluating validated honors methods and approaches." The staff also intended to undertake a new inventory of provisions for talented students, more broadly conceived than the inventories of 1961 and 1963.[117] However, these latter projects never materialized.

A final conference took place in Denver in April 1965, where attendees formed a successor organization to the ICSS, the National Collegiate Honors Council. Still based at Boulder and with Walter Weir as its director, the new group differed from the old in that individuals, rather than institutions, formed the membership (although later institutions also became members). The National Collegiate Honors Council held national conferences and eventually began its own newsletter.[118] The ICSS issued its final newsletter, an index issue, in mid-summer, 1965, and documents that ICSS produced or collected were housed permanently in the Western Historical Collection of the University of Colorado Libraries at Boulder.

The ICSS and the Reinvention of Honors

A wave of interest in honors education that arose in the late 1950s shifted the focus from junior-senior specialization to general education for first- and second-year students, the approach that has continued to this day. At the forefront of the movement was the Inter-University Committee on the Superior Student, which provided information, communication, and advocacy for the movement. According to Joseph Cohen, director of the ICSS, the number of honors programs at American colleges and universities tripled between 1957 and 1965 (Figure 4.1).[119] He noted, moreover, that "numbers alone give no idea of the spread of influence. The main purpose of the ICSS was to serve as an instigator of cross-fertilization."[120]

New program formation tapered off in 1961–1962 as saturation was achieved among its initial constituency of large public universities. According to the ICSS Inventory of programs, all but a few state universities (including land-grant state universities) reported having honors program by 1961. About 80 percent of these institutions had introduced general honors work, with the remainder still offering only departmental honors. Although some of these universities had

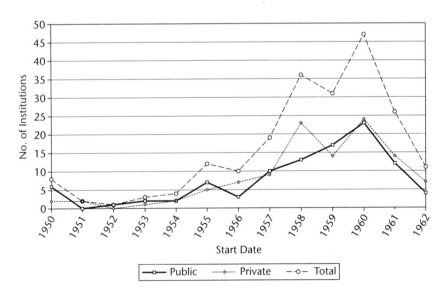

FIGURE 4.1 Inaugural Year of Current (1960s) Honors Program, 1950–1962

Source: ICSS Inventory, 1960–1963.

been experimenting with programs in the previous decade, the ICSS helped broaden their efforts to expand beyond the older, departmental model. Established programs, as at the University of Colorado, became stronger during the ICSS years. Other public universities introduced honors programs for the first time, now able to overcome obstacles that had previously prevented such initiatives, including "their inability to select students or limit their number, the pressures of public and legislative controls, and the struggle to establish an intellectual tradition."[121]

The 1957 launching of the Russian satellites was a catalyst for progress, but a desire to strengthen collegiate education, especially for the most talented students, had been growing since early in the decade. As Abraham Tannenbaum suggests: "the reaction to Sputnik might not have been so swift and strong if the critics' cries for change in our schools had not had a cumulative effect."[122] Institutions had embraced honors work primarily because of an ongoing dissatisfaction with educational standards (the lockstep), a recognition that talented students were needed in crucial fields, and concern for excellence in the face of increasing enrollments. Although the manpower perspective was influential in higher education, a humanistic perspective was a critical component of many honors programs, and democracy was now interpreted to mean differentiating between students in order to tailor education more closely to fulfill individual needs and potential. Honors advocates also argued for the cultivation of liberally educated individuals who could see beyond their specific disciplines and vocations to the broader interests of society.

The reform climate brought pressure on secondary schools to become better at identifying and nurturing academically talented students, and to improve the coordination of high school curricula and pre-college advising with higher education institutions. The National Merit Scholarship Program and Advanced Placement Program, along with state and local initiatives, encouraged higher standards in secondary education. Honors programs benefited as incoming freshmen were better prepared for college courses, and the connections that colleges and universities were building with local secondary schools facilitated recruitment of honors students. National testing and scholarship programs also tied in with the expansion of the higher education market away from primarily local and regional enrollment to national recruitment, which encouraged some academically talented students to seek more challenging post-secondary institutions further from home.[123] Honors education is credited with increasing graduate school attendance and the share of national fellowship awards at public universities.

As with any alteration of the status quo, there was some opposition. Critics felt that honors programs were elitist, detracted from the regular curriculum, and placed an unreasonable strain on institutional resources. Gaining faculty and administrative approval and participation could be a difficult process in the development of successful honors programs. However, anecdotal evidence supported Cohen's belief that honors programs could serve as "a nucleus of quality" that would improve standards throughout an institution.[124] Articles in the ICSS newsletter reported such effects within the authors' institutions. These effects naturally included the improvement of education for the students participating in honors options—or at least the perception of improvement, since learning was not measured in most programs. Faculty members involved with honors programs had the opportunity to depart from conventional approaches to their subject matter in classrooms with students who did not shy away from intellectual challenges. Honors programs could yield a general climate of increased respect for academic excellence among students and a spill-over of honors methods into regular courses. Students and faculty involved in honors work generally believed there was a spillover effect to the whole university.[125]

The claim made by leaders of the mid-century honors movement of a spill-over effect was more than a strategy to gain acceptance for their programs. Certainly, the immediate goal was to provide high-achieving students with appropriate intellectual challenges, and many organizers may have been content with that goal. The community benefit of improved institutional reputation that a strong honors program brings, and the resulting gains in recruiting and retaining high-caliber students and faculty, appear to have been explicit goals on some campuses. Numerous educators and administrators affiliated with the ICSS nonetheless viewed honors education as a source of innovation that could benefit more than the top 5 or 10 percent of students and their professors. The ICSS staff noted cases of honors approaches transferring into the regular curriculum and the honors spirit altering the campus climate. They believed such examples were not uncommon (though difficult to substantiate). A number of innovations in teaching and student life that honors programs brought have become commonplace in undergraduate education, including seminars, special first-year experiences, independent study, self-designed programs, and special interest housing. The current honors association, the National Collegiate Honors Council, similarly maintains that "the honors curriculum should serve as a prototype for educational practices that can work campus-wide in the future."[126]

A number of innovations advocated by the ICSS had not been achieved by the time the organization closed its offices. Although the widespread adoption of lower division and general honors offerings could be counted as a major success, little progress had been made in extending honors education beyond the liberal arts units of universities. After surveying 38 institutions with "all-university" honors programs, Dudley Wynn concluded that undergraduate professional schools in large public universities had not developed departmental honors programs, and that undergraduate professional college students were not participating significantly in general honors, despite all-university honors designations.[127] Furthermore, despite the longer tradition of departmental honors options, such opportunities were underdeveloped even within liberal arts units at many institutions.

The identification and recruitment of potential honors students continued to evolve during the 1960s. Although National Merit Scholarship lists helped institutions target finalists and semi-finalists, and improvements had been made in the design and utilization of testing, the recruitment and retention of honors students was an ongoing concern. According to Otto Graf, recruiting the best students to the University of Michigan could not be taken for granted:

> [T]he College was not totally successful in meeting competition for bright students from sister institutions within Michigan and from private and state-supported institutions elsewhere. Public and private universities and colleges were investing substantial sums for "academic tender," and a disappointingly large number of applicants admitted to our Honors Program chose to go elsewhere on generous scholarships and subsidies.[128]

Having successfully recruited students, institutions might soon find that some of them were not meeting expectations. Among the 11 Midwestern universities that formed the Committee on Institutional Cooperation (CIC), those that admitted students into honors programs as freshmen reported an attrition rate of 15 to 40 percent. A lower attrition rate of 5 to 10 percent was reported for students who entered honors programs after completing some college work first, which signaled an inherent problem for institutions offering freshman honors programs.[129]

Honors education has grown in surges since the mid-1920s. After the initial growth phase, programs did not flourish from the 1930s to the early 1950s due to low participation rates and their failure to "take root" in Arts and Sciences departments.

> About 1954, however, a new period of growth and development of honors programs began. The traditional departmental program continued, but it intersected with a whole series of new kinds of honors activities stimulated by a growing national concern for special treatment of gifted students in large public universities with ever-increasing enrollments.[130]

Despite the progress achieved during the ICSS period, Cohen and his colleagues did not feel that the honors movement had gone as far as it should. He wrote in 1965:

> Indeed, the honors movement is still in the explosive stage, as the final director of the ICSS, Dr. Philip I. Mitterling, avows. Some institutions are just coming to view honors programs as a possibility, others still have their doors closed to the idea. And many institutions with programs

formally labeled honors have far to go before they create programs of the [ICSS] type.... Meanwhile, the older programs encounter new problems calling for new solutions. There will be plenty to do in honors work for a long time to come.[131]

However, the decade of student rebellion after 1965 provided little encouragement for honors programs. A much larger growth period began around 1975 and continued to the late 1980s, after which the rate of new program formation leveled off. By 2000, the type of general honors programs championed and popularized through the efforts of Joseph Cohen and the ICSS had become a nearly universal feature at American colleges and universities.[132]

Appendix A: "Building an Honors Program"

1. Honors programs need to be adjusted to the problems and practicalities of each campus. There is no fool-proof program that will work everywhere.
2. Honors programs should develop with the understanding and support of the faculty. They should not be instituted by fiat.
3. Honors programs should not be separated from the total offering of the college. They should epitomize the aims of a true liberal arts education.
4. Honors programs require a structure and adequate budgeting in order to win a secure, recognized place within the university and in order to be effective.
5. Honors programs should start as early as possible, preferably in the freshman year.
6. Honors programs must involve thoughtful policies for identifying, selecting, retaining and advising students along with cumulative record-keeping.
7. Honors programs should have a central meeting place, like a lounge or library. They should provide honors students with library stack permits and other forms of special recognition.
8. Honors programs function more effectively when the honors counselor has authority in special cases to set aside, modify or substitute requirements in the best interest of the student.
9. Honors programs should include a built-in evaluation procedure so that errors can be detected and improvements devised.
10. Honors programs should involve liaison with the high schools, not only for recruitment purposes, but to encourage the creation of an honors attitude among the abler high school students.
11. Honors programs should be widely publicized to magnify their impact on the campus and elsewhere.

Source: "Building an Honors Program," The Superior Student 1, no. 1 (April 1958), 11

Appendix B: ICSS Conferences, 1957–1960

Founding meeting of the ICSS ("The Superior Student in the State University"), Boulder, Colorado	June 24–28, 1957
Southern Invitational Conference, Louisville, Kentucky	November 20–23, 1958
Eastern Invitational Conference, Ann Arbor, Michigan	June 14–17, 1959
"Conference on the Gifted Negro Student," Baton Rouge, Louisiana (co-organized with Southern University)	February 22–24, 1960
Western Invitational Conference, Berkeley, California	April 10–13, 1960

Sources and conference reports: *The Superior Student* 1, no. 7 (January 1959) for Louisville report; 2, no. 6 (October 1959) for Ann Arbor; 3, no. 3 (April 1960) for Baton Rouge; and 3, no. 5 (September 1960) for Berkeley.

Notes

1 Treated more fully in Julianna K. Chaszar, *The Reinvention of Honors Education in American Higher Education, 1955–1965*, Ph.D. diss., Pennsylvania State University, 2008. The author would like to thank Roger L. Geiger for assistance with this draft.
2 Rick Scott, "President's Column," *National Collegiate Honors Council Newsletter, Special Edition*, June 18, 2013.
3 Harvard University, *Annual Reports…, 1902–03*, 10–11.
4 Samuel Eliot Morison discusses this period of Harvard's curricular experiments in *Three Centuries of Harvard* (Cambridge, MA: Harvard University Press, 1936), 439–449.
5 Frank Aydelotte, *Breaking the Academic Lock Step: The Development of Honors Work in American Colleges and Universities* (New York: Harper & Brothers, 1944), 70–71. For a time, the tutorial system had two options, Plan A and Plan B. Plan A was intended for abler students and involved meeting more frequently with professors than in Plan B. As of 1944, honors at Harvard still required strong course records and results on the general exams—offered in 27 fields—and an honors thesis. In 1945 the A/B distinction was eliminated. Cohen noted that one-third of Harvard graduates took an honors degree in 1930, and by 1966 over 40 percent of students were taking honors. A strongly departmental approach to honors prevailed at Harvard, although special advising for high-ability freshmen and the Harvard Freshman Seminars showed that the institution was making some honors provisions for entering students: Joseph W. Cohen, in *The Superior Student in American Higher Education*, ed. Joseph W. Cohen (New York: McGraw-Hill, 1966), 14 (hereafter cited as *SSAHE*).
6 Aydelotte credited the introduction of the Rhodes Scholarships in 1904 with creating a greater awareness of English university practices among American scholars. As of 1944, Aydelotte counted over 1,000 ex-Rhodes Scholars in the United States and another 500 Americans who had attended Oxford or Cambridge on their own. Approximately one-third of these scholars had become teachers and administrators in higher education, and some of them were actively adapting British educational ideas to local circumstances—Aydelotte himself being the most renowned of these innovators: Aydelotte, *Breaking the Academic Lock Step*, 27–28.
7 Roger L. Geiger, *The History of American Higher Education: Learning and Culture from the Founding to World War II* (Princeton: Princeton University Press, 2015), chapter 9.

8 Cecil Rhodes, a former student at Oxford and believer in the value of British civilization, had provided in his will for a scholarship fund to bring outstanding students from the United States and the British colonies to Oxford.
9 Aydelotte, *Breaking the Academic Lock Step*, 21, 35. Aydelotte found that by 1944, most colleges at Oxford expected nearly all of their students to read for honors and that the pass degree was increasingly uncommon.
10 Ibid., 32–34.
11 For honors enrollments, see Burton R. Clark, *The Distinctive College* (New Brunswick: Transaction, 1992 [1970]), 188. Clark discusses the reinforcement of Swarthmore's new image (203–208).
12 National Academy of Sciences, *Report* (Washington, DC: Government Printing Office), (1920), 54, and (1921), 25. The annual reports document the evolution of the NRC's Division of Educational Relations' gifted student project, which resulted from a survey of research activities and capacities at colleges and universities that the Division began in 1919. The NRC, in collaboration with the American Association of University Professors, played a central role during the 1920s in promoting honors education: see Jane Robbins, "The 'Problem of the Gifted Student': National Research Council Efforts to Identify and Cultivate Undergraduate Talent in a New Era of Mass Education, 1919–1929," *Perspectives on the History of Higher Education* 24 (2005), 91–124.
13 Aydelotte warned that placing some institutions into the appropriate category based on printed descriptions was "almost impossible." The figures listed here are drawn from the 1925 edition: *Honors Courses in American Colleges and Universities*, 2nd edn, rev. [1st edn 1924], Bulletin of the National Research Council, vol. 10, part 2, no. 52 (April 1925), 12.
14 W. S. Learned, *The Quality of the Educational Process in the United States and Europe*, Bulletin no. 20 (Carnegie Foundation for the Advancement of Teaching: New York, 1927), 116–117, cited by Cohen, *SSAHE*, 12.
15 National Academy of Sciences, *Report* (1928), 57. By 1930, the Division of Educational Relations had become inactive.
16 American Association of University Women (AAUW), *Changes and Experiments in Liberal-Arts Education*, prepared by Kathryn McHale, part 2 of the *Thirty-First Yearbook of the National Society for the Study of Education*, ed. Guy Montrose Whipple (Bloomington: Public School Publishing Co., 1932).
17 Frank Aydelotte, "The Progress of the American College in Two Decades," *Bulletin of the Association of American Colleges* 21, no. 1 (March 1935), 26. The AAC was formed in 1914.
18 Aydelotte, *Breaking the Academic Lock Step*, 27–28.
19 Robert D. Clark, "Unsolved Problems in Honors," *The Superior Student* 7, no. 1 (November–December 1964), 5. The exceptions Clark noted were the University of Colorado's "General Honors" colloquia and "a scattering of successful departmental honors programs." Colorado's honors students were required to spend at least 200 hours reading works from a bibliography the departments provided. The top 30 percent of all students in Arts and Sciences were allowed to participate. The program had a slow start: of the 60 members of the class of 1932 who chose to enter the program in 1930, only 20 had remained during their senior year. Faculty were not sold on the idea either, since they did not receive reduced teaching loads in exchange for tutorial supervision under the honors program: Frederick S. Allen, *The University of Colorado, 1876–1976: A Centennial Publication of the University of Colorado* (New York: Harcourt Brace Jovanovich, 1976), 95–96.
20 Aydelotte, *Breaking the Academic Lock Step*, 90–105.
21 Ibid., 141–160. Aydelotte described exemplary programs for the first two years at Yale, Columbia, Stanford, and Chicago, but these approaches were not called "honors": Chaszar, *Reinvention*, 41–45.

22 Cohen, *SSAHE*, 10–11. Aydelotte's biographer, Frances Blanshard, wrote that Aydelotte would have preferred many small institutions federated in Oxford style as the means to accommodate the high demand for college education in the United States, rather than the development of large institutions: Frances Blanshard, *Frank Aydelotte of Swarthmore* (Middletown: Wesleyan University Press, 1970), 151.
23 Cohen noted that the war "was disastrous to many an honors program elsewhere." In order to maintain the Colorado program's momentum, the university established a series of "World Crisis Courses" and discontinued the requirement that students take both general and departmental honors—although about half of the honors students still chose both. Ibid., 22.
24 See Chapter 1, this volume.
25 Richard Hofstadter and C. Dewitt Hardy, *The Development and Scope of Higher Education in the United States* (New York: Columbia University Press, 1952), 115.
26 During these years, American colleges and universities began an extended process of "resorting" students on the basis of academic ability, made possible by the availability of information on students and institutions from national tests and from published handbooks: Caroline M. Hoxby, "The Changing Selectivity of American Colleges," National Bureau of Economic Research, Working Paper 15446 (October 2009).
27 The characterization of excellence as the "watchword" of the early 1960s comes from Louis Benezet, 44. He contrasts it to the watchword of the 1920s, progressive education, which was and remained controversial. Excellence, on the other hand, "has so far escaped nearly all controversy": Benezet, "The Trouble with Excellence," *Saturday Review*, October 21, 1961, 44. Nevertheless, it had many permutations, as a project of the Edgar Stern Family Fund showed. Its report, *Recognition of Excellence*, presented recent and ongoing research on excellence at all levels of schooling and phases of scholarly careers, as well as the current forms of recognizing excellence. The Fund's goal was to identify ways to improve the climate for "excellence of mind and spirit." The publication raised many questions and is a useful resource on how talent was being understood and rewarded: *Recognition of Excellence* (Edgar Stern Family Fund, The Free Press of Glencoe, 1960).
28 Committee on Government and Higher Education, *The Efficiency of Freedom* (Baltimore: The Johns Hopkins Press, 1959), 8. The report was written because of concern over increasing state control over higher education. Thus, although higher education was recognized as a matter of national survival, institutions felt that greater governmental control was unnecessary and unwise.
29 Cohen, *SSAHE*, vii–x, 20–23 (quotations from page ix).
30 Ibid., x. Cohen added: "It was a striking fact how many of the programs listed by Aydelotte in 1925 were practically nonexistent when I made my own first survey in 1952."
31 Ibid., 22–23. Cohen remembered D'Arms describing the role of honors director as "a thankless struggle with widespread noncompliance and consequent frustration."
32 Joseph Cohen, letter to Clarence Faust, President of the Fund for the Advancement of Education, December 11, 1952, Box 4, ICSS Papers, Archives of the University of Colorado at Boulder (henceforth UCBA). Cohen's survey data (1952–1953) are in three folders in the ICSS archives (UCBA), Box 4.
33 Ibid.
34 Also mentioned on this list were Stanford, Rutgers, Utah, Oregon, Florida State, and Ohio State universities. For Harvard, see Chapter 1, this volume. Wesleyan's Samuel Wadsworth Russell House, a prominent Greek Revival mansion completed in 1830, housed the Honors College from 1937 to 1996 and served as a hub of academic and cultural activity for the university and Middletown community: David B. Potts, *Wesleyan University, 1910–1970: Academic Ambition and Middle-Class America* (Middletown: Wesleyan University Press, 2015), 230–233.

35 Cohen to Faust, December 11, 1952.
36 Joseph W. Cohen to Edward D'Arms, August 1952, Box 4, ICSS Papers, UCBA. D'Arms became the first permanent, part-time director of the honors program after students and the Honors Council pressed for the creation of that position. He left the University during World War II for a government military post. During the few years he was director, writes Cohen,

> Professor D'Arms made a valiant effort at critical analysis of our first ten years. He pointed up the shortcomings of our awkward program, its promise, its dilemmas. He laid a firmer foundation for a series of honors offerings. Consultations with honors students became far more systematic.
> Cohen, SSAHE, 21

37 Cohen to D'Arms, January 12, 1956, folder 3806, box 445, series 200R, Record Group 1.2, Rockefeller Foundation Archives, Rockefeller Archive Center, Sleepy Hollow, New York (henceforth RF Archives-RAC).
38 Edward D'Arms, internal memo to RF staff, February 1, 1956, f. 3806, box 445, series 200R, RG 1.2, RF Archives-RAC.
39 John Marshall, penciled comment on D'Arms memo to RF staff, February 1, 1956, f. 3806, box 445, series 200R, RG 1.2, RF Archives-RAC.
40 Record of interviews at Boulder, Colorado, February 22–26, 1956, f. 3806, box 445, series 200R, RG 1.2, RF Archives-RAC.
41 Rockefeller Foundation, grant resolution, May 25, 1956: $18,000 was designated for the "administration and study of" the honors program at the University of Colorado, and $10,000 for "relations with other state institutions." f. 3806, box 445, series 200R, RG 1.2, RF Archives-RAC. A brief account of the grant and the early activities it supported appears in Cohen, SSAHE, 25–27.
42 Cohen later wrote:

> Without exception, there was intense listening and questioning at every institution – deans and associate deans, whole faculty committees, usually an Honors Committee and Educational Policies or Curriculum Committee, sometimes a General Education Committee, often all or some of the departmental heads, always specific selected individuals. I had to repeat the fundamental exposition frequently at the institution. I listened carefully to what they had to say about their own efforts.
> Cohen to D'Arms, January 28, 1957, f. 3807, box 445, series 200R, RG 1.2, RF Archives-RAC

43 Cohen to D'Arms, January 28, 1957, f. 3807, box 445, series 200R, RG 1.2, RF Archives-RAC.
44 Cohen to D'Arms, March 22, 1957, f. 3807, box 445, series 200R, RG 1.2, RF Archives-RAC.
45 D'Arms inter-office correspondence, February 21, 1956, f. 3806, box 445, series 200R, RG 1.2, RF Archives-RAC.
46 Regarding MSU: Paper by Stanley Idzerda, April 8, 1958, 2nd accession, Box 1, UCBA. Regarding OSU and Washington: Cohen, Letter to Robert Wert and Frederick Jackson, April 29, 1957, in Carnegie Corporation of New York Records, Columbia University Rare Book and Manuscript Library (henceforth CCNY Records), Series III.A (Grant files), Box 503, f. "Colorado, University of, Support of the Inter-University Committee on the Superior Student, 1957–1959."
47 Claude R. Rickman, *Trends in Provisions for Gifted Students in American Colleges and Universities, 1920–1955*, Ph.D. diss., University of North Carolina, 1956, 205–206.
48 Cohen to D'Arms, March 22, 1957, f. 3807, box 445, series 200R, RG 1.2, RF Archives-RAC.

49 D'Arms to Cohen, May 20, 1957, Box 4, f. "Rockefeller Foundation," ICSS Papers, UCBA. The Corporation had made a few grants related to honors and gifted education in the previous year. One was given to the University of Kansas for its honors program, one to the University of Louisville for a summer program for gifted high school students, and one in support of a conference on gifted education organized by the National Education Association: Carnegie Corporation of New York, *Annual Report* (New York: The Corporation, 1957), 79–80.

50 Jackson to Cohen, May 1, 1957, Box 4, f. "Carnegie Corporation," ICSS Papers, UCBA:

> You are in the middle of what seems to me to be one of the exciting developments in American public higher education today. We here at Carnegie Corporation will certainly want to keep in touch with you in the months ahead.
>
> Wert quotation: Robert Wert, Record of Interview, April 22, 1957, CCNY Records, Series III.A (Grant files), Box 503, f. "Colorado, University of, Support of the Inter-University Committee o the Superior Student, 1957–1959"

51 Cohen to Wert, May 22, 1957, Box 4, ICSS Papers, UCBA.

52 Cohen, form letter, undated, Box 3, f. "Carnegie Corporation Grant Steering Committee—Final Report," ICSS Papers, UCBA.

53 Council on Honors of the College of Arts and Sciences, Univ. of Colorado—Boulder, "Possible Topics for Discussion at Honors Conference," November 1956, Box 1, blue binder, ICSS Papers, UCBA.

54 "Decisions in Boulder," *The Superior Student* 1, no. 1 (April 1958), 10. Cohen wrote in *SSAHE*, 25–26, that 27 large public and private institutions were represented, with 43 attendees comprising both faculty and administrators.

55 "Decisions in Boulder," 11.

56 Cohen, *SSAHE*, 25.

57 "Decisions in Boulder."

58 Cohen to D'Arms, July 1, 1957, f. 3808, box 445, series 200R, RG 1.2, RF Archives-RAC.

59 "A New Beginning," *The Superior Student* 1, no. 1 (April 1958), 2.

60 "Decisions in Boulder," 10.

61 John Marshall, Record of phone call from Frederick Jackson, August 19, 1957, f. 3808, box 445, series 200R, RG 1.2, RF Archives-RAC. Foundations generally were hesitant to support projects in public universities, which were rapidly growing with state funds, preferring to compensate by favoring private institutions. Thus, Carnegie too would decline to maintain this successful project (see below).

62 Jackson suggested possible links to the Association of State and Land-Grant Universities or the American Council on Education. Record of phone conversation between Frederick Jackson and Joseph Cohen, October 9, 1957, CCNY Records, Series III.A (Grant files), Box 503, f. "Colorado, University of, Support of the Inter-University Committee on the Superior Student, 1957–1959." Cohen wrote a summary of the conversation: Cohen to steering committee members, October 9, 1957, Box 4, ICSS Papers, UCBA.

63 "Report to Carnegie Corporation," October 26, 1957, Box 4, f. "ICSS Materials," ICSS Papers, UCBA, 1.

64 The proposed name for that side of its operations was University Honors Information Service (UHIS).

65 "Report to Carnegie Corporation," 2–7. The internship program was originally envisioned as a semester-long experience. Due to budgetary constraints at interested institutions, however, this was reformulated as a two- to three-week seminar.

66 Ibid., 8–9.

67 Ibid., 9–11.
68 Jackson to Cohen, December 2, 1957, Box 4, f. "Carnegie Corporation," ICSS Papers, UCBA.
69 Jackson to Cohen, January 2, 1957 [*sic*—the letter must have been written in January 1958], Box 3, f. "Jackson, Frederick (2)," ICSS Papers, UCBA. The original budget request for $149,500 had included $16,000 in overhead for the University: Cohen, Letter to Jackson, November 26, 1957. Both the Anderson and Cohen letters are in CCNY Records, Series III.A (Grant files), Box 503, f. "Colorado, University of, Support of the Inter-University Committee on the Superior Student, 1957–1959."
70 Record of conversation between Jackson and Cohen in Chicago, March 3, 1958, CCNY Records, Series III.A (Grant files), Box 503, f. "Colorado, University of, Support of the Inter-University Committee on the Superior Student, 1957–1959."
71 Allen, *University of Colorado*, 166–168, 185. Enrollment reached a postwar low in 1951. From 1951 to 1963, the student body grew from 8,059 to 12,538.
72 Ibid., 204. An expansion of graduate education was part of this move toward greater visibility.
73 "A New Beginning," 2.
74 Cohen, *SSAHE*, 29.
75 "Report to Carnegie Corporation."
76 "Our First Six Months," *The Superior Student* 1, no. 4 (October 1958), 12–14.
77 "Notes and Comments," *The Superior Student* 1, no. 1 (April 1958), 16. The steering committee had suggested that all publicly supported four-year universities and private institutions with enrollments of 2,000 or more should receive the newsletter: "Report to Carnegie Corporation," 4.
78 "Report to Carnegie Corporation," 6. Michigan State and Penn State were named as examples of very large institutions in the target population. The steering committee noted that Colorado State, Michigan State, and Montana State had started honors programs.
79 An example of such a conference was the April 1957 meeting in South Dakota, where Cohen had been a speaker along with Everett Hunt of Swarthmore College. Ibid.
80 It was supposed to have taken place at the University of Texas–Austin, but the steering committee decided to look for another venue when conference arrangements became problematic due to segregation policies at UT: Joseph Cohen, Letter to Harry Ransom, May 15, 1958, Box 3, f. "Harry H. Ransom," ICSS Papers-UCBA.
81 Joseph W. Cohen, "Visit to the South," *The Superior Student* 1, no. 3 (June 1958), 19; and Cohen, "Some Notes on a Second Southern Visit," 1, no. 4 (October 1958), 11–12. Quotation from "Visit to the South," 19.
82 "ICSS Southern Invitation Conference," *The Superior Student* 1, no. 7 (January 1959), 1. This issue was devoted entirely to the Southern conference. Bish directed the NEA's Talented Youth Project, and Bryan was head of the NCA's Project on Guidance and Motivation of Superior and Talented Students.
83 "Notes and Comments," *The Superior Student* 2, no. 3 (April 1959), 19.
84 "ICSS Eastern Invitational Conference," *The Superior Student* 2, no. 6 (October 1959), 1.
85 Felton G. Clark to Frederick Jackson, February 5, 1959, Box 3, f. "Jackson, Frederick (2)," ICSS Papers-UCBA.
86 John Hope Franklin (Chairman, Dept. of History, Brooklyn College), "To Educate All the Jeffersonians" (Opening address at Baton Rouge conference), *The Superior Student* 3, no. 3 (April 1960), 6–8.
87 "Conference Follow-Up Notes," *The Superior Student* 3 no. 3 (April 1960), 27.
88 Stanley J. Idzerda (Dir. of Honors College, Michigan State University) to Cohen, November 17, 1959, and G. Robert Holsinger (Assistant Dean, Ohio State University)

to Cohen, January 8, 1960, both in Box 3, f. "Replies—Letter of Inquiry, First Set," ICSS Papers-UCBA.
89 James F. Davidson (College of Liberal Arts, University of Tennessee at Knoxville) to Cohen, December 21, 1959, Box 4, f. "Carnegie Proposal 1959–60," ICSS Papers-UCBA.
90 John O. Edison (Dean, Franklin College of Arts and Sciences, University of Georgia; includes comments by a colleague, Dr. C. Jay Smith, Jr.) to Cohen, December 22, 1959, Box 4, f. "Carnegie Proposal 1959–60," ICSS Papers-UCBA.
91 Jackson to Howard Quint, October 15, 1958, Box 3, f. "Jackson, Frederick (2)," ICSS Papers-UCBA.
92 "Agenda for ICSS Executive Committee Meetings, June 14 and 15, 1959, Ann Arbor, Michigan," CCNY Records, Series III.A (Grant files), Box 503, f. "Colorado, University of, Support of the Inter-University Committee on the Superior Student, 1957–1959."
93 Cohen, "Brief Survey of Results of ICSS to September 11, 1959," Box 4, f. "ICSS Materials," ICSS Papers-UCBA.
94 Ibid., 3.
95 Jackson, Letter to Cohen, October 20, 1959, CCNY Records, Series III.A (Grant files), Box 503, f. "Colorado, University of, Support of the Inter-University Committee on the Superior Student, 1957–1959."
96 Ewing P. Shahan, Dean, Vanderbilt University, to Cohen, December 22, 1959, ICSS Box 4, f. "Carnegie Proposal 1959–60," ICSS Papers-UCBA.
97 Blue sheet on conversations between Jackson and Cohen at the Carnegie Corporation offices, held on November 20 and 23, 1959, recorded by Jackson on November 24, 1959, CCNY Records, Series III.A (Grant files), Box 503, f. "Colorado, University of, Support of the Inter-University Committee on the Superior Student, 1957–1959."
98 Howard Quint, Letter to Jackson, December 31, 1959 (typed on January 2, 1960), CCNY Records, Series III.A (Grant files), Box 503, f. "Colorado, University of, Support of the Inter-University Committee on the Superior Student, 1960."
99 Jackson, Agenda sheet, February 25, 1960, CCNY Records, Series III.A (Grant files), Box 503, f. "Colorado, University of, Support of the Inter-University Committee on the Superior Student, 1960."
100 "Carnegie Grant to the ICSS," *The Superior Student* 3 no. 3 (April 1960), 1.
101 Chaszar, *Reinvention*, 135–144.
102 "ICSS 1961," *The Superior Student* 4, no. 5 (October 1961), 3.
103 Paula Fass termed this the "female paradox": *Outside In: Minorities and the Transformation of American Education* (New York: Oxford University Press, 1989), 156–188.
104 Margaret Mead (Associate Curator of Ethnology, American Museum of Natural History), "Gender in the Honors Program," *The Superior Student* 4, no. 4 (May 1961), 3.
105 Ibid., 4–5, and "Conflicting Views: Male and Female" (Responses to Mead's article), *The Superior Student* 4, no. 8 (March–April 1962), 16–23. Joseph Cohen had solicited responses to Mead's article in a general mailing posted in April 1961: Cohen, General mailing, April 17, 1961, CCNY Records, Series III.A (Grant files), Box 503, f. "Colorado, University of, Support of the Inter-University Committee on the Superior Student, 1961–1963."
106 Walter D. Weir, "Honors and the Liberal Arts Colleges," in Cohen, *SSAHE*, 90.
107 "Women in Honors," *The Superior Student* 4, no. 5 (October 1961), 10–11.
108 "Developmental Activities Program. Project Title: Talented Women and the American College: Needed Research on Able Women in Honors Programs, College and Society," Project proposal submitted to the US Commissioner of Education Under the Provisions of Public Law 53 (*c.* February 1964), Box 4, UCBA, 2. By this time, a number of important publications had highlighted the unique issues

of women. The project proposal cited Margaret Mead's *Male and Female* (1949), Simone de Beauvoir's *The Second Sex* (1953), Betty Friedan's *The Feminine Mystique* (1962), relevant chapters in Nevitt Sanford's *The American College* (1962), and Mabel Newcomer's *A Century of Higher Education for American Women* (1959). Other sources mentioned were Theodore Newcomb's studies of Bennington College, Katherine McBride's study of Bryn Mawr, US government publications, and the "literally hundreds of articles in both learned journals and popular magazines."

109 Walter B. Lovelace (ICSS Editorial Associate), "Talented Women," *The Superior Student* 6, no. 4 (May–June 1964), 36–37.

110 Florence Anderson, Notes on the conference on women, June 3, 1964, and Margaret Mahoney, Notes on the conference on women, May 27, 1964, both filed in CCNY Records, Series III.A (Grant files), Box 503, f. "Colorado, Univ. of, Support of the ICSS, 1964–1970." Cohen later expressed to Mahoney his regret that the book, *The Superior Student*, would not have a separate chapter about women: Cohen, Letter to Mahoney, January 25, 1966, CCNY Records, Series III.A (Grant files), Box 503, f. "Colorado, University of, 1961–1966."

111 In a survey of nonmembers on the mailing list, of 1,837 replies, 924 expressed the willingness to pay a subscription fee: *The Superior Student* 5, no. 1 (September–October 1962), 1–2. A list of members was published in the May–June 1962 issue, and additional members were listed in subsequent volumes, including the January–February 1964 issue which reported that 219 institutions and 19 associations had joined the ICSS: *The Superior Student* 6 no. 2, 46–47.

112 "A Continuing ICSS!" *The Superior Student* 4, no. 9 (May–June 1962), 1–2.

113 Cohen, *SSAHE*, 28 fn. Notes on Cohen's meeting at the Rockefeller Foundation, December 14, 1961, and "A Proposal for Federated Support," undated: Box 35, ICSS Papers-UCBA.

114 "Committee Sets Goals for Final Two Years of ICSS," *The Superior Student* 5, no. 3 (January–February 1963), 1, 40. Howard Quint expressed his doubt, however, that any educational organizations would want to take over the ICSS functions: HQ letter to Cohen, February 16, 1963, Box 4, ICSS Papers-UCBA.

115 Record of supplemental grant, April 15, 1963, CCNY Records, Series III.A (Grant files), Box 503, f. "Colorado, University of, 1961–1966."

116 Announcement in *The Superior Student* 5, no. 5 (May–June 1963), 3.

117 "The Final Year of ICSS," *The Superior Student* 7, no. 1 (November–December 1964), 1–2.

118 For an overview of the NCHC's evolution and recent activities, see: Chaszar, *Reinvention*, "Postscript: The National Collegiate Honors Council" in chapter 10.

119 For institutions and types of honors programs, see ibid., Appendix D.

120 Cohen, *SSAHE*, xii–xiii.

121 Ibid., 9.

122 Abraham J. Tannenbaum, "Pre-Sputnik to Post-Watergate Concern About the Gifted," in *The Gifted and the Talented: Their Education and Development*, ed. A. Harry Passow (Chicago: University of Chicago Press, 1979), 10.

123 Hoxby, "Changing Selectivity of American Colleges."

124 Cohen, *SSAHE*, vii–x, 20–23 (quotations from p. ix).

125 Wynn, in ibid., 135.

126 NCHC, thirteenth point from "Basic Characteristics of a Fully-Developed Honors Program," handout approved by the NCHC Executive Committee, March 3, 1994.

127 Dudley Wynn, "Honors and the University," in *SSAHE*, 135.

128 Otto G. Graf, "The Honors Program" (January 1980), in *The University of Michigan: An Encyclopedic Survey*, ed. William B. Shaw, http://quod.lib.umich.edu/u/umsurvey/, 8–9.

129 Arthur D. Pickett (Associate Director, University of Illinois Honors Program), "Honors Conference Reports: C.I.C.," *The Superior Student* 6, no. 3 (March–April 1964), 37.
130 George Waggoner, in *SSAHE*, 150.
131 Cohen, *SSAHE*, xiv.
132 David P. Baker, Sean Reardon, and Kate Riordan, "Creating the Upper Track in American Higher Education: An Organizational Ecology of the Rise and Spread of Honors Education," unpublished paper (2000).

5

COLLECTIVE BARGAINING AND COLLEGE FACULTY

Illinois in the 1960s

Timothy Reese Cain

Unionization is a significant part of modern American higher education, with more than 400,000 faculty and graduate assistants at over 1,100 colleges and universities covered by bargained contracts and thousands more otherwise affiliated with organized labor.[1] The unionization of college faculty has a long history, dating to the organization of the first American Federation of Teachers (AFT) local at Howard University in 1918, but it substantially grew and changed in the mid-to-late 1960s with significant efforts for and success in collective bargaining. Faculty became more militant, national organizations reconsidered their efforts, and collective bargaining became a primary goal and accomplishment of organized faculty.[2]

In this chapter, I examine the early efforts to collectively bargain in Illinois, a key state in the history of faculty unionization and labor organizing more broadly. Illinois was the birthplace of the AFT—it was founded by the joining of four Chicago-area teachers unions with one from nearby Gary, Indiana—and an early hotbed of teacher unionism.[3] It was the home to the second AFT college local, founded at the University of Illinois in 1919 to argue for improved remuneration and input into institutional governance.[4] And it has seen numerous efforts to organize college faculty in the years since. In the 1960s, it was an important battleground both for unionization and among the various groups trying to organize. Drives for membership and collective bargaining were undertaken at multiple institutions across the state. Some of these were unsuccessful as faculty at numerous institutions rejected unionization. At others though, the efforts bore fruit and resulted in some of the first negotiated contracts in higher education.

This chapter centers on the efforts of two unions at four institutions: the City Colleges of Chicago, Chicago State College, Northeastern Illinois State

College (NISC), and Belleville Junior College. Faculty at the first three joined the Cook County College Teachers Union (CCCTU). At the City Colleges, the majority of faculty were members and they successfully struck for bargaining rights in late 1966, and then again in early 1967 to facilitate negotiations for their first contract. In 1969, they struck once more when two faculty members were transferred between colleges in violation of the union contract. That strike resulted in a union victory and helped ensure the sanctity of union contracts. Faculty at Chicago State and NISC called a strike in spring 1968 but under different circumstances and with very different outcomes. Only a minority at Chicago State and NISC had joined the union. At the latter, only 30 union members of a faculty of approximately 240 showed up for the final strike vote and the decision to strike passed by a count of 17–13. Although Henry A. Patin, a CCCTU vice president, declared, "We will stay out until hell freezes over," the strike ended after two weeks, without securing bargaining rights.[5] At Belleville, the situation was different as faculty bargained under the auspices of the American Association of University Professors (AAUP), which was still determining its relationship to unionization. The resulting contract was the first ever by an AAUP chapter and was a key event in the association's shift toward accepting bargaining and, eventually, embracing unionism.[6]

When examined together, these two unions provide insight into the early years of collective bargaining in higher education. They reveal competing approaches to organizing and the divides that could arise among faculty on individual campuses, between different national organizations, and between different groups within individual national organizations. They point to issues of prestige that could inhibit or, alternatively, foster organizing. Finally, the efforts to involuntarily transfer faculty members between City Colleges to make them more diverse and culturally relevant for its largely African American student population highlight the severe tensions in American society and education at the end of the decade. Just as in the more famous battles in New York's Ocean Hill-Brownsville,[7] the AFT local clashed with administrators, seeking to protect the jobs of White educators who were being replaced in an effort for institutional and social change. For the union, many of whose members supported the ongoing changes at the colleges, it was a precarious situation.

Background and Context

The full history of faculty unionization has yet to be written but dates to the years just after World War I when faculty at almost two dozen institutions formed small locals affiliated with the AFT. These locals sought to provide faculty with voice in administrative decisions and to increase the remuneration afforded faculty during postwar economic difficulties. A combination of factors including faculty apathy and administrative antipathy doomed the first attempts to unionize the faculty, but in the late 1920s and 1930s new AFT college locals were formed for a variety of economic and social reasons. Many were highly involved in local political issues and advocated for rights for K-12 teachers, and the national AFT played a crucial national role in the development of modern academic freedom and tenure policies.[8] The combination of anti-communism and war pressures devastated faculty unionism in the AFT in the 1940s and early 1950s, but the AFT slowly re-emerged. In 1955, it fully committed to collective bargaining as a primary means of providing teachers with greater voice and better working conditions and remuneration. It was a shift, in the words of AFT Vice President Herrick S. Roth, from "collective begging" to "collective bargaining."[9] This commitment, combined with its historic ties to the American Federation of Labor (AFL), further emphasized the differences between the AFT and the National Education Association (NEA), a teachers' association still committed to a professional ideals and individual expertise. In its view, these were in opposition to unionization. The two organizations battled over the appropriate means and modes of teacher activity, with the former becoming militant earlier and leading the turn toward bargaining that the NEA would later adopt.[10]

The spark for the mass unionization of educational workers was the successful efforts of K-12 teachers to organize and negotiate a contract in New York City, which included an illegal November 1960 strike to force the school board to bargain. The following year, the AFT-affiliated United Federation of Teachers won a bargaining election and, after delays in negotiating, struck again, eventually garnering a precedent-setting formal contract with significant salary increases. The actions and their results had national consequences, as did the fact that the teachers had violated the anti-strike law without repercussions, leading to the need to rewrite collective bargaining legislation. In 1959, Wisconsin had legalized bargaining for public sector employees but it was in the 1960s that public sector bargaining came into its own, with President John F. Kennedy's executive order granting federal employees bargaining rights and 19 additional states likewise passing enabling legislation. As public sector bargaining is controlled by state law, the existence and specifics of this legislation mattered; where it did not exist, bargaining might be possible but was tenuous. Some states, including Illinois, did not consider such legislation, thereby requiring teachers interested in bargaining to force the issue through collective action.[11]

The first contracts in higher education were signed at Howard University, Fisk University, and Tri-State College in the late 1940s, but all were short-lived; widespread bargaining was a 1960s and 1970s occurrence.[12] Faculty at Milwaukee Technical Institute operated under a bargained contract beginning in 1963 but in 1966, the issue took on new urgency in higher education when faculty in the United Federation of College Teachers (AFT Local 1460) at St. John's University struck following the dismissal of 31 of their number. The strike failed to provoke immediate institutional change but galvanized college faculty in the union movement well beyond St. John's.[13] Shortly thereafter faculty at a number of institutions, including the City Colleges of Chicago, assumed a more aggressive stance, struck, and bargained for new contracts. By 1969, faculty at 21 two-year colleges and two four-year colleges, in addition to the 19 colleges of the City University of New York, were represented by the AFT in collective bargaining.[14]

As these events were unfolding and the AFT was achieving new successes, both the NEA and AAUP began reconsidering their professional approaches to promoting educators' rights. Leaders of both had long been opposed to unionization but internal and external pressures were causing them, over time, to change their models and began to support bargaining. For the AAUP, the shift began in the fall of 1964 with executive committee and council meetings beginning to take up the issue due to the increased efforts of the AFT, as well as specific inquiries into its stance on bargaining. The December 1964 Conference on the Representation of Economic Interests—which featured AAUP leaders and staffers, as well as external experts on collective bargaining—highlighted resistance to collective bargaining among the leadership, but also resulted in a begrudging acceptance that some of its efforts for faculty voice in governance were similar to some types of bargaining. As the increasing efforts of the AFT and then the stand-off between faculty and administrators at St. John's University raised the stakes, a Special Committee on the Representation of Economic Interests considered the issue and then drafted a policy on bargaining for consideration by the association's council. That policy, which was approved in 1966 after acrimonious debate, included that the AAUP remained opposed to exclusive bargaining, but that in "extraordinary circumstances" when in the absence of adequate provisions for faculty in governance, academic freedom, and economic interests,

> a faculty feels compelled to seek representation through an outside organization, the Association believes itself, by virtue of its principles and program, experience and broad membership to be the best qualified to act as representative of the faculty in institutions of higher education.[15]

This tentative acceptance of some form of participation in bargaining would be tested but, beginning with faculty at Belleville in early 1967, local units began to choose the AAUP as its representative. In October 1971, the AAUP's gradual acceptance of bargaining culminated with the Council's declaration that

> The Association will pursue collective bargaining as a major additional way of realizing the Association's goals in higher education, and will allocate such resources and staff as are necessary for the vigorous and selective development of this activity beyond present levels.[16]

When the NEA rewrote its constitution the following year, it too signaled a shift to collective bargaining.

Cook County College Teachers Union

Teacher unionization has a long and storied history in Chicago, dating to the late 1890s founding of the Chicago Teachers Federation and the militant action of its leader, Margaret Haley. It was joined by the Chicago Federation of Men Teachers and the Chicago Federation of Women High School Teachers in the 1910s, and by the Elementary Teachers Union and the Playground Teachers Union in the late 1920s. Although at first rivalrous—elementary teachers sought to ameliorate salary differences while high school teachers sought to maintain them, for example—the extreme pressures of the Great Depression brought together the unions, first as part of the broader Steering Committee of Teacher Welfare Organizations and the Citizens Schools Committee and then, in 1937, as the Chicago Teachers Union (CTU). The CTU was chartered as AFT Local 1 and by the following year was the largest teachers union in the country with 8,500 members. It was the only large city teachers union with the majority of all schoolteachers as members, and the first united teachers union in the country. Despite this strength in numbers, without the ability to collectively bargain and conflicted over whether to focus on bread-and-butter issues or larger social reform, the CTU struggled at first. In the 1940s, the CTU was able to achieve some success in campaigns for increased salaries, although was internally divided over whether female elementary school teachers should be paid the same wages as male high school teachers. Chicago teachers and the union suffered anti-communist pressures during the 1950s, though teacher remuneration improved in the era. By the late 1950s, some union members more aggressively pursued collective bargaining at first through advocacy for statewide legislation and then by appealing for the Board of Education to grant bargaining rights. Still, CTU president John Fewkes was at first hesitant and was viewed by many in the union to be too timid. By the early 1960s, momentum for bargaining was building and Walter Reuther, president of the United Auto Workers and head of the American Federation of Labor-Congress of Industrial Organizations' Industrial Union Department, supported teachers' efforts for collective bargaining, as did other labor organizations in a city where labor held sway. Reuther eventually convinced Mayor Richard J. Daley, who sought to consolidate his power and his Democratic machine in the face of challenges posed by the Civil Rights Movement, to support teacher bargaining. With Daley's support, the board granted some bargaining rights in 1964 and made them exclusive to the CTU in 1966.[17]

Organizing City Colleges

Amid these larger changes in teacher unionism in Chicago, the college teachers in the CTU's College Functional Group began to seek control of their own activities and pursue a more militant line than Fewkes. With the 1964 election of Norman Swenson as Vice President of the CTU (in charge of the College Functional Group), the college teachers challenged Fewkes and looked to sever themselves from the CTU in anticipation that the City Colleges soon would be separated from the school district. The college faculty appealed to Fewkes and CTU leadership to be made a priority within the union or to be allowed to leave the union to form their own AFT local. CTU leadership opted to let the college faculty go, and the CCCTU, with approximately 300 members, received a charter as AFT Local 1600 in November 1965. It was only four months after the passage of the Illinois Public Junior College Act set the stage for the separation of the City Colleges from the K-12 schools. The new union was aggressive, immediately demanding the right to bargain, picketing the college campuses to generate support and create pressure, and threatening a strike. William Lee, the president of the Chicago Federation of Labor, arranged for CCCTU leadership and Oscar Weil, president Illinois Federation of Teachers (IFT), to meet with Mayor Daley to discuss the situation. Daley requested patience and assured the union leaders that he would soon appoint the new board that had been authorized for the separated City Colleges; he guaranteed that it would be favorable to collective bargaining. When the new board was formed in the summer of 1966, it acceded to the request for a bargaining election, an election which the CCCTU easily won with more than 90 percent of the vote.[18]

Both sides recognized that the contract would attract significant attention as the first at a large college system and the union expressed some optimism that negotiations would proceed smoothly. Its demands included an unprecedented 12-hour course load, $2,000 salary increases, smaller class sizes, and paid insurance.[19] Yet despite the board's agreement to an election, it was not fully supportive of the effort. John F. Grede, an administrator at City Colleges, recalled that the institution "entered upon collective bargaining grudgingly but with considerable sympathy for the faculty who had been second class citizens under the common school system."[20] It first sought something akin to a company store model and negotiations that would not lead to a legally binding agreement. For CCCTU and the IFT, this was untenable. Establishing legally binding bargaining was as important as the content of the agreement itself. Yet, in Illinois, the legality of public sector bargaining remained an open question until November 8, 1966, when the state appellate court affirmed the rights of boards of education to enter into bargained agreements with teachers. Although important, the court could not require that boards negotiate, only enable them to do so. Negotiations remained stalled as the board's negotiator insisted on procedures that the union felt would handicap its efforts and lead to its ultimate failure. On November 30, the union struck in violation of state law with as much as 85 percent of the faculty staying off their jobs. As the union used the local media to emphasize that its demands were about improving working and educational conditions, the board responded with a court injunction ordering the faculty back to work. After three days, the sides reached a tentative agreement on significant issues and agreed to continue bargaining in good faith, with the faculty returning to work. This agreement was a key marker of the CCCTU's strength and assured it of its right to collectively bargain.[21]

Still, negotiations on economic issues remained slow, leading to a second strike on January 6, 1967. This second strike caused Mayor Daley's direct involvement two days later. Indicative of the linkages between public school and City College unionizing, he simultaneously intervened in CTU negotiations, forcing a new contract for K-12 teachers. At Daley's behest, the City College negotiators accepted CCCTU proposals on reduced class sizes and teaching loads. When the board negotiators hesitated on salary issues, Daley again intervened, offering $50 per month across the board pay increases on the condition that the strike was halted. The parties signed a memorandum of understanding and, over the ensuing months, met 37 times before finalizing the details of the contract. In addition to the workload, course size, and salary provisions, the first contract included new (though still problematic) grievance procedures, more favorable sabbatical and personal leave policies, health insurance provisions, and an agreement that the board would consult with the union in the event of unanticipated revenues. That final provision would lead to additional raises the following autumn.[22]

As the first contract at a large and multi-campus institution in the United States, the agreement was a significant step in the growth of faculty unionization—Grede would later term it a

> landmark event that opened a new era not only for the City Colleges of Chicago but for community colleges generally. Some collective bargaining had occurred previously but the sheer magnitude of the City Colleges involvement, spreading soon to encompass the surrounding community colleges in northeastern Illinois, was virtually unparalleled.[23]

Moreover, although the relatively small salary increase, the inclusion of a no-strike clause, and the lack of attention to broader physical and financial needs of the Colleges would be internally critiqued by AAUP associate general secretary Louis Joughin, even he recognized it as a victory. Perhaps as importantly, Joughin believed that the "situation in this group of junior colleges ... has in the past been really very bad and could, I think, be fairly characterized as the kind of mess which warranted the adversary approach in order to get improvement."[24] Although the AAUP remained publicly in favor of shared authority over exclusive bargaining, it was growing more aware that the current context could necessitate more activist approaches.[25]

Public Four-Year Colleges in Chicago

The efforts at the City Colleges were the most visible and dominated the activities of the CCCTU, but the union undertook political and legislative actions and, from its start, had a presence at the two four-year colleges that were separated from the city's Board of Education, as well. At its beginning, roughly one third of its membership were at the city's two teachers colleges, which would soon be renamed Chicago State University and Northeastern Illinois State College, though that membership briefly faded with the attention focused on bargaining at the City Colleges. The union's first significant battle at the four-year institutions involved Chicago State's 1967 efforts to hire Staughton Lynd, a labor, civil rights and anti-Vietnam war activist who was on leave from Yale University (from which he would be denied tenure for his political activity). He was recommended for hire by the faculty and president of the institution but the institution's board—the Board of Governors of State Colleges and Universities, which also oversaw two rural former teachers colleges, Eastern Illinois University and Western Illinois University—refused to do so, even over its own chairman's support. The board acknowledged that Lynd was a successful teacher and scholar but claimed that his activism, which included a recent trip to North Vietnam, had made him unfit for the position. The CCCTU, along with the AAUP, the American Civil Liberties Union, the Committee on Academic Freedom in Illinois, and other organizations, quickly came to Lynd's defense. The CCCTU publicly protested the decision and appeared before the board to argue for his position. More importantly, it offered to help fund a legal effort to gain him the position. The board at first refused to overturn its decision but in October, amid the on-going legal effort and the beginning of an AAUP investigation into the situation, it reversed course and agreed to pay Lynd his salary for the year. It allowed him to meet with graduate students, though not teach undergraduate courses. In exchange, Lynd agreed to drop his lawsuit and withdraw his request for AAUP assistance.[26] The CCCTU claimed responsibility for the partial victory, but the AAUP argued that it was the combined efforts of multiple organizations and the AAUP investigation that garnered the outcome.[27] Lynd, though, thanked CCCTU for being the first organization to come to his assistance and noted that he never could have funded the lawsuit without the union's help. He continued:

> I am more than ever convinced of the role of a teacher's trade union in protecting teachers' rights. Professional associations, civil liberties groups, ad hoc defense committees, all have their essential roles to play. But I believe my case demonstrates, if demonstrations were needed, that the prompt and militant support of fellow-teachers acting thought their union is an indispensible ingredient in the defense of academic freedom.[28]

As the ongoing battles to organize the faculty at Chicago State and NISC demonstrated, however, many on the faculty disagreed.

The CCCTU first requested that the board grant it bargaining rights in spring 1966, but was denied. In autumn 1967, the union tried again. Noting the need for better "cooperation and communication" that was highlighted by the Lynd case, Swenson asked for and received permission to appear before the board's November meeting to request an election.[29] In the ensuing two months, the CCCTU tried to organize the campuses, pointing to its efforts in the Lynd case and at the City Colleges. The apparent success of its efforts highlighted the changing understandings of the faculty and concerned the local AAUP chapter, which requested assistance from the Washington office, noting, "To argue that the AAUP is a professional organization and the union is not has not been effective."[30] At the November meeting, Swenson claimed to have the support of the majority of faculty at Chicago State and NISC—claims that the board and the AAUP would later rebut—and requested that an election be held immediately. He then introduced the union program, noting that its highlights were

> a thirty-six week calendar; a salary schedule ranging from $10,000 to $31,000; a class load of nine hours for undergraduate and six hours for graduate teaching; new and expanded fringe benefits; and an equitable grievance procedure providing for binding arbitration in all disputes.[31]

The board did not immediately act on the proposal but in the weeks afterward reached out to the AAUP's Washington office for guidance on and information about shared governance, its views on bargaining, and successful policies at other institutions. At its January meeting, the board released its own plan to improve shared governance at the four institutions that it oversaw, hewing closely to the materials that the AAUP had provided. It then rejected the CCCTU request, knowing that the union had threatened a strike vote if the election was not granted. In so doing, the board argued that collective bargaining was antithetical to academic freedom, could poison relations, would not work with existing mechanisms for governance, and would disenfranchise faculty who were not in the union.[32] The CCCTU representative at the meeting was incensed but Charles M. Larsen, the president of the AAUP chapter at San Jose State College who attended the meeting to help support the local AAUP chapter's efforts to counter collective bargaining, expressed his approval, especially in light of longstanding concerns about the faculty role in governance at the institutions. He pointed to the recent 1966 Statement on Government of Colleges and Universities as the guiding document in the area and noted that the AAUP was "not so much opposed to 'collective bargaining' as it was in favor of something which we regard as much better."[33] In the ensuing weeks and months, the AAUP Washington office and local chapters lauded aspects of the board's statement and continued to work on efforts to improve faculty roles in governance and to enact provisions for a faculty senate.[34]

The CCCTU, however, declared that the board's policy statement was merely a front to make it look like it had considered the issue carefully and followed through with its strike vote. By a two-to-one margin faculty at the two institutions voted to strike if no election was agreed upon by March 1, 1968, though only a minority of the faculty at each institution voted; at NISC, fewer than a third of the faculty voted and less than 20 percent of the total faculty voted in favor of the strike. The union held informational pickets arguing for its case but when the board refused to reconsider an election, it moved forward with strike plans setting up a showdown not just between the faculty and board, but within the faculty itself.[35] In preparation for a March 25 visit by board chair Richard J. Nelson, Jerome Sachs, president of NISC, wrote to the faculty that the union's strike threat was entirely about its desire to force bargaining, not about other issues of improving the two institutions. He argued:

> The way to improve college government is by working through the faculty and its constitution. The Union position seems to be that the only way to improve college government is to by-pass it and work through confrontation and an exclusive bargaining agreement.[36]

When Nelson addressed the joint faculties of the two institutions he acknowledged the difficult situation and expressed his understanding that they were dissatisfied and had reasons to be so. At the same time, he pointed to the 1965 shift in governance that had removed the institutions from the Chicago Board of Education and placed them under control of his board. He claimed it was a key turning point that had brought new resources and possibilities to the institution, even if there was still work to do. Highlighting a central argument in the ongoing debates over faculty unionization, he continued:

> In light of these problems I have recited I suppose it is not too surprising that the activists in your ranks have had some success in pushing the union as a solution. This has been a source of genuine regret to all of us on the Board. Believe me, we are not so Neanderthal in outlook that we are simply anti-union. The Board has a long record of negotiating and administering agreements with non-academic unions. It is our belief, however, that a union of faculty members is not compatible with the idea of a true college or university. An institution of higher learning is a community of scholars. Individualism is prized. I suppose I am suggesting in large part that the issue is one of your perception of yourselves. Are you scholars, or are you rote teachers? We want very much for you to think of yourselves as scholars and academicians.[37]

In ensuing weeks, the AAUP tried to forestall and then end a strike. It polled the faculty at the two institutions and found that while the majority (56 percent) approved of bargaining, the CCCTU was not their top choice. With an 85 percent response rate, it found that 32.8 percent favored the senate as the bargaining agent, 31.8 percent favored the union, 21.5 percent favored the AAUP, and 3.2 percent favored either the AAUP or the senate. When, on April 3, the CCCTU struck the two institutions, the AAUP argued for negotiations between the senate and the board, rather than the union or any other group.[38] The union stayed away from work for more than two weeks, timing the strike for the end of the term in belief that the threat of withholding grades would provide leverage. The union claimed to largely shut down the institutions but the colleges claimed that the vast majority of classes were held; at NISC, at least, it appears that they were. And while numerous people picketed the institutions, many were faculty from the City Colleges, not from Chicago State or NISC. Despite aggressive rhetoric, the strike was inopportune. IFT president Weil tried to convince the union not to strike, recognizing that the membership was not prepared and that it would not be successful excepting the unlikely intervention from the governor. Moreover, although Nelson was sympathetic to faculty concerns, the board as a whole was against unionization for philosophical, political, and pragmatic reasons. The threat to withhold grades created tension but little leverage as the board asserted its legal right to assign grades without the striking faculty's input. After 15 days, and an agreement that the board would meet with representatives of the faculty and that there would be no punitive action against the faculty, the CCCTU ended the strike and returned to work. The union declared victory, averring that its action had made the board agree to consider bargaining. The board disagreed, noting that it had always agreed to meet with any and all faculty groups.[39]

In addition to emphasizing the importance of preparation when undertaking a strike, the battle over collective bargaining at Chicago State and NISC highlights several important aspects of the contested nature of faculty unionization in an era of great change in American higher education. Most obvious were the competing perspectives on exclusive representation, including its relationship to academic freedom and professionalism. Throughout the period, board chairman Nelson maintained that an exclusive bargaining agent threatened academic freedom and academic tradition, although Larsen expressed concern that the argument was not working.[40] Moreover, when the AAUP stood for election as a bargaining agent in other state systems in 1969, the union would use its willingness to do so as an explicit rebuttal of the board's arguments that academic freedom and collective bargaining were incompatible.[41] In the build up to the strike, Swenson appeared on a panel on unionization sponsored by the Illinois Association of Junior Colleges, and, in the words of the AAUP representative at the event, "expressed his 'regret' at the AAUP's insufficient militancy."[42] Additionally, while the strike was unsuccessful and it would be years before the colleges could collectively bargain, the union's activities highlighted faculty discontent and helped set the stage for broader changes in faculty governance.

Just as it had in the 1930s, the efforts of a minority of activist union faculty helped push administrators to work with the more conservative AAUP to otherwise improve the conditions of faculty work. Indeed, throughout the union's battle for bargaining and even after it was concluded, the board and college presidents turned to the AAUP for advice on how to address union concerns while maintaining its resistance to bargaining.

Faculty Transfers Threaten CCCTU

The defeat at the four-year colleges was not the only challenge for the CCCTU in the late 1960s as the City Colleges faced a crisis involving race and racism which threatened to upend the union's hard won gains. Chicago, with large and growing African American and Hispanic populations, was highly segregated, as was its K-12 school system. By the mid-1960s, 90 percent of Chicago's Black elementary school students attended segregated schools and, in 1968, the city began a controversial and ultimately unsuccessful school busing program. Facing a federal mandate, it also sought to shift faculty between schools to desegregate teaching staffs and help shift the perception of schools as either being Black or White, though it faced significant resistance from the CTU. Indeed, retaining teachers in their existing positions was a key priority for the union but one that further alienated many African American teachers, who already felt mistreated by both the schools and the CTU. A multi-year struggle culminated in an agreement between the CTU and the board in 1972, but the schools failed to meet federal standards throughout much of the 1970s.[43] Like the K-12 schools, the City Colleges faced severe challenges over the racial make-up of its faculties. Some of the pressures and issues were different, but the transfer of faculty around racial issues was a vital social and civil rights concern set against a backdrop of a racially and politically divided city. It was likewise a key union concern, especially when it was in explicit violation of a contract.

The City Colleges were sites of significant protest in Chicago in the late 1960s. Crane College, which had a substantial underserved Black student population, especially, was a center of political activism, with its older students pushing for changes in the institution, city, and nation. The Black Panthers had a significant presence among students on campus, including for a time, Fred Hampton, the Illinois Black Panther leader whose killing by Chicago police in December 1969 has had lasting political and social influences. Students organized on- and off-campus protests, formed a rifle club to arm themselves amid heightened tensions, and, in May 1968, issued a list of ten demands to the institution, including a Black president, a more relevant curriculum, and additional Black faculty and staff. The institution found the demands "reasonable, moral, and just," and quickly agreed to them, including hiring Charles Hurst, a dean at Howard University, as its new president.[44] Soon, after a contentious campaign that implicated White fears over radicalism in the colleges, the institution was renamed Malcolm X College and charted a course to increase the relevance of the curriculum and change the racial make-up of the faculty. Part of that change—the part that aroused significant angst in the union—was the transfer of numerous older White faculty to other institutions in the city. The union voiced concern, with its vice president Otto K. Benca declaring "Many of the faculty at Malcolm X College seem to feel that their revolution comes ahead of our bargaining agreement.... We are also concerned about losing control of academic standards, since students are determining who will teach what."[45] Still, the transfers from Malcolm X were at least somewhat voluntary, with White faculty opting to leave in the face of discord and threats rather than being moved by administrators.[46]

The specific concerns at the City Colleges began with Black students' demands for greater relevance in the college curriculum and concerns that the overwhelming White college faculty were unable to meet students' needs. At Wilson Junior College, two months of meetings between the administrators and the student members of the Afro-American Club culminated in the administration agreeing to recommend to the faculty that more Black authors be included in courses' required reading lists. When the faculty did not take action on the recommendation, the students did. On March 2 and 3, 1968, student members of the Afro-American club held sit-ins and teach-ins in three classrooms in the social sciences department. The college president, Charles Monroe, not only decided not to call the police to disperse the students as some faculty wanted, but joined some of the sit-in activities. An all day faculty meeting on Saturday, March 4, resulted in the social science faculty agreeing to the demand, an agreement that would soon be matched by other departments.[47]

The following fall, two faculty members, Leon Novar and Noel Johnson—both of whom served in leadership roles in CCCTU—offered courses without the requisite materials. When informed of the shortcomings, both added readings by Black authors, though neither appeared to comply with the list. Both Novar and Johnson claimed it was a misunderstanding due to the fact that neither had been on-campus when the agreement was made the previous fall and that neither had been given the list of required readings until well after the term had begun. Still, students held sit-ins in their classes, prevented them from teaching, and demanded their resignations. The faculty council, noting the two had not met the "spirit of the agreement" recommended that they be transferred away from Wilson to restore peace; the full faculty voted 36 to 32 to support the decision. With that justification, the City Colleges chancellor, Oscar Shabot, ordered their removal from their classes and requested their transfer to other institutions.[48] The two faculty members and their union filed a grievance, with Swenson charging that the administration was attempting to "divide, weaken, and polarize the faculty and students."[49] The board at first refused to act on the requested transfers, giving the union a temporary victory, but in early January, transferred the two against their wishes.[50] Though Novar and Johnson lost their desired positions, the union seized on the situation to insert a clause into its new contract—which it was negotiating that fall and early winter—preventing unilateral faculty transfers by the administration during an academic term.[51]

Protests continued throughout the winter at Wilson Junior College. In March, students forced its closure and students demanded the removal of Molly Bruckner, a social sciences faculty member and CCCTU officer whom they claimed was racist. Although the social sciences faculty voted 19–2 in favor of removing Bruckner, college president Charles R. Monroe rejected the request to transfer Bruckner, citing the union's agreement with the board banning mid-semester transfers. The next day, Shabot relieved Monroe of his duties and removed Bruckner from her classroom, but did not reassign her to another institution.[52] He claimed that Bruckner was taken out of the classroom because she was in danger:

> She could have been seriously hurt in the situation. You might say "Don't say that because you could have done something to protect her." What I could have done would have been to have so many police that there would have been a different problem, namely that the college wouldn't open.[53]

The union publicly condemned the removal and formed a committee to investigate the situation. These actions fell far short of Bruckner's expectations and, on April 25, she resigned from the union, noting her disappointment that the union had not punished its members who were implicated in her removal. She called it "a travesty of unionism and professionalism" and wrote that she would "not support and organization which has proved itself so weak and ineffectual any longer."[54]

When, in August, R. Stephen Nicholson, president of Bogan Junior College, requested that two department heads, Michael G. Kaufman and Bernard F. McArdle, the former of whom was influential in the union, be transferred to other campuses for impeding administration plans, the union decided to take action. Although the contract allowed for transfers prior to a school year with adequate notice and offered a grievance procedure to appeal such a transfer, union leaders believed that the action was a direct attack on the CCCTU. They held that Shabot's plan was to stall grievance procedures and force the sides into expensive arbitration that could threaten the union's viability. Although it was in explicit violation of the union contract, the union struck on September 16 and 17, demanding a reversal of the transfers. The board responded by pursuing a court injunction to force the teachers back to work. The judge ordered the striking faculty back to work but, at the same time, ordered that no disciplinary action be taken during arbitration. A week later, the union celebrated another minor victory when the arbiter ordered the board to keep the faculty on "detached status with pay" rather than expecting them to report to their new assignments. After six weeks of hearings, the union finally received the victory it had sought when the arbiter ruled that the two faculty be returned to their positions. Though the arbiter noted that it was "still possible that Kaufman and McArdle are serious sources of infection," the institution had overreached by disciplining the two through transfer.[55]

These battles over the transfer of faculty were serious for the union. Issues of seniority and, especially, upholding contract provisions were crucial. If contracts could be circumvented without repercussions or if the process of getting the board to adhere to them was too onerous, the union's condition was dire. At the same time, the racial situation was fraught. Many in the union recognized the challenges facing the colleges and supported the changes being made—it was the role of union members in her removal that most angered Bruckner—and the larger political disagreements threatened to divide the union. Indeed, in January 1970, the local's board approved a motion calling on a moratorium on the union publicly advocating on political or social issues not directly tied to its interests, in hopes of reducing divisions.[56] Moreover, union leadership recognized that it was in a precarious position as it did not want to alienate students, nor appear to not support racial progress. It sought a strategy of advocating for changing the racial make-up of the faculty moving forward with new hires rather than by shifting current faculty. Although Weil later argued that the policy helped the union navigate a difficult situation, it was not enough to placate some Black leaders including, for example, Malcolm X president Hurst, who supported Shabot when the union voted no confidence in his leadership during the struggles over Kaufman and McArdle.[57]

The AAUP's "Wayward Chapter"[58]

The events at Belleville Junior College contrasted sharply with those in Chicago, in terms of the initial actions taken, the affiliations chosen, and the larger organizational approaches. Moreover, they reveal the internal tensions in the AAUP as it, along with the NEA, struggled to come to terms with collective bargaining—at the same time that the AAUP was working against bargaining at four-year colleges in Chicago, it was supporting efforts at the two-year college downstate. The institution's roots dated to a post-World War II temporary extension center of the University of Illinois designed to provide educational opportunities to returning soldiers. Almost immediately, though, the Board of Education of the Belleville Township High School District 201 voted to turn the extension center into Belleville Junior College.[59] The new institution shared space, faculty, and a budget with the high school, and continued to do so in a new a new multi-building campus, which opened in 1963. By 1965, when the Illinois Public Junior College Act allowed for the creation of separate junior college districts, the institution had a full-time equivalent enrollment of 2,600 students; that same year, the faculties of the high school and junior college, which had had substantial overlap, were formally separated. In October 1966, a referendum to create what became Belleville Junior College District 522 passed with more than 80 percent voting in the affirmative. A new board was appointed in December and, in 1967, Hugo J. Haberaecker, the superintendent of District 201, was hired as the first president of what would be re-launched as Belleville Area College.[60]

Labor activity among educators in Belleville dated to at least 1936, when, in response to the non-renewal of several teachers and an ensuing mass student strike, a group of teachers obtained a charter for Local 434 from the American Federation of Teachers. The local did not garner collective bargaining rights but the district did recognize it as the voice of the teachers and formed an advisory committee on salaries made up of representatives from the local and administration. The arrangement continued into the mid-1960s, when the faculty of the high school and junior college began to be more assertive in their relations. In spring 1964, they negotiated a three-year contract with the board and, two years later, after the legal ruling allowing school boards to collectively bargain, the local's leaders of circulated petitions seeking to become the formal bargaining agent of the faculty. Failing to gain agreement from the board, the local then held an election in September, which resulted in a 223 to 12 victory in favor of bargaining under the auspices of the AFT. The election, combined with public hearing in a heavily unionized town, led to the recognition of Local 434 as the bargaining agent for the teachers. When the junior college separated from the high school in the immediate aftermath, its new board allowed the faculty to maintain the same right to negotiate.[61]

The AFT's presence and strength in Belleville did not preclude junior college faculty from looking elsewhere for additional support in their efforts. In 1963, a small group of eligible faculty members formed a branch of the AAUP, indicating their status as college teachers. The separation of the junior college from the high school then made many more faculty eligible by removing their high school responsibilities, and the chapter expanded.[62] When the faculty members, most of whom had been transferred from the K-12 to the community college district, voted on representation on February 1, 1967, voters selected the AAUP by a 32–6 margin. The Board recognized the AAUP as the exclusive bargaining agent the following month.[63] The choice of the AAUP as the agent was significant in several ways. First, it spoke to the faculty's desire to claim prestige amid the separation from the high school. As Genevieve Snider, the first president of the AAUP chapter later recalled, "We were anxious to be as college-like as we could. The AFT would just put us back in the high school bracket. The AAUP was the only way to go."[64] Snider claimed that the choice of the AAUP was not a rejection of the AFT and claimed that the two groups still worked together on campus, but the move was indicative of the faculty's desire to avoid the more aggressive stance that was associated with AFT unionization.[65] Whereas at City Colleges, the faculty had immediately pursued formal bargaining, at Belleville, the faculty sought collegial and somewhat informal relations—especially with a board that they worried might be more conservative than the high school board—and believed that they would be better served by the AAUP's approach and principles. Indeed, the intended approach to working with the board was so seemingly collegial that attendees at a statewide AAUP junior college conference in May 1967 would question whether they even could be considered "'collective bargaining' in the sense ordinarily associated with that term."[66]

Although the Belleville faculty's decision was an affirmation of the AAUP's more professional approach, it simultaneously pushed at the leading edge of the association's policies and, in at least one way, exceeded them. The 1966 statement allowing for AAUP units to bargain in "extraordinary circumstances" included the requirement that they receive approval from the general secretary prior to seeking such a role, something the Belleville group did not do.[67] As AAUP president Clark Byse noted in a speech later that year,

> Thus did collective bargaining come to the AAUP—in Belleville, Illinois, without the knowledge, encouragement, or consent of the General Secretary or the officers or the Council of the AAUP. Indeed, had the request been made to the General Secretary, I know not what the answer would have been.[68]

There is no evidence that the Belleville faculty recognized this overstepping, and they certainly did not understand the uniqueness of what they had done nor how it might be received. Snider attended the association's annual meeting in May intending to inform the AAUP of the action, believing that other chapters had undertaken the same action. But she arrived to a contentious meeting at which the AAUP roundly rejected the New York AFT leader Israel Kugler's call for the two organizations to merge. She later recalled that it was "no time or place to tell them we had voted for them as our bargaining unit."[69] Snider and her successor as chapter president, Jan Milligan, informed AAUP associate secretary Robert Van Waes of the decision by phone on May 24, shortly after her return. The decision was met with surprise and discord. Though some AAUP leaders supported the move, others vehemently disagreed.[70] Still, the AAUP national allowed the chapter to proceed with what Van Waes termed an "interesting experiment" that could "offer guidance" to the national association.[71]

The First AAUP Contract

Three months later, on August 25, Snider made another significant call to the AAUP, further engaging the national association in bargaining. She reported that the faculty and board at Belleville had been negotiating all summer but remained unable to bridge differences in salary proposals. Moreover, the board had agreed to found a faculty senate but was reluctant to give it any significant power. Snider highlighted that the negotiations remained cordial but feared that the tone could change with the beginning of classes in September, and she asked Bertram Davis, AAUP general secretary, for assistance.[72] At Davis's request, Walter Franke, an associate professor of labor and industrial relations and the president-elect of the AAUP chapter at the University of Illinois, met with the Belleville AAUP's negotiating committee 12 days later to provide advice regarding the ongoing negotiations. He reported back that the major issues involved governance provisions, concerns that the board's proposed salary schedule was identical to that the high school teachers had negotiated, and what he viewed as a minor difference in compensation for summer teaching. For the faculty, though, the summer salary issue was quite significant both as the board's proposal would have decreased compensation relative to previous years and as the chapter believed a victory on the issue would be symbolically significant. Just as importantly, the collection of differences highlighted concerns about the status of the faculty.[73] They had chosen the AAUP as a claim for collegiate faculty status but believed that the board continued to view the institution as analogous to a high school and the faculty as an "unprofessional employee group."[74] For Franke, the experience highlighted that if the AAUP was going to allow its chapter to bargain, the national office would both need to be more involved throughout the process, not just at an impasse, and would need to consider ways of applying more pressure on recalcitrant administrations. This more assertive stance, Franke argued, could help serve institutions similar to Belleville and, in so doing, help attract them to the AAUP, rather than the AFT. As such, Franke pointed to perhaps the central issue with which the AAUP wrestled in the late 1960s, and the one that increasingly led it toward full acceptance of collective bargaining.[75]

At the September 14, 1967 meeting of the board, the AAUP negotiating committee was granted the opportunity to present its concerns, and did so in a largely deferential manner. Professor D. C. Edwards addressed the board on the committee's behalf and emphasized "we have no desire to usurp the power of the Board" and "no desire to bankrupt this district." Still the faculty found it inconceivable that they would not have a role in governance. Edwards stated, "In the interests of the students and the community that the college serves, we feel that we should be a part of the team, not some appendage which is somehow 'on the other side'." Edwards concluded his speech with claims for both the professional status and loyalty of the faculty:

> [T]his faculty is a competent one, chosen because of their training and experience, and retained because they have accomplished the tasks assigned to them. They are concerned for the proper and orderly development of the college. They are concerned about the student, his requirements, and aspirations. They are concerned as tax-paying citizens of

this community about the proper development of public institutions. As professional people they want to serve this school in the way that their training and conscience indicates. You would have it no other way.[76]

Although the meeting started off cordially, it was ultimately unproductive and confirmed some of the chapter's concerns. Snider declared an impasse and requested more direct AAUP assistance. The AAUP Washington office agreed to send Davis and Larsen to help with negotiations but internally expressed uncertainty about the action it could take in this evolving situation. They were unsure of the legal implications of their work with Belleville, or even the relevant bargaining laws in Illinois and appealed for assistance to Matthew W. Finkin, a recent law school graduate and addition to the AAUP staff. Finkin assured Davis and Larsen that they could legally assist in the negotiations but cautioned that it was less clear if AAUP policy allowed it.[77]

Davis and Larsen spent September 19 and 20 in Belleville, meeting with the AAUP negotiation committee, college president Haberaecker, the full board, and other members of the faculty and administration. At the formal meeting with the board, Davis noted how close the sides were to agreeing and presented the faculty's remaining concerns: their role in developing tenure policy; the request for $100 in additional salary for each faculty member; and the change in summer salary formula. The board responded to the salary concerns by agreeing to insert a clause that no faculty member would receive a lower salary for summer teaching than he or she had in previous years, but declined other increases in salary. The board claimed that it had been forced to borrow money and, for the first time in the school's history, to charge tuition just to meet the requirements of the salary schedule it had proposed; it had done so as an act of good faith to match the increases that high school teachers had received. The faculty were more successful in achieving concessions on the tenure issue, with the board readily agreeing for a faculty committee to design the policy in conjunction with a representative of the administration, pursuant to board approval.[78]

Within the week, the board had fulfilled its side of the agreement.[79] The faculty did, as well, based on the board's concessions on tenure and promise to completely revise the salary schedule for the following year, though it did note, in a letter conveying its decision, its "many reservations about the inappropriate and unsatisfactory salary provisions presently offered." At the same time, the letter noted, "We are hopeful that our future negotiations will be perhaps more fruitful, but none the less, carried out in the same atmosphere of mutual respect."[80] Edwards hand delivered the letter in, according to Milligan, "an apparently successful attempt to keep things cordial."[81] Indeed, this cordiality was key for all of the participants, including the members of the AAUP Washington office, to whom Milligan gave significant credit for the outcome.[82] The AAUP's first contract had been "negotiated," though, indicative of the nature and tone of the process, it was referred to simply as a "Faculty Personnel Policy," a fact noted in the Washington office.[83]

The faculty senate was formed in early 1968 and new tenure and academic freedom policies were created. Salary negotiations in spring 1968 proceeded amicably, with the faculty garnering 10–22 percent increases in salary based on seniority.[84] Larsen, who assisted in the negotiations, praised President Haberaecker and the senior administration for their efforts and for the "atmosphere of cooperation" that existed between the administration and faculty. He continued, "We believe that this approach will continue to serve the best interests of all components of the college community and the students and the community which the college serves."[85] That belief was misplaced.

Increasing Militancy

Amid increasing national turn to unionization and a larger sense of unrest, the negotiations that began in spring 1969 took on a decidedly adversarial tone and quickly assumed a more formal bargaining approach than had previously existed at Belleville. The difficulties appear to have been precipitated by a combination of factors, including the board's efforts to expand vocational programs at the seeming expense of the existing transfer programs.[86] For the faculty, who largely taught transfer courses, this appeared to threaten their professionalization efforts and posed significant challenges to the limited budget. Throughout the negotiations, the creation of occupational programs was pitted against significant raises for existing faculty—the "real 'bread and butter issue'" to the faculty.[87] Moreover, the creation of the new programs without faculty support pointed to the limitations of shared governance on the campus.[88] Faculty were also concerned about the workload of counselors, who were part of the bargaining unit. The administration had agreed that their workload was negotiable but had failed to do so, instead imposing harsher conditions than had previously been in place. Moreover, the AAUP believed that the Haberaecker was attempting to cause dissension among the counselors and split them off from the AAUP unit.[89] Finally, faculty remained concerned about the summer salary schedule.[90]

Perhaps as significant as the substantive issues were procedural concerns. After several months of negotiating, the administration and the faculty were still at odds over the proposed contract, including due to disagreements about the financial wherewithal of the institution. The board then requested the administration's latest proposal and signaled an inclination to accept it. Rather than requesting the AAUP submit its latest proposal as well, the board invited the committee to a board meeting to respond to the administrative proposal on short notice, thereby offending the faculty and forcing them into a defensive stance.[91] The board formally proposed the administration's recommendations at its May 12 meeting and called a meeting for May 26 to engage in negotiations with the faculty. It was at that meeting, which was attended by AAUP staff associate Albert Sumberg, that the nature of bargaining changed at Belleville and, hence, in the AAUP.[92] Though Sumberg provided advice to the Belleville chapter throughout the negotiations,[93] the key public figure was Robert Carr, a lawyer whom the faculty had recently retained and whom had played an important role in the previous year's successful teachers union strikes in nearby East St. Louis. In front of a large audience composed mostly of faculty members, Carr was introduced to the board and immediately sought control of the conversation. His first step was to request—and then help enact—a reorganization of the physical space of the meeting room so that the two sides would sit across a table from each other on equal footing.[94] The meeting highlighted the discrepancies in the negotiating positions—the faculty were demanding more than $2,000 more per person in regular salary than the board and argued that summer pay should be higher, not lower, than school year pay—as well as the changed relations between the sides. As Carr told the board, the faculty "would not have hired me if they had not been put upon. People who hire me are desperate."[95]

Carr's negotiations with the board remained contentious at ensuing meetings. Disagreements over the differences in faculty and administrative salaries, which were influenced by misleading reports in the *Belleville News-Democrat*, turned personal when Carr questioned the credentials of a highly paid administrator, openly disparaging his Doctorate of Education. The administrator resigned two month later, indicating a lack of respect was the cause. Carr also accused Wayne Stumpf, the Dean of Business Services who had been singled out for praise by the AAUP in the previous year's negotiations, of misleading the board on the financial situation.[96] The board pushed back, threatening to implement their proposed salary structure over faculty objections, noting that they had hundreds of applicants for positions and that dissatisfied faculty could be easily replaced. When board members personally challenged Carr, he retorted, "I don't wear horns."[97] This more aggressive stance by the bargaining unit did not immediately result in a contract and negotiations remained stalled at the beginning of the school year. In response, the faculty, which just more than two years earlier had chosen the AAUP in part for its professional, rather than labor, approach, moved closer to the latter's tactics. Although it equivocated by calling it a "boycott" rather than a strike, a substantial portion of the faculty—estimates range from 25–57, or roughly one-third to more than two-thirds—stayed away from campus during the first week of classes. This act led directly to a new contract—termed a "Memorandum of Understanding" rather than the more nebulous "Faculty Personnel Policy"—which was agreed to on September 15, 1969 and included substantial raises for the faculty.[98] The increased militancy and work stoppage were crucial. Still, the faculty lauded the AAUP for its "strength and prestige" and Sumberg in particular for his "time," "counsel," and "moderating influence behind the scenes."[99] For its part, the AAUP remained quiet about what Larsen had termed its "favorite faculty bargaining agent," not mentioning it in its *AAUP Bulletin* until 1971.[100]

Discussion and Conclusion

These instances of faculty unionization in late 1960s Illinois highlight the contentious and varied nature of collective bargaining during the period of significant societal and educational upheaval. They point to the long standing issues of differentiation of K-12 and higher education that implicate both organizational structure and prestige. Each of the institutions was separated from its K-12 school board in the middle of the decade and provided with a higher education-specific governing board; and each of the faculties sought new routes of influence in the new arrangement. At the City Colleges, faculty chose to organize and collectively bargain under the auspices of AFT, benefitting from the advances already made by the CTU. At Belleville, even though they were able to negotiate in part because of the AFT's earlier school board negotiations, the faculty worried that maintaining ties to the AFT would be a hindrance rather than a help. They intentionally sought status as college faculty and believed that aligning with the AAUP would identify them as such. In a stratified field, they sought differentiation. At Chicago State and NISC, the equation was somewhat different, as were the results. The choice was between bargaining through the AFT or pursuing shared governance through a faculty senate based on AAUP principles. Though the faculty was divided, it ultimately pursued the latter.

These institutional differences also point to the importance of local and state contexts. As employees of public institutions, faculty unionized based on provisions in state law, rather than under the auspices of the National Labor Relations Board. Without guarantees of the right to bargain Illinois—indeed, without even initial clarity that it was legal—faculty and teachers had to apply pressure through assertive action. Both in Belleville and in City Colleges, strong organized labor movements in the cities provided backing that contributed to successes. In different contexts—if Daley was not, for example, trying to consolidate his power or if the broader labor movement had not been as strong locally—the outcomes may have been very different. So, too, might they have been in states with enabling or restricting legislation or in private institutions operating under a different legal environment.

An additional theme is the ongoing conflict between the AFT and the AAUP (and to a certain extent, the NEA, though it was a much less significant participant in these Illinois battles). The two organizations had disagreed on key issues of policy and approach since their proximate founding in the 1910s and, as the AAUP was beginning to accept bargaining, those disagreements continued. In some respects, they returned to the height of the tensions that surrounded the two organizations in the battles over academic freedom and tenure in the late 1930s. They pursued different tactics and policies and, at NISC and Chicago State, battled openly. The local AAUP chapters confronted the CCCTU and accused it of multiple exaggerations and outright lies, while simultaneously worrying that CCCTU might overtake, and even take over, them. The CCCTU, though, saw its way as path breaking and believed that other faculty organizations would follow; Norman Swenson pointed to the Belleville case chapter and foretold that the larger AAUP would be "driven" by its membership "into a stronger a stronger attitude and into collective bargaining."[101] Indeed, even Belleville became more militant and pursued more traditional bargaining at the end of the decade.

The cases likewise show the fraught political environment of the late 1960s, with faculty, both individually and in their organizations, having to deal with difficult political and social challenges while navigating for their own rights in the context of broader struggles. The fact that they were unionizing was tied to the larger social upheaval—the activism on campuses and in society influenced the activism of college faculty. The battles over teachers' rights and community control in Ocean Hill-Brownsville are among the most important and controversial in the history of teacher unionism in the twentieth century. There, the AFT-affiliated United Federation of Teachers undertook successful citywide strikes to force the reinstatement of teachers dismissed in violation of the union contract when a locally controlled school board took over the newly created district. Pitting many Jewish unionized teachers versus African American community advocates, Ocean Hill-Brownsville simultaneously bolstered and entrenched union rights, and fractured the left in New York City and beyond. The City Colleges difficulties were ultimately less dramatic, although they caused dissension within the union. Just as in New York, the union was ultimately successful in having its contracts upheld and teachers' rights emboldened, though without nearly the same level of collateral damage.

A final consideration that needs to be explored further is the difficulties that the organizations faced when considering faculty rights and options for influence in multi-campus systems. As they were in New York, California, and elsewhere in the period, the AFT and AAUP were wrestling with how best to promote the interests of faculty that existed within larger systems. The AAUP approach was for multi-campus senates, an approach on which it worked closely with governing board president Nelson. NISC and Chicago State shared the same board with two other institutions in the state, and the national AAUP sought to find excuses to get the faculty on those four institutions to get together as a way of promoting its statewide faculty governance goals. The CCCTU had little interest in such activities and worried that doing so would diminish its power and influence—the other two institutions were not in Chicago and its faculty were not members of the local chapter. For individual faculty, CCCTU's efforts to organize on multiple campuses were conflicted. The faculty at NISC, where support for unionization was weakest, were especially fearful of having their interests and negotiations driven by those at Chicago State. Though looking across campuses to unite faculty offered possibilities for strength, it also raised challenges and complications.

Taken together, then, these cases are a step toward providing a fuller picture of the battles over unionization in the crucial period when bargaining began to take hold of American higher education. They highlight the local, statewide, and national nature of the debates. They demonstrate the shifting organizational positions and allegiances, and, especially, the conflict within and between organizations as they sought to garner power and protections for the faculty. They further point to alternate models of organizing and disagreements over which were the most appropriate for college faculty, if indeed any were. These questions of whether to bargain and, if so, through which approaches and affiliations were at the heart of the debates over faculty unionization in the late 1960s and, in fact, remain so today. Whereas some viewed unionization as antithetical to professional professorial status, others viewed it a necessary guarantor of rights and roles. Yet, context matters, too. Amid evolving views on bargaining, different institutional and political situations called for, and allowed, different faculty responses.

Notes

1 Joe Berry and Michelle Savarese, *Contracts and Bargaining Agents in Institutions of Higher Education* (New York, 2012).
2 Timothy Reese Cain, "'Only Organized Effort Will Find the Way Out!': Faculty Unionization at Howard University, 1918–1950," *Perspectives on the History of Higher Education* 29 (2012): 113–150.
3 Marjorie Murphy, *Blackboard Unions: The AFT and the NEA, 1900–1980* (Ithaca, 1990), 81–84.
4 Timothy Reese Cain, "'Learning and Labor': Faculty Unionization at the University of Illinois, 1919–1923," *Labor History* 51, no. 4 (2010): 543–569.
5 "Union to Keep up Strike," *Chicago Tribune*, April 5, 1968.
6 Philo A. Hutcheson, *A Professional Professoriate: Unionization, Bureaucratization, and the AAUP* (Nashville, 2000), 100–101.
7 Dianne Ravitch, *The Great School Wars: A History of the New York City Public Schools* (Baltimore, 2000); Jerald E. Podair, *The Strike that Changed New York: Blacks, Whites, and the Ocean Hill-Brownsville Crisis* (New Haven, 2003); Charles S. Isaacs, *Inside Ocean Hill-Brownsville: A Teacher's Education, 1968–69* (Albany, 2014).
8 Timothy Reese Cain, "The First Attempts to Organize the Faculty," *Teachers College Record* 112, no. 3 (2010): 875–913; Timothy Reese Cain, *Establishing Academic Freedom: Politics, Principles, and the Development of Core Values* (New York: Palgrave Macmillan, 2012).
9 Carl J. Megel, "Collective Bargaining v. Collective Begging," *The American Teacher* 41 (October 1941): 11–12, 11.
10 Murphy, *Blackboard Unions*, 210–231; Wayne J. Urban, *Gender, Race, and the National Education Association: Professionalism and Its Limitations* (New York, 2000), 171–209.
11 Murphy, *Blackboard Unions*; John F. Lyons, *Teachers and Reform: Chicago Public Education, 1929–1970* (Urbana, 2008), 163–164.
12 Cain, "'Only Organized Effort'," 136–139; Jeannette A. Lester, "The American Federation of Teachers in Higher Education: A History of Union Organization of Faculty Members in Colleges and Universities, 1916–1966" (Ed.D. diss., University of Toledo, 1968), 152–155.
13 Israel Kugler, "The 1966 Strike at St. John's University, A Memoir," *Labor's Heritage* 9, no. 2 (1997): 4–19.

14 Lester, "American Federation of Teachers."
15 Hutcheson, *Professional Professoriate*, 69–96; "Representation of Economic Interests," *AAUP Bulletin* 52, no. 2 (1966): 229–234, 230.
16 "Council Position on Collective Bargaining," *AAUP Bulletin* 58, no. 1 (1972): 46–61, 52.
17 Lyons, *Teachers and Reform*, 9–170.
18 Oscar Weil, *Teachers Beyond the Law: How Teachers Changed Their World* (Bloomington, 2012), 221–225. Audio recording, Norman G. Swenson Oral History Interview by Daniel Golodner. File 1. AFT Oral History Project. Archive of Labor and Urban Affairs, Detroit, MI; Norman G. Swenson, "Historic Collective Bargaining Victory," October 8, 1966, Box 3, Folder System-wide Senate Chicago State & WISC, Western & Eastern Ill. Univs, Committee N Papers [hereafter Committee N Papers], American Association of University Professors Archives, Gelman Library, George Washington University. Enid Hill, Minutes, Meeting of the House of Representatives, June 15, 1966, Box 1, Folder June 1966–May 1967, Cook County College Teachers Union, Local 1600 Papers [hereafter CCCTU Papers], Archive of Labor and Urban Affairs, Wayne State University.
19 Norman G. Swenson, "Progress Report on CB Negotiations," October 17, 1966, Box 3, Folder REI Specific Institutions Chicago City Colleges (Illinois), Committee N Papers.
20 John F. Grede, "Further Observations on Collective Bargaining." Paper prepared for the Continuing Education Division of the University of Florida (1976): 3, ED426717.
21 Weil, *Teachers Beyond the Law*, 230–248; William King, "Mayor Calls Strike Talk," *Chicago Tribune*, January 8, 1967.
22 Weil, *Teachers Beyond the Law*, 250–261; Donald Janson, "Strike of College Teachers in Chicago is Settled," *New York Times*, January 10, 1967; Ronald Koziol, "City College Teacher Union Sign Contract," *Chicago Tribune*, May 4, 1967; "College Teachers Get Raise," *Chicago Tribune*, October 11, 1967; Norman G. Swenson and Leon Novar, "Chicago City College Teachers Strike," *Junior College Journal* 37, no. 6 (1967): 19–22.
23 John F. Grede, "Final Observations on Collective Bargaining" (1998): 3, ED426716.
24 L. J. [Louis Joughin] to File, February 28, 1967, Box 3, Folder REI Specific Institutions Chicago City Colleges (Illinois), Committee N Papers.
25 Hutcheson, *Professional Professoriate*, 100–102.
26 Donald Janson, "Lynd Rebuffed on Application to Join Chicago State College," *New York Times*, July 18, 1967; "Lynd Says He'll Sue on College Rejection," *Chicago Tribune*, August 1, 1967; Casey Banas, "Professors Demand Lynd be Given Post," *Chicago Tribune*, August 10, 1967; "Illinois Board Ends Opposition to Hiring Lynd as a Professor," *New York Times*, October 19, 1967; "O.K. Lynd for College Post," *Chicago Tribune*, October 20, 1967.
27 C. [Charles] M. Larsen to Earl John Clark, November 2, 1967, Box 3, Folder Northern Illinois State College, Committee N Papers.
28 Staughton Lynd to Norman Swenson, October 19, 1967, Box 3, Folder Northern Illinois State College, Committee N Papers. CCCTU provided the lawyers and paid one-third of the legal fees. The remainder was covered by the Committee on Academic Freedom in Illinois. Arnold E. Charnin to Norman Swenson, November 22, 1967, Box 3, Folder REI: Chicago State College and Northeastern Illinois State College, Committee N Papers.
29 Norman G. Swenson to Richard Nelson, September 27, 1967, Box 3, Folder Northern Illinois State College, Committee N Papers.
30 Earl John Clark to Bertram H. Davis, October 27, 1967, Box 3, Folder Northern Illinois State College, Committee N Papers. On the challenges to the numbers, see,

for example, NISC Chapter, AAUP to the Students of Northeastern Illinois State College, Box 3, Folder Northern Illinois State College, Committee N Papers.

31 Norman G. Swenson, "State College Division Presentation to Board of Governors of State Colleges and Universities," November 27, 1967, Box 3, Folder Northern Illinois State College, Committee N Papers.

32 Policy Statement of Board of Governors of State Colleges and Universities with regard to Faculty Representation," January 1968, Box 3, Folder Board of Governors, Committee N Papers; Board of Governors of State Colleges and Universities, Press Release, January 15 [1968], Box 3, Folder Board of Governors, Committee N Papers; "Union Vote Denied for Two City Colleges," *Chicago Tribune*, January 16, 1968.

33 C. M. L. [Charles M. Larsen] to File-REI, ND [Feb 1968], Box 3, Folder Chicago Schedule-Jan 1968, Committee N Papers; 1966 *Statement on Government of Colleges and Universities* (Jointly formulated by the American Association of University Professors, the American Council on Education, and the Association of Governing Boards of Universities and Colleges). Retrieved from www.aaup.org/report/1966-statement-government-colleges-and-universities.

34 REI Control Sheet; Bertram H. Davis to Richard Nelson, February 5, 1968, Box 3, Folder Board of Governors, Committee N Papers; Northeastern Illinois State College, American Association of University Professors, "Chapter Policy for Representation of Faculty Interests," January 25, 1968, Box 3, Folder Chicago State College, Committee N Papers; William W. Allen to Earl John Clark, February 13, 1968, Box 3, Folder System-wide Senate Chicago State & WISC, Western & Eastern Ill. Univs, Committee N Papers.

35 Richard J. Nelson to Norman G. Swenson, February 2, 1968, Box 3, Folder Northern Illinois State College, Committee N Papers; Henry Patin and Don Seigel, "Report on the Strike Vote," January 29, 1968, Box 3, Folder Northern Illinois State College, Committee N Papers; Cook County College Teachers Union, State College Division, "Why We Are Picketing Today," [Flyer], Box 3, Folder System-wide Senate Chicago State & WISC, Western & Eastern Ill. Univs, Committee N Papers; NISC Chapter, American Association of University Professors to the Students of Northeastern Illinois State College, April 4, 1968, Box 3, Folder Northern Illinois State College, Committee N Papers.

36 President [Jerome] Sachs to All Full-time Members of the Faculty, March 19, 1968, Box 3, Folder Northern Illinois State College, Committee N Papers.

37 Richard J. Nelson, "Remarks to Faculties," March 25, 1968, Box 3, Folder Board of Governors, Committee N Papers.

38 C. M. L. [Charles M. Larsen] to B. H. D. [Bertram H. Davis], L. J. [Louis Joughin], C. B. [Clark Byse], R. S. B. [Ralph S. Brown], April 3, 1968, Box 3, Folder Chicago State College, Committee N Papers; "Union to Keep Up Strike at Two Colleges," *Chicago Tribune*, April 5, 1968.

39 "Teachers Strike 2 State Colleges in City," *Chicago Tribune*, April 4, 1968; "Union to Keep Up Strike at Two Colleges," *Chicago Tribune*, April 5, 1968; "College Board Chief Raps Faculty Union," *Chicago Tribune*, April 12, 1968; "Teachers Union Votes to Return to Work," *Chicago Tribune*, April 18, 1968; "Rejects Demands of Union," *Chicago Tribune*, April 19, 1968; Weil, *Teachers Beyond the Law*, 580–585; Norman G. Swenson to David Selden, April 18, 1968, Box 6, Folder Board of Governors State Colleges and Universities, 1967–1973, CCCTU Papers; Milton Byrd to All Faculty Members, April 18, 1968, Box 3, Folder Board of Governors, Committee N Papers; "Statement of Richard J. Nelson," April 18, 1968, Box 3, Folder Chicago Schedule-Jan 1968, Committee N Papers.

40 See, for example, "Statement by Richard J. Nelson," April 11, 1968, Box 3, Folder Northern Illinois State College, Committee N Papers; Richard J. Nelson to Norman G. Swenson, February 2, 1968, Box 3, Folder Northern Illinois State College,

Committee N Papers; C. [Charles] M. Larsen to Richard Nelson, March 20, 1968, Box 3, Folder Western Ill. University, Committee N Papers.
41. Norman G. Swenson to W. I. Taylor, May 13, 1969, Box 6, Folder Board of Governors State Colleges and Universities, 1967–1973, CCCTU Papers; F. H McKelvey to Norman G. Swenson, April 18, 1969, Box 6, Folder Board of Governors State Colleges and Universities, 1967–1973, CCCTU Papers.
42. Philip Denefeld to C. [Charles] M. Larsen, March 23, 1968, Box 3, Folder General Chicago State Etc, Committee N Papers.
43. Dionne Danns, *Desegregating Chicago's Public Schools: Policy Implementation, Politics, and Protest, 1965–1985* (New York, 2014), 19–89; Lyons, *Teachers and Reform*, 171–205.
44. Martha Biondi, *The Black Revolution on Campus* (Berkeley, 2012), 101–113; See also, Sharon Johnson, "The Miracle of Malcolm X," *Change* 3, no. 3 (1971): 18–21; Philip W. Semas, "Malcolm X College Aim: Black Community Self-Determination," *Chronicle of Higher Education*, May 31, 1971, p. 5.
45. Peter Negronda, "Bold City College Plan Stimulates Both Hope and Fears," *Chicago Tribune*, September 7, 1969.
46. "City College Transfers 20 in Racial Feud," *Chicago Tribune*, June 3, 1969.
47. Arthur Siddon, "Toil and Trouble Stirred as Wilson Student Power Cauldron Boils Over," *Chicago Tribune*, December 15, 1968.
48. Ibid.
49. "Shabat's Bid to Shift Two Delayed," *Chicago Tribune*, November 26, 1968.
50. Ibid.; "Lack of Funds, Strike Plans Vex Schools," *Chicago Tribune*, January 22, 1969. The new contract, which was negotiated under a strike threat by the union, also included salary increases of $1,750 to $2,250 over two years. "City College Grants Teachers Pay Raise," *Chicago Tribune*, January 25, 1969.
51. The provision, first proposed at an emergency meeting of the local's legislative body, initially specified "in response to student ultimatums or invasions of the classroom." Cook County College Teachers Union, Local 1600, House of Representatives, Recessed Emergency Meeting Minutes. Johnson and Novar would unsuccessfully sue the district, with a final ruling coming in 1975. *Johnson v. Board of Junior College District No. 508*. 31 Ill. App. 3d 270 (1975) 334 N.E.2d 442.
52. "Wilson Students Halt Classes, Want Prof Fired," *Chicago Daily Defender*, March 13, 1969; "Who Runs City College?" *Chicago Tribune*, March 15, 1969; Arthur Siddon, "Black Protest Wins Changes at Wilson," *Chicago Tribune*, March 14, 1969; "Chicago State is Closed by Negro Protest," *Chicago Tribune*, March 15, 1969; "City College Chief Clashes with Faculty," *Chicago Tribune*, March 15, 1969.
53. "Shabat Praises Patience in Handling of Wilson, Southeast Campus Disorders," *Chicago Tribune*, March 23, 1969.
54. "Statement of Molly Bruckner, April 25, 1969, Box 1, Folder June 1968-May 1969, CCCTU Papers.
55. "City College Asks Court to Halt Strike," *Chicago Tribune*, September 16, 1969; "Truce Shaky in College Dispute," *Chicago Tribune*, September 18, 1969; "City College Ordered to Pay Two Teachers in Transfer," *Chicago Tribune*, September 24, 1969; "City College Told to Reinstate Pair," *Chicago Tribune*. See also, Weil, *Teachers Beyond the Law*, 477–479. Weil tells a slightly different version of these events that condenses the action in ways that the chronology does not fully support.
56. Tom Eckstein, Cook County College Teachers Union, Executive Board Meeting Minutes, January 9, 1970, Box 2, Folder June 1969–May 1970, CCCTU Papers.
57. Weil, *Teachers Beyond the Law*, 477–479; "Dr. Hurst Backs Shabat in Union Row," *Chicago Defender*, October 22, 1969.
58. B. H. D. [Bertram H. Davis] to File, September 12, 1967, Box 3, Folder REI Specific Insts. Belleville Junior College (Illinois), Committee N Papers.

59 Phil Krebs, "Illinois Community Colleges: Their History and System," *Community College Journal of Research and Practice* 23, no. 1 (1999): 19–41, 23.
60 Gerald W. Smith, *Illinois Junior-Community College Development 1946–1980* (Springfield, IL, 1980), 133–135, ED195296. Wayne Lanter, *Defending the Citadel: Confronting Corporate Management and Corruption in an Illinois Community College* (Freeburg, 2012); Genevieve Snider, "Belleville Junior College Chapter of AAUP," Box 3, Folder REI Specific Insts. Belleville Junior College (Illinois), Committee N Papers. The creation of the district was itself highly problematic, as the boundary lines were drawn in a way to intentionally exclude the predominantly Black East St. Louis from the predominantly White Belleville. Ishwanzya Rivers, "Rising from the Bricks: The Historical Development of East St. Louis State Community College, 1969–2004" (Ph.D. diss., University of Illinois, 2011), 108–117.
61 Herbert E. Baum and Kenneth Pyatt, "History of AFT," Box 3, Folder REI Specific Insts. Belleville Junior College (Illinois), Committee N Papers; Weil, *Teachers Beyond the Law*; R. V. W. [Robert Van Waes] to Staff, May 24, 1967, Box 3, Folder REI Specific Insts. Belleville Junior College (Illinois), Committee N Papers.
62 "Organizational Notes," *AAUP Bulletin* 49, no. 2 (June 1963): 203–207, 2037; Lanter, *Defending the Citadel*; R. V. W. [Robert Van Waes] to Staff, May 24, 1967, Box 3, Folder REI Specific Insts. Belleville Junior College (Illinois), Committee N Papers.
63 Lavette Grovesteen, "Certificate"; Orison R. Seibert to Bertram H. Davis, 20 September 1967, Box 3, Folder REI Specific Insts. Belleville Junior College (Illinois), Committee N Papers.
64 "75 Years: A Retrospective on the Occasion of the Seventy-Fifth Annual Meeting," *Academe* 75, no. 3 (1989): 4–33, 16.
65 Genevieve Snider, "Belleville Junior College Chapter of the AAUP."
66 R. V. W. [Robert Van Waes] to Staff, May 24, 1967, Box 3, Folder REI Specific Insts. Belleville Junior College (Illinois), Committee N Papers.
67 "Representation of Economic Interests," *AAUP Bulletin* 52, no. 2 (1966): 229–234, 230.
68 Clyde Byse, "Collective Bargaining and Unionism in American Higher Education: Some Preliminary Comments." Address delivered at the Danforth Foundation Workshop on Liberal Arts Education, Colorado Springs, Colorado. In Hutcheson, *Professional Professoriate*, 100–101.
69 "75 Years," 16.
70 Ibid.; "President of First AAUP Collective Bargaining Chapter Dies," *Academe* 86, no. 4 (2000): 8.
71 R. V. W. [Robert Van Waes] to Staff, May 24, 1967, Box 3, Folder REI Specific Insts. Belleville Junior College (Illinois), Committee N Papers.
72 B. H. D. [Bertram H. Davis] to File, September 12, 1967, Box 3, Folder REI Specific Insts. Belleville Junior College (Illinois), Committee N Papers.
73 Walter Franke to Bertram H. Davis, September 8, 1967, Box 3, Folder REI Specific Insts. Belleville Junior College (Illinois), Committee N Papers; C. M. L. [Charles M. Larsen] to File (REI), September 14, 1967, Box 3, Folder REI Specific Insts. Belleville Junior College (Illinois), Committee N Papers.
74 B. H. D. [Bertram H. Davis] to File, September 18, 1967, Box 3, Folder REI Specific Insts. Belleville Junior College (Illinois), Committee N Papers.
75 Walter Franke to Bertram H. Davis, September 8, 1967, Box 3, Folder REI Specific Insts. Belleville Junior College (Illinois), Committee N Papers.
76 Untitled. Folder Belleville Junior College, Box 3, Folder REI Specific Insts. Belleville Junior College (Illinois), Committee N Papers. For evidence that it is Edwards' speech, see Untitled report of meeting, Box 3, Folder REI Specific Insts. Belleville Junior College (Illinois), Committee N Papers.

77 M. W. F. [Matthew W. Finkin] to B. H. D. [Bertram H. Davis] and C. M. L. [Charles M. Larsen], September 18, 1967, Box 3, Folder REI Specific Insts. Belleville Junior College (Illinois), Committee N Papers.
78 C. M. L. [Charles M. Larsen] to File, October 30, 1967. Box 3, Folder REI Specific Insts. Belleville Junior College (Illinois), Committee N Papers. Bertram H. Orison Seibert, September 25, 1967, Bertram H. Davis to H. J. Haberaeker, September 26, 1967, Box 3, Folder REI Specific Insts. Belleville Junior College (Illinois), Committee N Papers.
79 C. M. L. [Charles M. Larsen] to File, September 25, 1967, Box 3, Folder REI Specific Insts. Belleville Junior College (Illinois), Committee N Papers.
80 D. C. [Clark] Edwards to Board Negotiating Committee, September 28, 1967, Box 3, Folder REI Specific Insts. Belleville Junior College (Illinois), Committee N Papers.
81 Jan Milligan to Charles M. Larsen, October 19, 1967, Box 3, Folder REI Specific Insts. Belleville Junior College (Illinois), Committee N Papers.
82 Jan [Milligan] to Bertram H. Davis, September 21, 1967, Box 3, Folder REI Specific Insts. Belleville Junior College (Illinois), Committee N Papers.
83 Untitled document attached to Faculty Personnel Procedures, Box 3, Folder Belleville Junior College, Committee N Papers.
84 C. M. L. [Charles M. Larsen] "Control Sheet. REI Area. Representation of Economic Interests." Undated, Box 3, Folder REI Specific Insts. Belleville Junior College (Illinois), Committee N Papers.
85 C. [Charles] M. Larsen to President H. J. Haberaecker, May 31, 1968, Box 3, Folder REI Specific Insts. Belleville Junior College (Illinois), Committee N Papers.
86 Lanter, *Defending the Citadel*, 34–36.
87 "JC Staff Asks Big Raise," *Belleville News-Democrat*, May 27, 1969, Box 3 Folder, Belleville 8/29/69, Committee N Papers.
88 Lanter, *Defending the Citadel*, 34–36.
89 "Salary Committee Minutes," April 23, 1969, Box 3, Folder Belleville Junior College (2), Committee N Papers; "Report on Negotiations (Salary, etc.), Spring 1969," May 6, 1969, Box 3 Folder, Belleville 8/29/69, Committee N Papers.
90 "JC Staff Asks Big Raise," *Belleville News-Democrat*, May 27, 1969, Box 3 Folder, Belleville 8/29/69, Committee N Papers.
91 Wayne Stumpf to D.C. [Clark] Edwards, May 8, 1969, Box 3, Folder Belleville Junior College (2), Committee N Papers; Genevieve Snider to Mr. [Alfred] Sumberg, May 10, 1969, Box 3, Folder Belleville Junior College (2), Committee N Papers.
92 "JC Staff Asks Big Raise," *Belleville News-Democrat*, May 27, 1969, Box 3 Folder, Belleville 8/29/69, Committee N Papers. Lanter, *Defending the Citadel*, 40–41.
93 Alfred D. Sumberg to D. Clark Edwards, August 26, 1969, Box 3 Folder, Belleville 8/29/69, Committee N Papers; Bill [William R. Keel?] to Al [Albert Sumberg], September 15, 1969, Box 3, Folder Belleville Junior College, Committee N Papers; William R. Keel and Grace M. Brashier to Alfred D. Sumberg, September 22, 1969, Box 3, Folder Belleville Junior College, Committee N Papers.
94 "JC Staff Asks Big Raise," *Belleville News-Democrat*, May 27, 1969, Box 3 Folder, Belleville 8/29/69, Committee N Papers; Lanter, *Defending the Citadel*, 40–41.
95 "JC Staff Asks Big Raise," *Belleville News-Democrat*, May 27, 1969, Box 3 Folder, Belleville 8/29/69, Committee N Papers.
96 Lanter, *Defending the Citadel*, 46–49. C. [Charles] M. Larsen to President H. J. Haberaecker, May 31, 1968, Box 3, Folder REI Specific Insts. Belleville Junior College (Illinois), Committee N Papers.
97 "College Salary Talks Stalemated," *Belleville News-Democrat*, June 12, 1969, Box 3 Folder, Belleville 8/29/69, Committee N Papers.

98 Bill [William R. Keel] to Al [Albert Sumberg], September 15, 1969, Box 3, Folder Belleville Junior College, Committee N Papers; William R. Keel and Grace M. Brashier to Alfred D. Sumberg, September 22, 1969, Box 3, Folder Belleville Junior College, Committee N Papers; Lanter, *Defending the Citadel*, 50–51.
99 William R. Keel and Grace M. Brashier to Alfred D. Sumberg, September 22, 1969, Box 3, Folder Belleville Junior College, Committee N Papers.
100 C. [Charles] M. Larsen to Jan Milligan, January 31, 1968, Box 3, Folder REI Specific Insts. Belleville Junior College (Illinois), Committee N Papers; Hutcheson, *A Professional Professoriate*.
101 Denefeld to Larsen, March 23, 1968.

6

BRAVE SONS AND DAUGHTERS TRUE

1960s Protests at "The Fundamentalist Harvard"

Adam Laats

At first glance, the goings-on at Wheaton College in Illinois may seem typical of turbulent campuses throughout the late 1960s and early 1970s. Student leaders demanded more freedom of speech. African American students marched into deans' offices and demanded more inclusive courses and programs. Faculty were divided, with significant numbers supporting the radical students and equally significant numbers opposed.

But although it boasted a similar postcard-perfect campus and similarly elite academic statistics as schools such as Cornell, Wisconsin, and Berkeley, the protests and counter-protests at Wheaton took place in a markedly different environment. While Mario Savio at Berkeley insisted on free speech as a fundamental right of true democracy, Wes Craven at Wheaton insisted on free speech to spread the "joy and love of Christ … [in] the Fundamental Christian world."[1] And whereas members of the Afro-American Society at Cornell occupied Straight Hall to demand a Black Studies program, the "Black and Puerto Rican Students of Wheaton College" organization wanted both a Black Studies program and an official "black students' chapel" service.[2] And while faculty members at many colleges and universities agonized over their role in support of or in opposition to student protests, at Wheaton the discussion took on a distinctly evangelical tone, with sympathetic faculty agreeing that White racism had no "Biblical or theological grounds."[3]

If we hope to understand the full complexity of American higher education in the 1960s and early 1970s, we must include the unique experiences of conservative evangelical schools such as Wheaton College. Tempestuous debates about racism, patriotism, and moral citizenship roiled Wheaton as they did other schools, but in a wholly different environment. In order to make sense of Wheaton's "Sixties,"[4] we need to understand the context of evangelical higher education. In some ways, Wheaton operated much like secular, pluralist, or liberal religious colleges. In others, however, Wheaton's fundamentalist legacy left it with a very different set of challenges.

Thanks to nearly four decades of intense academic attention, we know quite a bit about leftist student protests in the 1960s and 1970s.[5] Indeed, for many younger history students, 1960s and 1970s protests as a whole have come to be synonymous in their historical imaginations with "anti-Vietnam War" student protests.[6] Happily, we also have a newer but growing historiography of the "other" Sixties on campus. In the face of popular images of hippies and anti-war protests, buttoned-down students in organizations such as Young Americans for Freedom and the Intercollegiate Studies Institute held conferences and waved signs in support of traditional values and patriotic ideals.[7] We even have our first glimmers of the ways "the Sixties" played out at conservative denominational Protestant schools such as Pepperdine College,[8] and of the ways some evangelical students jumped head-first into activism on both the left and the right.[9]

A Great Fundamentalist University

Things were notably different, however, at Wheaton College and other interdenominational colleges and universities that emerged in the 1920s as part of a new movement known as fundamentalism. As historian George M. Marsden has defined it, early fundamentalism was best understood as "militantly anti-modern Protestant evangelicalism."[10] Conservatives in denominations such as the Northern Baptists and Northern Presbyterians protested against liberal theology among their leaders. They fretted that missionary boards and college administrations had abandoned traditional fidelity to core Christian ideas. Throughout the early 1920s, they fought hard for control of denominational organizations, under the somewhat ambiguous banner of a loosely defined fundamentalist movement.

From the very beginning, anxiety about trends in higher education fueled that emerging movement. By the 1910s, conservative Protestant theologians, scholars, and activists had worried for decades about developments at elite schools such as Chicago and Yale. In 1919, at the founding meeting of the World [or World's] Christian Fundamentals Association, President Charles Blanchard of Wheaton College offered his fundamentalist colleagues an analysis of the need for determined educational activism. "It is the duty of Christian pastors and teachers," Blanchard reported,

> to publicly protest against the teaching of men and secular or Christian institutions which deny the inspiration of the Bible, the truth of the miracles which it records, the account of the creation of man, the virgin birth and the redemptive work or our Lord Jesus Christ.[11]

Too many schools, Blanchard worried, had followed secularizing trends without considering the theological costs. They had allowed their faculty to have their heads turned by modern skepticism and—in Blanchard's opinion—by shallow and soulless false science.

The answer seemed obvious. Throughout the early 1920s, fundamentalist activists and scholars battled for control of colleges and universities. Leaders such as William Jennings Bryan and William Bell Riley contested the leadership at public universities such as the University of Wisconsin and the University of Minnesota. Headline-grabbing evangelists such as J. Frank Norris and T. T. Martin battled for control of denominationally affiliated schools such as Baylor University and Wake Forest. When those fights failed, as they generally did, fundamentalists opened their own schools. In some cases, as with Wheaton College, they converted existing religious colleges to their movement. New schools such as Bob Jones College (now Bob Jones University (BJU)) and Bryan University (now Bryan College) promised theologically and culturally conservative educations to children from fundamentalist families.[12]

To many fundamentalists, the situation seemed dire. Without theologically safe schools, fundamentalist children faced a harrowing prospect of skeptical teaching and soul-destroying doubt. Only by establishing intellectually and spiritually safe schools could fundamentalism save America's future. As Minneapolis-based fundamentalist leader William Bell Riley put it in 1925, "America needs a Fundamentalist University at this moment as she needs nothing else."[13]

Fundamentalists often believed the fix would be fairly simple. In defiance of changing trends at mainstream colleges and universities, fundamentalist schools would insist on a rigid orthodoxy among faculty members. Without liberals in the classroom, many naive fundamentalists believed in the 1920s, students would be safe from intellectual challenges to their orthodox upbringing. Soon after he founded his new college in 1926, evangelist Bob Jones Sr. promised, "fathers and mothers who place their sons and daughters in our institution can go to sleep at night with no haunting fear that some skeptical teacher will steal the faith of their precious children."[14]

As school leaders and fundamentalist activists discovered to their chagrin over the next 50 years, higher education was never so simple. Nor was the impulse toward theologically safe education restricted to Protestant fundamentalists. Alongside schools such as Bob Jones College and Wheaton College that identified as part of the fundamentalist movement, conservative denominational schools also strove to offer students a reliably orthodox education in the Reformed tradition, or in any of the Lutheran traditions, or Anabaptist, or Catholic, or a host of other denominational and denominationally affiliated possibilities. And conservatives—just as with non-conservatives—chose among an ever-expanding menu of higher-educational opportunities. Not only colleges and universities, but Bible institutes and seminaries offered conservative Protestant students a variety of school structures and professional training possibilities.

It can be tricky to draw a bright line between denominational colleges and seminaries and interdenominational ones, but during the 1920s and for decades thereafter, conservative evangelical Protestants tended to put their interdenominational schools in a different category. In distinction to existing conservative denominational colleges and universities, fundamentalist schools hoped to offer a broadly conservative evangelical education, shorn of any affiliation with distinct denominational doctrines. Fundamentalist leaders hoped to build a network of colleges, universities, institutes, and seminaries that would serve to mold new generations of fundamentalists from a variety of denominational backgrounds. These schools would educate the entirety of the conservative evangelical community, not restricted by the wishes of any particular denomination.

Among this complex and expanding world of conservative religious higher education in the United States, Wheaton College emerged as a unique leader. Alone among the fundamentalist schools, Wheaton had a long tradition as an established four-year liberal-arts college. It offered a lineage and campus that start-up fundamentalist schools could not match. As historian Michael S. Hamilton has argued, "Wheaton was the flagship liberal arts college of fundamentalism, one of its most important and prominent institutions."[15]

Wheaton's unique role and influence resulted from the unusual decision of President Charles Blanchard to pull his school into the fundamentalist network. Like other 1920s fundamentalists, Blanchard imagined the move could be a fairly easy one. The primary requirement, Blanchard believed, was to purge the institution of any theological liberals. To that end, Blanchard interrogated his existing faculty. He asked current and potential teachers about their religious and scientific beliefs. He also questioned them about their lifestyle practices. He wanted to know if they smoked, danced, played cards, went to movies, or even "associate[d] with worldly people in other amusements." Blanchard insisted that faculty members sign an eight-point statement of faith that included such fundamentals as a belief in an inerrant Bible, in a creation as told in Genesis, in a truly divine Christ, and in the authenticity of miracles. Anyone who objected was encouraged to seek employment elsewhere.[16]

Blanchard's optimism seemed well founded. After leaping onto the fundamentalist bandwagon, Wheaton College experienced enormous growth in the 1920s and 1930s. Before it declared itself as the "Fundamentalist Harvard," Wheaton had mostly served local and regional students. In 1917, for example, 60 percent of Wheaton students hailed from Illinois. By 1938, only 25 percent of students did.[17] Between 1916 and 1928, the college grew by over 400 percent in terms of student attendance. In contrast, a similar group of 27 Methodist colleges also grew during that same period, but only by 46 percent.[18]

Leading the pack of fundamentalist colleges and universities, however, also brought its own set of challenges. In the 1940s, a small group of fundamentalist intellectuals led by Wheaton alumnus Carl Henry began arguing for needed reforms in the fundamentalist subculture. In fits and starts during the 1940s and

1950s, Henry and other fundamentalist scholars pushed for profound reform of American fundamentalism, for a "neo-evangelical" (or simply "evangelical") identity that retained the steadfast theological orthodoxy of fundamentalism without fundamentalism's cultural separatism and dour social pessimism.[19]

Speaking broadly, the fundamentalist/evangelical split of the 1950s also split the network of fundamentalist schools. Some institutions, such as Wheaton and Fuller Theological Seminary in Pasadena, California, became the leading institutions of evangelicalism, famous for their relative openness to ideas beyond the fundamentalist subculture. Students at Wheaton and Fuller, for example, were encouraged to read the works of non-fundamentalist scholars such as Karl Barth and Reinhold Niebuhr. They were encouraged to challenge rigid fundamentalist thinking about the Bible and American culture.[20] Other schools, such as BJU, denounced the emerging evangelical movement in no uncertain terms. In 1958, for example, BJU provoked a controversy with a proposed full-page advertisement in the *Moody Monthly*, a magazine from Moody Bible Institute (MBI) in Chicago. The editors at Moody balked when they read the copy: BJU lumped together followers of the "New Evangelicalism" with the worst of their traditional foes, "modernists" and "infidels." If some schools hoped to attract the world's attention by embracing liberal, "evangelical" thinking, the leaders of BJU promised, their school would cling steadfastly to fundamentalist tradition.[21]

The editors at *Moody Monthly* hoped for more congenial relationships within the wider fundamentalist and evangelical family. So, too, did the leaders of Wheaton College. The evangelical reform had put them in a bind. Wheaton's leaders wholeheartedly supported the call for a new vibrant evangelical intellectualism. They wanted their students to encounter a greater breadth of authors and ideas than those from the restricted fundamentalist canon. In order to maintain their status as a leading American liberal-arts school, they felt they had to. Yet Wheaton had come to rely on its cachet as the premier college of American fundamentalism. It relied on its ability to select from highly qualified applicants attracted to its reputation as a thoroughly conservative, proudly fundamentalist school. The turbulence of the 1960s and early 1970s brought this unresolved tension to the fore.

Protests and Counter-Protests

In evangelical and fundamentalist higher education just as in mainstream schools, the 1960s and early 1970s were a period of profound changes. One factor in this campus unrest was a continuing postwar enrollment boom. Between 1960 and 1972, the percentage of American evangelicals who had attended college tripled.[22] Of course, not all of these educated evangelicals attended evangelical schools, but many did.

Unlike mainstream schools, evangelical colleges, universities, seminaries, and institutes during the 1960s and 1970s faced continuing anxiety over their status as "evangelical" or "fundamentalist" schools. A few schools, such as BJU or Tennessee Temple University, damned all evangelical innovation and insisted on unquestioned fundamentalist orthodoxy. Many more schools, however, embraced the new cultural and intellectual freedoms of evangelicalism while insisting on their continuing adherence to the theological truths that had animated the fundamentalist movement.

Schools such as Wheaton, nonetheless, were generally suspected for ditching their fundamentalist roots in favor of evangelical openness. Yet the broader Wheaton community usually assumed that their school still served as a leader of both evangelical and fundamentalist higher education. For example, in 1963, one Wheaton alumnus wrote to President Raymond Edman to insist on Wheaton's continuing status as *"the* fundamentalist college."[23] Wheaton students also recognized the school's continuing role as an intellectual leader in the "Fundamental Christian world."[24] At Wheaton as at other conservative evangelical institutions of higher education, there was no simple solution to these definitional dilemmas. On the one hand, evangelical colleges hoped to welcome thoughtful, earnest, positive, evangelical dissent. On the other hand, though, they feared what might happen to their school if they lost the confidence of the wider American evangelical public, including those many conservative evangelical students and parents who continued to think of themselves as fundamentalists.

Across the network of conservative evangelical schools, administrations responded differently to the challenges of the Sixties. At staunchly fundamentalist BJU, for example, leaders insisted upon a uniform and unquestioned political conservatism among both students and faculty. At other schools, however, students, faculty, and administration struggled to define what it meant to be a conservative evangelical school in a time of rapid social change. Chicago's MBI and Biola College (now Biola University) in suburban Los Angeles both experienced struggles similar to those of Wheaton College. In each case, students and faculty were split on questions of racism and civil-rights activism, the wars in Southeast Asia, and student lifestyle rules. Administrators generally felt more freedom than did administrators at public schools to crack down on dissent. They also generally felt that such dissent represented a more profound threat to their school than did administrators at non-evangelical schools. Unlike the leaders of rigidly fundamentalist schools such as BJU, however, most administrators at evangelical schools recognized the possibility of legitimate dissent among their students, even if they attempted to quash it.

At leading evangelical schools such as Wheaton College and Calvin College—widely considered the flagship school for students affiliated with Dutch Reformed traditions—some students protested vigorously against US policy in Vietnam and Cambodia during the late 1960s and early 1970s.[25] The atmosphere at fundamentalist BJU remained starkly different throughout the Sixties. Indeed, in the words of BJU's in-house institutional historian, "student radicalism was nonexistent on the campus."[26] Yet BJU students did engage in political activism. In 1966 and again in 1970, students conducted letter-writing campaigns to express their support for American troops and for an aggressive American military policy in Southeast Asia.[27]

The top leadership of BJU never shied away from radical statements about both the Vietnam War and anti-war protests. Perhaps most memorably, President Bob Jones Jr., son of founder and first president Bob Jones Sr., tongue-lashed student protesters at other universities even in the immediate aftermath of the shootings at Kent State University. With four students dead at the hand of nervous National Guard members and many more wounded, many commentators—even those who did not agree with the protesters—felt that the crackdown had gone too far. Not Bob Jones Jr. The day after the shootings, President Jones used his weekly chapel talk to denounce the protesters in provocative terms. The protesters, Jones informed the BJU community, "should have been shot." The country as a whole was better off without them. College campuses and administrators had a duty to dole out merciless punishment to students who flouted the most basic proprieties of church and society. The blame, Jones continued, was not with the National Guard, but rather with

> ungodly professors who have taught those kids the wrong kind of ideology, parents who haven't had the guts to rear those kids right and teach them some discipline and the value of money, and the preachers who have given them stones for bread and have encouraged violence and lawlessness.[28]

Whereas some administrators and school leaders pandered to a dissipated and slovenly post-Christian morality, Jones promised, his school would always stand for stern, uncompromising enforcement of traditional values.

If there were any glimmers of dissent among BJU students, faculty, or alumni, no trace has survived in the archival record. Officially, the school community embraced President Jones's take-no-prisoners approach to school discipline. To emphasize their endorsement of school policy, in early 1970 the alumni association issued a statement of support. Too many schools—even conservative evangelical schools—the alumni claimed, had allowed themselves the sinful luxury of moral laxity. "Whereas," the association resolved,

> we note the tragic results of tolerant, soft-core administrators who are permitting the breakdown of principles and policies which in years past brought pride to students and alumni; and Whereas many graduates of these restless institutions are shocked and stand in disbelief at destruction of buildings, property, discipline, and moral integrity ... we declare our continued allegiance and loyalty to the school.

The BJU Alumni Association sided proudly with BJU's top leadership, in spite of "unwarranted attack by the Neo-Evangelical forces and liberals."[29]

Most other conservative evangelical schools did not insist on such uniform political and cultural conservatism among their students and faculty. Yet the fundamentalist/evangelical network remained notably more politically conservative than mainstream schools. At Chicago's MBI, in 1968, a majority of 54 percent of students supported a more aggressive bombing campaign in Southeast Asia, compared to only 21 percent at higher-educational institutions nationwide.[30]

Some MBI students wanted their conservative evangelical school to take a stronger stand against the perception that all college students opposed the war. Student Dave Broucek wrote in the pages of the student newspaper that he was "more than just a little disgusted with student 'anti' demonstrations that grab all the headlines." Like President Nixon, Broucek wrote, he believed that a "silent majority" of Americans—young and old—hoped and prayed for a measured, dignified withdrawal from Vietnam. Radical leftist students, Broucek warned, thought they fought for freedom, but in reality they only created "furrows of division among Americans."[31]

MBI's administrators agreed that thoughtful evangelicals should support American policy in Vietnam. President William Culbertson announced in a chapel talk that Christian pacifism certainly deserved respect. However, Culbertson intoned, on the eve of a national moratorium protest against the war, it was also a Christian duty to support duly elected leaders and to fight communism at every opportunity. "We would not be," Culbertson concluded, "among those who would give encouragement to the enemy, nor would we discourage our own men."[32]

Students at fundamentalist and evangelical schools worried about more than just the war in Vietnam, they also pressed for a relaxation of draconian lifestyle rules. Of course, students nationwide at all sorts of colleges fought against traditional *in loco parentis* rules. Yet at evangelical colleges, those rules tended to be far stricter and tended to be considered a central part of their schools' distinctive nature. At evangelical and fundamentalist colleges, most students were not allowed to smoke, drink, dance, gamble, or attend movies. Students endured a strict curfew rule as well as severe restrictions on acceptable clothing. Many fundamentalists and evangelicals viewed these rules as part of the theological *raison d'être* of their institutions, not merely convenient and practical administrative guidelines.

At MBI and other conservative evangelical and fundamentalist schools, students mobilized in the Sixties for a relaxation in those rules. Yet at MBI as at many schools, the student body was by no means unified on the desirability of big changes. By the end of 1970, many students thought changes were in the works at MBI. The administration had announced a willingness to re-examine the thick student-life rulebook. Student Council President Don Wipf declared his support for lifestyle-rules relaxation in the pages of the *Moody Student*. Rules are good, Wipf agreed, but "a person will not mature nor be able to face today's world if he is not free to make choices."[33]

Other MBI students disagreed. One student insisted that she did not want to change the rules. She only wanted to submit to "God's Word and let it change me."[34] The editor of the student paper agreed. Though it was frustrating at times to be held to seemingly inconsistent rules, he wrote, maturity did not come from rebellion, but from obedience. The best thing for students to do, he thought, was to "work more on changing our attitudes than on changing the rules."[35]

At Biola College in suburban Los Angeles, California, students, faculty, and the administration confronted similar questions of student life and protest in the context of a staunchly conservative evangelical institution. And, just as at MBI, Biola students and administrators showed a profound anxiety about perceptions of left-wing student activism.

In late 1968 and early 1969, student editors of *The Chimes* protested mildly against US policy in Southeast Asia. Todd Lewis worried that too many patriotic Christians gleefully threatened to bomb Vietnam back into the Stone Age. A more Christian policy, Lewis argued, would mean caring more deeply for all victims of war, whatever country they hailed from.[36]

Biola President Samuel Sutherland did not approve. He quietly and privately urged Lewis to write another column, one that clarified Biola's support for American policy.[37] Lewis pushed back, quietly and privately.[38] His fellow student editor, Bob Guernsey, did so loudly and publicly. In his next column, Guernsey condemned Biola's administration and student body both, the former for high-handed, unchristian militarism, the latter for "sheep-like" acquiescence.[39]

Sutherland kicked Guernsey out, at least for the rest of the academic year.[40] Other students, too, who protested against Biola's unofficial pro-war, conservative political stance found themselves out. In total, President Sutherland expelled or suspended 11 students in 1969, for a range of offenses from drug use, to movie attendance, to inappropriate male–female socializing, to having a vaguely unacceptable "attitude."[41]

In contrast to what we might have found on non-evangelical campuses, many students approved and even encouraged stiff penalties for non-conservative students. Students at the Biola-affiliated Talbot Seminary wrote a group letter to President Sutherland encouraging him to take a harder line against leftism on campus. Visiting speakers should be vetted more thoroughly, the students wrote, to be sure they were free from "Neo-Evangelicalism's pseudo-Christianity." The dress code—especially for women—should be strictly maintained, ensuring students did not enter campus wearing skirts shorter than one-and-a-half inches above the knee. Music on campus must be regulated to keep it from veering too wildly into the world of "the popular beat of the day." In conclusion, the students wrote, "May God help all of the administration and faculty at Biola Schools to become more alert in detecting danger signs and in taking action to prevent the deterioration that has begun here."[42]

President Sutherland sympathized. He hoped to promote an image of his campus as utterly free from left-wing student activism. In April 1969, he publicly announced that Biola did not welcome any "militant organizations such as the Black Student Union or Students for Democratic Society." He noted that Biola students were "interested in strengthening rather than destroying the democratic process. Progress and change at Biola College will continue to be achieved through an orderly rather than a destructive process."[43]

Clearly, in spite of his public stance, President Sutherland knew that some Biola students were friendly to the ideas of leftist groups. In public, however, President Sutherland presented a picture of a unified conservative campus. He listened to complaints from conservative seminary students and apparently took them to heart. It seems President Sutherland assumed that those conservative students represented a powerful constituency, and he acted harshly in order to retain the confidence of fundamentalist and conservative elements in the wider evangelical community.

Free (Evangelical) Speech Movement

At Wheaton College, students and faculty found themselves profoundly divided on issues such as free speech and civil rights. The administration recognized the changing times—at least privately—but felt overwhelming pressure to reassure the wider fundamentalist public that their school remained true to the impulses of President Blanchard in the 1920s.

As always, contingent factors such as personality and temperament often played an outsized role in the ways broader social trends unfolded. On Wheaton's campus, the top leadership changed just as campus protests were heating up. Since 1941, V. Raymond Edman had held the presidency. In many ways, Wheaton was the center of his life. Indeed, just two short years after his retirement in 1965, Edman suddenly and shockingly died during a campus chapel talk. The top leadership passed to Hudson Armerding, who guided Wheaton until 1982. As the leading historian of Wheaton College has pointed out, both Edman and Armerding defied simple stereotypes of twentieth-century fundamentalism. Both of them were earnest and uncompromising evangelicals, but both of them usually put consensus above conflict. Both of them had long careers as administrators and both understood the difference between impossible theological compromise and healthy institutional compromise. Certainly, if Wheaton had been led during "the Sixties" by more personally pugnacious leaders, events on campus could have played out much differently.[44]

For example, another sort of campus leader might have had a very different reaction to Wheaton's unique free-speech movement. In the early 1960s, students on campuses nationwide mobilized in the name of free speech. Most memorably at the University of California—Berkeley, leftist students and their allies fought for more openness to a range of political ideas on campus. At Wheaton, students fought for a distinctly evangelical version of political and literary openness.

In 1962, students published a gently satirical unofficial student newspaper, *Brave Son*. The name poked fun at one of current President Raymond Edman's favorite descriptions of the Wheaton student body, "brave sons and daughters true." From a non-evangelical twenty-first century perspective, it can be difficult to understand why the rebellions hinted at in this newspaper were so controversial. Most of them, after all, pushed for more and better evangelical religion, not less. For example, student writer Glen Watts protested against the intellectually stultifying traditions of fundamentalism. Education in too many evangelical colleges, Watts argued, represented nothing more than fundamentalism's "negativisms, clichés, and basic inferiority complex." Students were not taught to think for themselves, Watts charged, but rather were "herded down an educational ramp and out into the world more like cattle than men." Yet Watts did not call for less evangelical religion, but more. He encouraged Wheaton students to fight for a more truly evangelical education, a more truly Christian vision. As he put it, the solution could not be found in more empty "talk about Christ, but [in] an encounter with Him."[45] At Wheaton College in 1962, however, these evangelical sentiments were intensely contentious.

The editors and writers of *Brave Son* were not the only Wheaton students to fight for evangelical free speech. Adding fuel to the fire were the provocative tactics of student editor Wes Craven at the student literary magazine *Kodon*. Craven, who went on to enormous mainstream success as the director of the *Nightmare on Elm Street* horror movies, insisted that his magazine would be "controversial." In order for evangelicals to produce decent literature at all, Craven argued, they must be free of any "'party-line'" attitude. They must overcome the intellectual limitations of fundamentalist tradition and be guided only by "the criteria and boundaries of artistry." In Craven's opinion, "the Fundamental Christian world, and more specifically Wheaton, is sadly short of its potential, and far behind its contemporaries."[46] In the first edition of *Kodon*, Craven included two stories that challenged the traditions of Wheaton's buttoned-down fundamentalist past. In one, a teenage girl wrestled with the moral ambiguity of her unmarried pregnancy. In another, a White woman pondered her sexual attraction to an African American man.

Craven's stories unleashed a firestorm. Though resoundingly tame by today's standards, those stories pushed Wheaton's administration into action. Control of *Kodon* was removed from student editors.[47] *Brave Son* was banned. A mortified President Edman scrambled to reassure outraged alumni that the tone of the magazine did not have official approval. *Kodon*, Edman wrote to interested parties, veered from its earlier "approved" status, and had therefore been suspended.[48]

Board member Herman Fischer responded with a more vitriolic denunciation of the tone and spirit of *Kodon*. Craven, Fischer told Wheaton's student council president, had taken cowardly refuge behind evangelical-sounding phrases. Fischer was personally offended by Craven's condemnation of "fundamental Church culture." Fischer insisted that real Christianity, real evangelicalism, had no need to write about "human degradation," since the Bible was entirely clear about humanity's essentially degraded condition. Craven's bad-faith error, Fischer insisted, was to "speak of artistically portraying degradation," since that was merely a "contradiction in terms."[49]

In the short term, the administration managed to shut down Wheaton's evangelical free-speech movement. Yet both Craven and the *Brave Son* editors managed to fire a few parting shots. In an interim edition of *Kodon*, sent to print before the administration ruled to remove student leadership, Craven again blasted the presumptions of fundamentalism. Too many Wheaton students and too many fundamentalists in general, Craven wrote, "feel we have the answer to everything in Christianity. This is not so."[50] His protest, he insisted, was not against true evangelical Christianity, but rather against the accreted falsehoods of fundamentalism. "We are not rebelling against Christianity," Craven claimed, "but against make-believe."[51]

The student editors of *Brave Son*, too, attempted a brief and ill-fated revenge. In March 1963, a group of five students distributed an independent newsletter on campus, *Critique*. This self-financed publication attacked Wheaton's tradition of force-feeding fundamentalist verities down students' throats. In one article, Philip McIlnay blasted President Edman for misunderstanding the basic premises of both true Christianity and a true liberal-arts education. Edman had come to him, McIlnay reported, to insist that Wheaton must retain its ability to reassure evangelical parents of its continuing fidelity to fundamentalist tradition. "This college," Edman reportedly told McIlnay, "will be a place Christian parents can send their children to with the confidence that their faith will be established and not shaken."[52] Edman and other leaders, McIlnay charged, failed to grasp the true nature of real Christian education. "We must note," McIlnay wrote,

> that the 'protective' approach proscribes the natural freedom of man to seek truth where he will.... Christian education must exist in the free atmosphere of such a perspective or we will have no choice but to reject Christian education.[53]

For their parts, McIlnay and his named co-editor Jack Hommes apparently underestimated the strength of fundamentalist influence at Wheaton College in 1963. Both students were suspended for a full year. Technically, they had broken no school rules, since none existed to cover such a situation. Nevertheless, the administration kicked them out for "insubordination." Some faculty members protested—privately and after approving the suspensions—that such a penalty was woefully out of proportion to the crime. Students who drank alcohol or engaged in sexual misconduct, Professor Gerald Hawthorne reminded the administration, had been suspended for a week or two. Did Wheaton really want to punish students so severely for thinking critically and writing candidly about central issues of evangelical culture?[54]

The harshness of the sentences revealed the high stakes involved for Wheaton's leaders. In order to sustain itself as the flagship college for fundamentalists and evangelicals, Wheaton needed to root out any students or faculty who might damage that image. McIlnay may or may not have stretched the truth with his description of President Edman's warning, but the tone rings true. Only if Wheaton could maintain its reputation as a culturally and theologically safe space for conservative evangelical parents and students could it continue to exist. Unlike free-wheeling students or even respected faculty members, administrators had to worry about parents' "confidence" that the institution would enforce traditional evangelical and fundamentalist behavior and belief.

In the long run, Wheaton's attempt to quash evangelical dissent only fed the flames of student discontent. Years later, a roster of 46 students signed the masthead of a revived *Brave Son*. In 1970, the students no longer claimed to represent true evangelical religion, true striving for a closer relationship to Jesus. Instead, by that time student protesters had adopted the secular language of free-speech protesters at non-evangelical colleges. The new *Brave Son* featured mainly a single word in enormous font: "Censored." When administrators had closed down student publications in 1963, the new generation of student protesters insisted, they violated students' inalienable American right to free speech. For true freedom, the students wrote, Wheaton must revise its draconian policy toward student publications.[55] By this time, Wheaton's faculty and administration did not debate the issue. They immediately crushed the upstart student newspaper.

All God's Children

Much of the free-speech debate at Wheaton was tied intimately to questions of race and racism. One of the most controversial elements of the early incarnation of *Brave Son* was its inclusion of a faculty call to greater anti-racist activism on campus. In frustration, one faculty member had resorted to publishing his analysis of Wheaton's flawed record on race relations in the pages of that rebellious publication. Yet the faculty report in question had originally been solicited by the Wheaton administration itself. As we'll see in this section, the tempestuous back-and-forth served as a painful example of Wheaton's complicated relationship to questions of racism, civil rights, and evangelical social activism.

No one in the extended Wheaton community could forget Wheaton's oft-told legacy. Campus leaders and alumni celebrated the fact that Wheaton College had been founded in 1860 as a hub of anti-slavery evangelical activism.[56] Perhaps for that reason, when White Wheaton students mobilized 100 years later to help desegregate a local barber shop, their activism was generally accepted as part of Wheaton's anti-racist legacy.[57]

Indeed, in the early summer of 1960, President Raymond Edman asked a group of Wheaton professors to study and report about Wheaton's progress on healing racial divides. The committee, led by Gordon S. Jaeck of the sociology and anthropology departments, assisted by Professor Lamberta Voget, Assistant Professor James O. Buswell III, instructors Alvin Moser and David Winter, and "special instructor" James Murk, found that Wheaton had lost its way on issues of race and social justice.[58]

As did later student protesters, the faculty committee expounded its opinions not in secular terms, but in terms of honing and improving Wheaton's status as an evangelical Protestant institution. Yes, the committee concluded, the school had been founded in an earlier evangelical era of moral leadership on racial questions, but since then, Wheaton had become far more conservative, far more accommodating to dominant social trends toward White racism. Between 1860 and 1960, the faculty group wrote, "minority groups, particularly Negroes, were for a time excluded from admission … [later] they were restricted in regard to housing and certain social activities." The evangelical church had a special duty to buck the trends of secular society. In this case, "evangelical white people" had allowed themselves falsely to wrap their racial privilege and social prejudice in the language of Christianity. To right this historic wrong, the committee suggested, Wheaton College should initiate a series of educational programs about racial problems. It should aggressively recruit a "colored person" for the faculty. It should encourage the nearby town of Wheaton to fight racial prejudice and ban racial segregation. It should do a better job in teaching students from other nations. It should re-examine its admissions policies to recruit more non-White students. And it should clarify that dating and marriage rules did not support bans—or even imply support for bans—on interracial dating.[59]

President Edman had solicited this faculty report, but he quickly buried it.[60] In frustration, committee member James Murk published an essay with a similar tone in the controversial April 1962 edition of *Brave Son*. Murk repeated the action steps the committee had recommended. He made his case in a more staunchly evangelical tone than had the original committee report. "Prejudice," Murk wrote, "is sin."[61] There were no "Biblical or theological grounds" for racial prejudice.[62] Because of Wheaton's unique role as the flagship college of conservative evangelicalism, Murk argued, "we are in a singular position to make a positive and constructive impact on our evangelical churches."[63] If Wheaton could reverse its lamentable recent history of White racism, it could re-direct a wayward White evangelical tradition in the United States.

Throughout the 1960s and early 1970s, the Wheaton community struggled with questions of racism and social activism. Its multi-headed constituency and multi-voiced community created some awkward compromises. For example, in

1966 evangelical activist John Alexander joined the Wheaton faculty. Alexander had emerged from the world of White fundamentalism as a committed fighter against White racism in the evangelical community. In 1966, he moved to the Chicago area and began teaching at Wheaton.[64] By most accounts, Alexander's fervent evangelical anti-racism proved popular among Wheaton students. The administration, however, remained deeply ambivalent. For example, the Wheaton bookstore was not allowed to display Alexander's anti-racist newsletter, *Freedom Now*. The bookstore could, however, keep semi-illicit copies under its counter, and sell them if students asked for them. It didn't take long for Alexander to grow frustrated with this sort of hesitancy. In 1970, he moved to Philadelphia to engage in full-time anti-racist evangelical activism.[65]

Wheaton's students, too, joined college students nationwide in pushing for more radical anti-racist measures on their evangelical campus. In late 1968, a group of non-White students organized as the Black and Puerto Rican Students of Wheaton College. They presented the administration with a short list of typed demands. They insisted on new academic programs at the college. Proposed new courses would help non-White students get in touch with "cultural antecedents which have been minimized and ignored." Their call was not only in the name of "African, Afro-American and Latin American studies," however. They insisted that they made their demands in order not only to improve Wheaton's academic education as a whole, but specifically to improve Wheaton's "Christian education relevant to our cultural heritage."[66]

The administration was cautiously supportive of these demands. New President Hudson Armerding initiated a plan to hire more non-White faculty. He instituted a special chapel service for African-American students. He encouraged liberal faculty members to engage their colleagues with talks about the relationship of White evangelicalism to the history of White racism.[67] In one of his chapel talks, President Armerding insisted that Wheaton College did not have and had never had any sort of ban on interracial dating or marriage.[68]

At the same time, however, President Armerding warned that it would not be easy to reverse the long legacy of White racism. It would only harm the school to hire in haste, he wrote in a public memo. It was difficult to find what he called "*qualified* faculty" from minority backgrounds.[69] When it came to student life, too, Armerding waffled. Yes, students at Wheaton were free to date and marry across the color line. But all students would be given mandatory counseling about the social difficulties that could be expected for interracial marriages.[70]

In the end, he approved a plan to initiate new courses of study. Instead of offering programs specifically focused on African history, African-American history, or Latin American history, however, Armerding presented a watered-down proposal. He was in "sympathy" with student protests, Armerding wrote. But it would be better for the Wheaton community—and more practical given the ever-present difficulties of finding qualified instructors—if the school offered instead of specific Black Studies courses more general classes about "various racial minorities."[71]

Student activists were not impressed. African American leader Ron Potter agreed to meet with President Armerding. But whereas President Armerding insisted it would be a very private, one-on-one meeting, Potter declared that it would be public and he would bring a handful of his fellow African American activists. Potter strove to explain to Armerding that Wheaton's hesitant reforms still resonated with the echoes of White privilege and racism. It was not enough, Potter told Armerding, to allow interracial dating, while still warning students that such relationships would lead to ostracism and despair. It was not enough to put off hiring African American professors due to a perceived difficulty in finding highly qualified candidates. It was not enough, in short, for White evangelical institutions to allow African American participation grudgingly and under pressure. The solution, Potter told Armerding, was for people like himself to desert schools like Wheaton and build their own institutions.[72]

To the wider Wheaton community, Potter defended his separatism even as he sought to explain it to well-meaning White evangelicals. Too many White evangelicals, Potter wrote in a column in the student newspaper, accommodated African American complaints as long as they came wrapped in the traditional patronizing trappings of special pleadings. Whenever African American evangelicals protested more stridently, Potter lamented, those same self-satisfied White evangelicals accused them of "bitterness or hatred." Such small-mindedness was nothing short of "pitiful," Potter charged. "White evangelicals" had a duty to move more forcefully beyond their traditional racial blinders in order to "understand larger issues that divide us."[73]

Faculty Divides

For their part, the faculty at Wheaton remained profoundly divided. Some teachers, such as James Murk, John Alexander, and James O. Buswell III, continued to push for more anti-racist institutional reform. Others worked quietly to encourage the administration to move in an anti-racist direction. Arthur Rupprecht of the language department, for example, wrote to Armerding in May 1970 to continue efforts to recruit more evangelical African American students, "despite the problems that have arisen."[74]

Throughout the 1960s and 1970s, however, other powerful voices urged Wheaton's leaders to move slowly and cautiously. In 1960, for instance, when President Edman first requested the faculty report on race and racism, Merrill C. Tenney urged restraint. At the time, Tenney was the influential dean of Wheaton's graduate school. He was shocked to learn that Wheaton had ever banned African American students and encouraged Edman to clarify that such discrimination was a black mark on Wheaton's record. He agreed, too, that interracial marriage was not a sin. It was, however, a very difficult and dangerous thing for White leaders in 1960 to endorse. Even, or especially, if those White leaders ran evangelical institutions. As they had done with questions of student free speech, administrators like Tenney and Edman recognized that Wheaton faced an existential threat when it came to such questions. If parents thought any of Wheaton's policies implied any sort of "danger to their children," Tenney warned, they might decide to send their children—and their tuition dollars—elsewhere.[75] It was not an idle worry. As did most evangelical colleges during the period, Wheaton relied far more than did mainstream colleges on tuition and fees to support itself. Any loss of paying students represented a real and immediate threat to the life of the institution itself.[76] Not for theological reasons, then, but for these vital nuts-and-bolts issues of institutional survival, Tenney agreed that Edman ought not to release the provocative antiracist faculty report.

Less influential members of the far-flung evangelical community also hoped to push the administration in one direction or the other. One of President Armerding's former students from Gordon College, where Armerding had worked until 1965, wrote to him in alarm in 1970. The former student had heard at a recent student conference that Wheaton did not allow interracial dating. He hoped it was not true, and urged Armerding to take steps to clear Wheaton's name of such charges.[77]

Another alumnus wrote to Armerding to urge restraint. On a recent visit to campus in early 1970, this alum reported, he had been shocked to see the militant tone of African American activism. Surely an evangelical student—whatever his or her race—could be made to understand that evangelicals did not accost each other with demands and issue bitter "bulletins," this alum fretted.[78]

Weighing all of these influences from the campus and wider evangelical community, Wheaton's administrators eventually moved moderately to meet students' demands. By early 1971, Wheaton had initiated a series of specific curricular changes that it hoped would satisfy activists' complaints. The school hired an African American instructor to teach new courses in Urban Sociology and People of Africa. The school added a course called "Black Americans in American Society." Teachers of a required course in American Civilization had agreed to add more content specifically relevant to African American history.[79]

The moves did not permanently solve the vexing problem of White racism in an evangelical institution, but they did quiet the immediate student protests. The deeper tensions, however, remained at the heart of "Sixties" controversies at Wheaton College. As at many non-evangelical colleges and universities, students, faculty, and even administrators were often split about questions of free speech, racism, and civil rights. And, as at many non-evangelical schools, over the course of the 1960s student demands grew more strident and more indignant.

Funding Fundamentalism

At Wheaton College, however, such common campus controversies remained mired in evangelical history and tradition. When student and faculty protesters pushed for change, they did so in the language of evangelical Protestantism. Free speech was not only an American right, they argued, but a Christian imperative. Racism was not only a social blight, they insisted, but a grievous sin. Also, the administration of Wheaton College found itself restrained in uniquely evangelical ways. As did leaders of non-evangelical schools, Wheaton's top leadership fretted that a reputation for an unsafe campus would drive away tuition-paying students. Unlike non-evangelical school administrators, however, Wheaton's leaders faced the legacy of fundamentalist tradition. Their school—like other conservative evangelical colleges and universities—had been founded explicitly to safeguard the spiritual, cultural, and intellectual traditions of fundamentalism. If Wheaton was seen as straying too far from those strict traditions, it faced the very real possibility of alienating its traditional conservative constituency.

Throughout the 1960s and early 1970s, Wheaton's top administrators worried about more than just student protests. Anxious administrators fretted about a sudden and mysterious drop in new student applications. While earnest evangelical students worried about moving the school closer to true anti-racist evangelical Christianity, or while they pushed to have their voices heard without the fetters of conservative administration censorship, the school's top administration wondered if the school was on a path to financial insolvency.

From a peak of 8,528 new applications in 1964,[80] by 1967 the admissions office reported a dismal and alarming 1,101 applications.[81] Numbers rebounded somewhat in the ensuing years, with 1,376 in 1968,[82] up to 1,519 in 1975.[83] Such numbers represented a new institutional reality for the administrators of Wheaton College. They could no longer rely on a captured market of ambitious, intelligent conservative evangelical students. They had to compete with a growing number of conservative evangelical colleges and universities, and they had to prove that they were still a safe school for conservative evangelical students.

Like admissions officers everywhere, Wheaton's bureaucrats looked frantically for reasons for their sudden drop in applications. And like admissions officers at non-evangelical colleges, they found a long list of likely suspects. For example, in 1966, Wheaton enforced for the first time new requirements for high-school graduation among applicants. Admissions Director Charles Schoenherr wondered if Wheaton's history of strict admissions standards had begun to deter borderline applicants. He mused that Wheaton's weak athletic teams might be dissuading qualified applicants. Schoenherr also had worries unique to Wheaton's evangelical/fundamentalist history. He fretted that Wheaton might be losing out to both new and established fundamentalist schools.[84]

In 1966, the admissions office reported that more and more potential Wheaton students were likely applying to and attending other evangelical colleges.[85] Since the 1920s, the population of fundamentalist institutions of higher education had grown significantly. New schools such as Tennessee Temple College (1946) and Clearwater Christian College (1966) did more than simply increase the total number of conservative evangelical colleges. Each of them opened as staunchly fundamentalist schools, and, like BJU, promised conservative parents a more conservative alternative to evangelical colleges like Wheaton. Could it be, Schoenherr asked President Armerding in a 1966 memo, that Wheaton had an "image" problem among its conservative evangelical constituency? "To what extent," Schoenherr wondered, "have rumors about Wheaton going 'liberal' hurt?"[86]

Wheaton's leaders at the time could not find a quantifiable answer to that question. It seems beyond doubt, however, that Wheaton's willingness to entertain student and faculty protests in the Sixties, even as grudging and beleaguered as it was, led to severe criticism from the conservative evangelical and fundamentalist communities. At BJU, for example, top administrators reeled at what they saw as Wheaton's precipitous decline into liberalism and apostasy. Longtime BJU administrator Gilbert Stenholm, for instance, was shocked and dismayed at Wes Craven's controversial 1962 issue of *Kodon*. In the margins of his copy, where Craven insisted his magazine would be "free and limited only by the criteria and the boundaries of artistry," Stenholm penned in three emphatic exclamation marks. And in the margins of one of the magazine's edgy stories, a shocked Stenholm wrote a single word: "Profanity!"[87] By the mid-1970s, Bob Jones Jr. used Wheaton as a negative example of what could happen to evangelical schools that wavered from strict fundamentalist rules.[88]

Fundamentalists at BJU were not the only ones to criticize Wheaton's supposed liberalism. Robert Ketcham, by 1967 an elder statesman of separatist fundamentalism, expressed his outrage to President Armerding over the *Kodon* affair. Even five years later, Ketcham was still dismayed that Wheaton's leaders had allowed a student publication to include profanity and to take the name of the Lord in vain. Ketcham warned Armerding that fundamentalists would not support a school in which a rebel student was not "brought on the carpet immediately."[89] Ketcham had allies and sympathizers at the very top levels of Wheaton's leadership. A member of the Board of trustees, David Otis Fuller, expressed his sympathy with Ketcham's complaint. In a private response to Ketcham, Fuller agreed that he, too, had been "disturbed" by trends at Wheaton. However, he assured the senior fundamentalist that "Doctor Armerding is doing his best to try and keep Wheaton from going the way of so many other educational institutions which began as orthodox and fundamental as any group could be."[90]

Fundamentalist scrutiny of Wheaton's status as a trustworthy school was not limited to competitors such as Bob Jones or influential leaders such as the

Reverend Ketcham. Throughout the late 1960s and early 1970s, alumni, parents, and even people with no apparent immediate connection to the school flooded President Armerding's inbox with dire warnings about the dangers of creeping liberalism. To cite just one example, in late 1968 one earnest fundamentalist with no personal links to Wheaton expressed her worries about the school's direction. "Recently after a church meeting," she wrote to Armerding, several members of her conservative evangelical congregation began to discuss recent developments at Wheaton. "Some said," she continued, "your school now teaches 'theistic evolution' and has departed from the fundamentals of the Bible. Is this true? Would you please investigate your curriculum?"[91] Due to Wheaton's unique history as the "Fundamentalist Harvard," the flagship liberal-arts college for conservative evangelicalism, fundamentalists from around the country shared this sort of proprietary concern for Wheaton's status.

The Evangelical Sixties

Wheaton's leaders could never dismiss such correspondence as merely nosy intrusions by fundamentalist busybodies. By the 1960s, conservative evangelical students had many more evangelical schools to choose from. If the administrators of Wheaton ignored the anxieties of the broader fundamentalist community, they risked alienating potential students and losing their potential tuition dollars.

These pressures shaped the responses of Wheaton's top administrators to student and faculty protests throughout the Sixties. Just as at non-evangelical schools, Wheaton's leaders hoped to encourage thoughtful, moral, informed critical debate on their campus. And, just as at non-evangelical schools, some of Wheaton's leaders personally sympathized with both anti-racist and free-speech activism. Unlike the leaders of non-evangelical institutions, however, Wheaton's administrators faced a unique evangelical institutional dilemma. If they veered too sharply away from conservative traditions, they faced the real threat that their students would desert to fundamentalist schools.

From the perspective of the twenty-first century, it is clear that the worst 1960s worries of Wheaton's top administrators were unfounded. These days, Wheaton continues to thrive and to enjoy its reputation as the leading school of American evangelicalism. Yet such hindsight should not distract us from the substantial anxiety Wheaton's leaders experienced in the 1960s. When students and faculty protested during "the Sixties," Wheaton's leaders had to consider many of the same worries as did leaders of non-evangelical schools: Were students hurting their school's reputation? Could schools combat racism? Should schools welcome protests against the Vietnam War? Against traditional sexual mores?

At Wheaton, however, such questions were made even more difficult by the lingering tensions within the family of fundamentalist and evangelical institutions. Wheaton had long been accused by fundamentalist rivals of straying too far from traditional theological and cultural certainties. If Wheaton's leaders leaned too far to support "Sixties" protests, they worried—with good reason— that they might lose their valuable reputation as the "Fundamentalist Harvard." In the end, their school rebounded and thrived, but between roughly 1963 and 1973, Wheaton's unique status as the flagship school for conservative evangelical students put its leaders in a uniquely difficult situation.

Notes

1 Wesley Earl Craven, "A Warning from the Editor," *Kodon* 17:1 (Fall 1962): 3.
2 Hudson Armerding to Rev. Grover Wilcox, March 12, 1970, President Hudson T. Armerding Papers, Wheaton College Archives, Office of the President Records; Box 9, folder 12, Black Students Black Studies, 1969–71, contained within the Archives of the Billy Graham Center, Wheaton, Illinois.
3 James M. Murk, "The Race Question," *Brave Son* 1:2 (April 1962): 10.
4 Of course, much of the campus unrest popularly associated with the "Sixties" happened in the 1970s. In this chapter I will follow the convention of referring to the period roughly from 1963–1975 as "the Sixties" when it matches historical experience—a coherent period of campus activism in favor of more student freedom and civil rights, and against American militarism in Southeast Asia. In places where more specificity is called for, I will refer to specific dates. For a discussion of the difference between the 1960s and "the Sixties," see, for example, Andrew Hartman, *War for the Soul of America: A History of the Culture Wars* (Chicago: University of Chicago Press, 2015), 9–37.
5 The literature on leftist protest in the 1960s and 1970s is vast. Key titles include the following: Kirkpatrick Sale, *SDS* (New York: Vintage, 1974); Todd Gitlin, *The Sixties: Years of Hope, Days of Rage* (New York: Bantam Books, 1987); Robert Cohen, *Freedom's Orator: Mario Savio and the Radical Legacy of the 1960s* (New York: Oxford University Press, 2002); Martha Biondi, *The Black Revolution on Campus* (Berkeley: University of California Press, 2012).
6 See Sam Wineburg, "Making (Historical) Sense in the New Millennium," in *Historical Thinking and Other Unnatural Acts: Charting the Future of Teaching the Past* (Philadelphia: Temple University Press, 2001), 232–255.
7 Molly Worthen, *Apostles of Reason: The Crisis of Authority in American Evangelicalism* (New York: Oxford University Press, 2014), 63–65; George H. Nash, *The Conservative Intellectual Movement in America Since 1945*, Thirtieth-Anniversary Edition (Wilmington: ISI Books, 2008), 40–42; John A. Andrews III, *The Other Side of the Sixties: Young Americans for Freedom and the Rise of Conservative Politics* (New Brunswick: Rutgers University Press, 1997); Gregory L. Schneider, *Cadres for Conservatism: Young Americans for Freedom and the Rise of the Contemporary Right* (New York: New York University Press, 1999); Rebecca E. Klatch, *A Generation Divided: The New Left, the New Right, and the 1960s* (Berkeley: University of California Press, 1999).
8 Darren Dochuk, *From Bible Belt to Sun Belt: Plain-Folk Religion, Grassroots Politics, and the Rise of Evangelical Conservatism* (New York: Norton, 2011).
9 For leftist evangelical student activism, see David R. Swartz, *Moral Minority: The Evangelical Left in an Age of Conservatism* (Philadelphia: University of Pennsylvania Press, 2012); for more conservative campus activism among evangelical students, see John G. Turner, *Bill Bright & Campus Crusade for Christ: The Renewal of Evangelicalism in Postwar America* (Chapel Hill: University of North Carolina Press, 2008).
10 George M. Marsden, *Fundamentalism and American Culture: The Shaping of Twentieth-Century Evangelicalism: 1870–1925*, second edition (New York: Oxford University Press, 2006), 4.

11. Charles A. Blanchard, "Report of Committee on Correlation of Colleges, Seminaries and Academies," *God Hath Spoken* (Philadelphia: Bible Conference Committee, 1919), 19–20.
12. Adam Laats, *Fundamentalism and Education in the Scopes Era: God, Darwin, and the Roots of America's Culture Wars* (New York: Palgrave Macmillan, 2010), 43–60, 121–138.
13. William Bell Riley, "William Jennings Bryan University," *Christian Fundamentals in School and Church* 7 (October–December 1925): 52.
14. Bob Jones Sr., *Bob Jones Magazine* 1 (June 1928): 3.
15. Michael S. Hamilton, *The Fundamentalist Harvard: Wheaton College and the Continuing Vitality of American Evangelicalism, 1919–1965* (Ph.D. Diss., University of Notre Dame, 1994), 28.
16. Charles A. Blanchard, "Questionnaire for possible teachers" and "Fundamentals of the Christian Faith," [April 15, 1923?] Box #2: College-related; File: "Student Recruitment"; Blanchard papers, Wheaton College Archives, Archives of the Billy Graham Center, Wheaton, Illinois.
17. Hamilton, *Fundamentalist Harvard*, 37.
18. Ibid., 32.
19. Joel A. Carpenter, *Revive Us Again: The Reawakening of American Fundamentalism* (New York: Oxford University Press, 1997).
20. George Marsden, *Reforming Fundamentalism: Fuller Seminary and the New Evangelicalism* (Grand Rapids: Eerdmans, 1987).
21. Bill Boyle to Bob Jones Jr., June 2, 1958; Bob Jones Jr. to Boyle, September 6, 1958, Turner Box, Bob Jones U and Moody Monthly folder, Bob Jones University Archives, Greenville, SC.
22. Swartz, *Moral Minority*, 16.
23. Richard W. Anderson to Raymond Edman, undated. [Edman's response was dated February 5, 1963.] Box 6, folder 11: Kodon, 1948–1949; 1959–1964, President V. Raymond Edman Papers, Wheaton College Archives, Office of the President Records; Archives of the Billy Graham Center, Wheaton, Illinois. Emphasis in original.
24. Craven, "A Warning from the Editor," 3.
25. Swartz, *Moral Minority*, 62.
26. Daniel L. Turner, *Standing Without Apology: The History of Bob Jones University* (Greenville: Bob Jones University Press, 1997), 209.
27. "BJU Stages Write-in" *BJU Bulletin*, May 1966, 15; "BJU Student Leaders Protest Anarchy," *Voice of the Alumni*, June 1970, 2.
28. Bob Jones Jr., "Chapel Talk," May 5, 1970, typescript. Stenholm papers, Bob Jones University Archives, Greenville, South Carolina.
29. Resolution passed by BJU Alumni Association, April 2, 1970, Stenholm papers.
30. Michael Jay Sider-Rose, *Between Heaven and Earth: Moody Bible Institute and the Politics of the Moderate Christian Right, 1945–1986* (Ph.D. Diss., University of Pittsburgh, 2000), 187.
31. Dave Broucek, "Let's End Peaceniks' War," *Moody Student*, November 14, 1969, 2.
32. "Culbertson Chapel Announcement," October 13, 1969. Typescript, Box 1, Folder: Culbertson, Wm. Policies while at MBI, William Culbertson Papers, Moody Bible Institute Archives, Chicago, Illinois.
33. "Students, Deans to Revise Rules," *Moody Student*, November 20, 1970, 1.
34. Ibid.
35. Mike Farrell, "Are We Fighting the Wrong Fight?" *Moody Student*, December 16, 1970, 2.
36. Todd Lewis, "The Times They Are…" *The Chimes*, January 15, 1969, 3.
37. Samuel H. Sutherland to Todd Lewis, January 21, 1969. Folder: Chimes, The, Student Newspaper Publication Biola, Samuel Sutherland papers, Biola University archives, La Mirada, California.

38 Dick Chase to Samuel Sutherland, n.d., Folder: Chimes, The, Student Newspaper Publication Biola, Samuel Sutherland papers.
39 Bob Guernsey, "Why It's So Quiet," *The Chimes*, March 12, 1969, 2.
40 Memo, n.d., Folder: Chimes, The, Student Newspaper Publication Biola, Samuel Sutherland papers.
41 Memo, "List of Suspensions, Fall 1969," Folder: Student Problems, Samuel Sutherland papers.
42 Memo to Samuel Sutherland from Students of Talbot Theological Seminary, n.d., typescript, Folder: Chimes, The, Student Newspaper Publication Biola, Samuel Sutherland papers.
43 Memo, "Policy and Procedure Re: Militant Organizations Effect on Biola College Campus," April 10, 1969, Folder: Militant Organizations and their Effect on Biola Campus, Samuel Sutherland papers.
44 Hamilton, *Fundamentalist Harvard*, 18.
45 Glen Watts, "The Mumbling Majority," *Brave Son* 1:2 (April 1962): 3–4.
46 Craven, "A Warning from the Editor," 3.
47 Hamilton, *Fundamentalist Harvard*, 249–250.
48 V. Raymond Edman to Paul M. Saxton, February 7, 1963. Edman papers.
49 Herman A. Fischer to Harry E. Cawood, February 9, 1963, Edman papers.
50 Wesley Earl Craven, "From the Editor: To the Woman Who Came to My Office and Wept," *Kodon* 17:2 (Winter 1962): 4.
51 Ibid., 6.
52 Philip K. McIlnay, "Academics and the Faith," *Critique* 1:1 (March 1963): 1.
53 Ibid., 2.
54 Hamilton, *Fundamentalist Harvard*, 251–252.
55 "For Wheaton and Its Freedom," *Brave Son*, May 22, 1970, 1.
56 Hamilton, *Fundamentalist Harvard*, 29.
57 Swartz, *Moral Minority*, 40.
58 Gordon S. Jaeck to Raymond Edman, July 11, 1960. "Wheaton College Statement on Race Relations," Edman papers.
59 Ibid.
60 Raymond Edman to Executive Council, July 22, 1960, Edman papers.
61 James M. Murk, "The Race Question," *Brave Son* (April 1962): 11.
62 Ibid., 10.
63 Ibid., 12.
64 Swartz, *Moral Minority*, 29–31.
65 Ibid., 38.
66 Dr. Veltman to Hudson Armerding, November 17, 1968. Armerding papers.
67 Armerding to Donald Fay, March 18, 1970. Armerding papers.
68 Armerding, "Chapel Statement," March 26, 1970. Armerding papers.
69 Armerding, "Minority Groups," February 21, 1969. Armerding papers. Emphasis in original.
70 Armerding, Chapel statement, March 26, 1970. Armerding papers.
71 Armerding, "Minority Groups," February 21, 1969. Armerding papers.
72 Armerding to Rev. Grover Wilcox, March 12, 1970; Ron Potter to Armerding, March 17, 1970. Armerding papers.
73 R. Potter, "The 'Black Problem' Is Your Problem," *Wheaton Record*, February 27, 1970, 4.
74 Arthur Rupprecht to Armerding, May 18, 1970. Armerding papers.
75 Merrill C. Tenney to Edman, July 29, 1960. Edman papers.
76 Robert Burkinshaw, "The Funding of Evangelical Higher Education in the United States and Canada in the Postwar Period," in Larry Eskridge and Mark A. Noll, eds.,

More Money, More Ministry: Money and Evangelicals in Recent North American History (Grand Rapids: Eerdmans, 2000), 275.
77 Laurence H. Taylor to Armerding, June 11, 1970. Armerding papers.
78 Donald Fay to Armerding, March 11, 1970. Armerding papers.
79 Peter Veltman to Armerding, January 27, 1971. Armerding papers.
80 Robert O. DeVette to Peter Veltman, September 1, 1967. Armerding papers.
81 Box 3, folder 12: admissions, 1968–69. Armerding papers.
82 Box 3, folder 13: admissions, 1969–70. Armerding papers.
83 Box 3, folder 19: admissions, 1976–77. Armerding papers.
84 Charles W. Shoenherr to Armerding, April 15, 1966. Armerding papers.
85 Report to the President from the Admissions Office, July 15, 1966. Armerding papers.
86 Charles W. Shoenherr to Armerding, April 15, 1966. Armerding papers.
87 *Kodon* copy (Fall 1962), Gilbert Stenholm papers, Bob Jones University archives.
88 Bob Jones Jr. to Jim Walton, August 10, 1976. Bob Jones University archives.
89 Robert T. Ketcham to Armerding, April 3, 1967. Armerding papers.
90 David Otis Fuller to Ketcham, March 10, 1967. Armerding papers.
91 E. L. Eddy to Armerding, October 21, 1968. Armerding papers.

7

THE STUDENT PROTEST MOVEMENT IN THE *1968 ERA* IN THREE ACTS

Inception, Confrontations, and Legacies

Roger L. Geiger

More than a half-century has passed since the formation of Students for a Democratic Society in 1960 (SDS) and its 1962 manifesto, the *Port Huron Statement* (*PHS*). A mountain of literature has described the events and people of the ensuing "long 1960s," extending by some reckonings to the fall of Saigon in 1975. This literature has in fact given rise to a multitude of understandings, inconsistent if not contradictory. That the student movement interacted with far larger developments in American society and indeed the world makes interpretation all the more challenging. American society and culture experienced a sea change in the decade of the 1960s. Many of these changes had been advocated by the New Left, including undermining the Cold War mentality, obtaining greater inclusion of minorities in American life, and enlarging personal freedom against societal constraints. However, the violent confrontations at many universities from spring 1968 to spring 1970—what is here identified as the *1968 Era*—were in several ways counterproductive toward those ends. The radical Left expounded ideologies far more rigid than the doctrines it opposed, endorsed expressions of Black nationalism that tended to poison race relations, and adopted lifestyles that precluded cooperation with more moderate reformers. Hence, the student movement of the 1960s can be interpreted as either a progenitor of ideological extremism and politicization or as a force for achieving a more humane and tolerant society.[1]

The cultural revolution experienced by the United States in the 1960s has since been, at once, assimilated, transmogrified, and contested. Universities played a central role in this revolution as the locus for articulating fundamental challenges to the prevailing culture, incubating them, and providing a base for their propagation. Although the revolution transcended universities, they experienced deep and long-lasting effects. And, the underlying themes of this revolution have been subsequently relabeled and reformulated in response to social change in the decades since the 1960s.

Accordingly, this chapter first seeks to identify the constituent elements of the student movement and the cultural revolution that comprised the student rebellion. Second, it examines the radical phase of the *1968 Era*, when the student movement embraced revolutionary political strategies and provoked violent confrontations. Finally, it explores the longer-term consequences of these developments on American universities and society.

Antecedents

Students for a Democratic Society (SDS) was the self-defined organization of the "New Left" and the center of the student movement from the mid-1960s to its crack-up in 1969. A loose, protean organization with independent local chapters, its evolution nonetheless defined the path of mounting student radicalism. The origins and early development of SDS reveal the forces that gave rise to the student movement and the core ideas or beliefs that informed its development.[2]

SDS was organized in 1960 largely by a University of Michigan (sometime) graduate student, Al Haber, as the resuscitation of the student wing of the League for Industrial Democracy—an Old Left socialist party with a strong anti-communist and anti-Soviet stance. Haber was soon joined by Tom Hayden, editor of the *Michigan Daily* (1960–1961), who shared the vision of SDS becoming the vehicle for a national student movement. In the summer of 1960, before assuming the *Daily* editorship, Hayden had hitchhiked to the hearth of student activism, the University of California, Berkeley, and acquired a tutorial on current issues and protest actions. Following graduation the next year, he became the (sole) field secretary for SDS, based in Atlanta, and liaison with the Student Nonviolent Coordinating Committee (SNCC)—the student activist group formed to combat racial segregation in the South. There he experienced the brutality of diehard segregationists, and came away with a resolve to make SDS into the SNCC for the rest of the country. Now a dedicated activist for social change, he began writing a manifesto for the organization, "an agenda for a generation." A founding convention was set for June 1962 at a labor union camp outside of Port Huron, Michigan.[3]

The *Port Huron Statement* (*PHS*), based on Hayden's draft, is the most detailed and coherent expression of the original ideas, ideals, and aspirations of the New Left.[4] It posited the ideal of "participatory democracy," generally regarded as the most original political doctrine of the student movement. Inspired by a charismatic Michigan philosophy professor, Arnold Kaufmann,[5] it sought "a democracy of individual participation," that would allow an individual to "share in those social decisions determining the quality and direction of his life" (p. 3). Participatory democracy was intended to address and redress underlying problems in American society. By "bringing people out of isolation and into community," a more robust and active democracy would combat alienation by helping people "find meaning in personal life." The *PHS* promised a new political order in which private problems would find public resolutions. And this included the "economic experience," where the authors argued that "the means of production should be open to democratic participation and subject to democratic social regulation" (p. 4).

In calling for the creation of a new Left, the *PHS* echoed another movement hero, sociologist C. Wright Mills, who argued that leadership of the Left could no longer come from workers, the mainstay of Marxist theory, but from intellectuals.[6] The new Left should consist of, and be oriented toward, "younger people who matured in the postwar world." Thus, it would mobilize students chiefly, but also faculty, to create "a left with real intellectual skills" capable of "action … informed by reason" (p. 29). This new Left "must include liberals and socialists," and build bridges to "an awakening community of allies." However, this emphasis also made "the university the potential base and agency in a movement of social change."

In words that might have been written by University of California President Clark Kerr (below), the *PHS* extolled the university as "the central institution for organizing, evaluating, and transmitting knowledge," thus creating the "reliance by men of power on the men and storehouses of knowledge." Moreover, the university is "open to participation," "permits the political life to be an adjunct to the academic one," is distributed throughout the country, and is the obvious locus for the recruitment of young people.

SDS was "committed to stimulating this kind of social movement, this kind of vision and program in campus and community across the country," even if it appeared "to seek the unattainable." However, underlying the unattainable goals was a pervasive psychological reality. Throughout the document there are repeated references to alienation, apathy, and powerlessness affecting Americans, particularly the postwar generation. C. Wright Mills had published an influential volume, *The Power Elite* (1956), emphasizing the monopolization of power by unaccountable elites in the military, corporations, and government. He had also written earlier on powerlessness and alienation among the "white-collar" middle class. The *PHS* interpreted this loss of control by citizens in relation to national politics, corporations, or bureaucratic universities as a major source of discontent—the problem for which participatory democracy was the answer. In addition—and more importantly—this powerlessness was exacerbated by "the hypocrisy of American ideals." This case could be readily made. Racial segregation and discrimination made a mockery of American democracy. The power of Southern Democrats in Congress hobbled the Democratic Party—and American democracy. The military-industrial complex propelled the Cold War and the arms race according to no less authority than President Dwight D. Eisenhower. And American foreign policy opposed democratic movements in the developing world in favor of reliable, anti-communist dictators. The official image of the United States as a paragon of democracy and defender of the "Free World" could scarcely stand against these realities. Rather, their hypocrisy stood as proof of the need for a true democratic movement, for Students for a Democratic Society.[7] Thus, the student movement from its outset embraced "democracy" as its cause and rationale.

The bulk of the *PHS* in fact analyzed the issues cited above from this point of view, providing a snapshot of American politics, circa 1962.[8] No exaggeration was needed to portray the denial of basic civil rights in the South. There private citizens, law enforcement authorities, and governments employed violence and legal subterfuge to prevent African Americans from voting, having access to public facilities, or obtaining equal education. Black students had opened a new front of protest in 1960 with lunch counter sit-ins, which had soon been followed by the formation of SNCC and more aggressive tactics. Hayden had been among the first Northern activists to personally experience segregationist violence, but others followed in his path and were radicalized in the process. There could be no doubt in the Civil Rights Movement who was on the side of American democracy.

Other paramount issues revolved around the Cold War. The existing peace movement was still focused on disarmament, and the *PHS* rhetorically invoked the fear of living under the threat of nuclear annihilation. Although President Eisenhower had with difficulty maintained some moderation against exaggerated calls for military preparedness, Sputnik (1957) had demonstrated a Soviet advantage in rocketry, or at least rocket thrust. John F. Kennedy was elected president in 1960 on promises to overcome an alleged missile gap, and Republicans backed the arms race even more fervently, nominating bellicose Barry Goldwater for the presidency in 1964. Pressures for building more and more sophisticated nuclear weapons were never greater than in the early 1960s. This state of mind nourished the "military-industrial complex"—"the most spectacular and important creation of the authoritarian and oligopolistic structure of economic decision-making in America" (p. 8). These developments were fueled by a pervasive anti-communism. McCarthyism had self-destructed in the mid-1950s, but the far-right John Birch Society, founded in 1958, kept right-wing paranoia alive, as did the House Un-American Activities Committee, and its clones in several states, which continued to harass liberals and leftists. Against the authoritarian tendencies of the anti-communism campaigns of the Dixiecrat–Republican coalition, the New Left could again plausibly present itself as the champion of American democracy.[9]

Anti-communism had a further dimension in Cold War foreign policy, where it pitted the United States against the "colonial revolution." Throughout the developing world the CIA was rumored to be implicated in supporting dictatorial regimes in order to promote corporate investments and military alliances. The crude policies to overthrow or isolate Fidel Castro in Cuba seemed further to expose American hostility to revolutionary change. Support for Cuba, in fact, became a litmus test for the Left to demonstrate adherence to "anti-anti-communism." Given the Cold War consensus in American society, these issues may have appeared somewhat academic in 1962, but not for long.

In sum, the *PHS* portrayed an array of real problems afflicting American society. If some of the aspirations were utopian—global disarmament, "eliminating the disparity between have and have-not nations" (p. 19), and much else—the direction of reform advocated was far more consistent with the ideals of American democracy than the positions they opposed. Whether a citizen in 1962 would choose to support the New Left or the political establishment might well depend on how perilous she or he regarded the situation. However, in the years to follow, these conditions became more dire; and the prescriptions of the New Left became correspondingly more relevant and cogent, especially to students.

Thus, the *PHS* articulated sentiments that would become fundamental tenets of the student movement for the remainder of the 1960s:

1 An indictment of the social, political, and economic order of the United States that incorporated the Old Left rejection of capitalism.
2 Adoption of the rubric of democracy as the fundamental means and mission of the student movement, contrasted with American hypocrisy.
3 A commitment to the Civil Rights Movement, and more broadly the goals of racial equality and an end to discrimination.
4 Opposition to the pathology of the Cold War, soon magnified by the war in Vietnam.
5 Growing identification with all aspects of the anti-colonial and radical movements in the Third World.

Interestingly, the *PHS* expresses no animus against universities. They are in fact the only institution portrayed positively. Indeed, SNCC, the putative model, used historically Black southern colleges and universities as precarious bases in carrying the campaign against Jim Crow to Southern society.[10] Similarly, the first concerted action project of SDS was the Economic Research and Action Project, in which a number of early members sought to address issues of race and poverty by embedding themselves in urban ghettoes.[11] This was an effort by young people (former students) to tackle what they regarded as a major failing of American society—the Northern analogue to Jim Crow. The student movement was soon refocused on higher education by the Free Speech Movement (FSM) at the University of California, Berkeley—its first and in many ways defining triumph.

SDS was absent from this epic Berkeley confrontation, and scarcely needed among the multitude of student political organizations. The drama began at the opening of the 1964 fall semester, when the Berkeley administration withdrew the rights of student groups to man tables and distribute leaflets outside the main gate to campus. But much lay behind this arbitrary injunction.[12] Berkeley students had waged a campaign of civil disobedience to force an end to racial discrimination by San Francisco businesses that refused to hire Blacks. FSM leaders, like Mario Savio, had participated in the 1964 "Freedom Summer" in Mississippi working for civil rights. It has long been alleged that local business interests pressured the administration to suppress student civil rights activists, but no such link has been proven. Chancellor Edward Strong probably needed no external prompting: he and his top administrators convinced themselves that left-wing student groups were dominated by communists and intent on destroying the university. However, by attempting to muzzle their political activities, he created the perfect morality play for the student movement—student free speech against university repression.

As events unfolded during the fall, the university attempted to uphold the untenable position of denying "free speech" and imposing punishments on student protesters. Offended students, organized into the FSM, made two significant contributions to the emerging student movement. The first was to employ the techniques of civil disobedience, perfected in the Civil Rights Movement, against the university. The initial instance was unplanned. When a FSM activist was arrested in Sproul Plaza, a crowd spontaneously surrounded the police car, prompting a legendary 32-hour stand-off in which the university ultimately backed down. However, a later occupation of the administration building employed well-rehearsed protest protocol, forcing the police to drag out each of the hundreds of non-resisting protesters. The spectacle was a public relations fiasco for the Berkeley administration and helped to convince the faculty to support the FSM.

Second, in the course of the struggle students demonized the university in terms that went far beyond regulations about where students could distribute leaflets. The rhetorical assault on the University of California was inspired in part by Old Left groups on campus, particularly the Independent Socialist Club founded by a university librarian and Old-Left Troskyite, Hal Draper. The night before the Sproul Plaza affair he had given a talk, attended by FSM leaders, characterizing the university as a knowledge factory—an image repeated in the next day's speeches. Moreover, the FSM was able to personify the message in the president of the UC System, Clark Kerr—a scholar of industrial relations who had brilliantly characterized the modern "multiversity" in *The Uses of the University* (1963). Kerr spoke often and eloquently on the contributions of the university to the modern economy, and vice versa.[13] These views were soon pilloried in a Draper pamphlet, *The Mind of Clark Kerr* (October 1964). Draper easily distorted Kerr's nuanced arguments to claim that the university had become a knowledge factory in service to the capitalist power structure of a "monster-bureaucratic state." This diatribe was predicated on the premise that "capitalism is an outlived system ... based on a Permanent War

Economy, it perpetuates poverty, unemployment, racism, and imperialism." Draper was a minor figure, but his rhetoric was readily incorporated into the FSM. Its leader, Mario Savio, who was more a moralist than an ideologue, consistently invoked the image of the university "as a factory, a knowledge factory" designed to turn its students into conforming products. Far from being non-political (as it demanded students to be), he charged, the university was dominated by "reactionary" regents and engaged in building "newer and better atom bombs." Ultimately, he famously charged, "the operation of the machine [the university] becomes so odious, makes you so sick at heart, that you can't take part."[14] This was a far cry from the relatively open university depicted in the *PHS*. On the other hand, the FSM was portrayed by Savio and others as embodying the values of the New Left—individuality, freedom, and participatory democracy, exemplified in its own interminable deliberations.

In December the FSM achieved a heady victory—elimination of the restrictions on political activity on UC campuses. Rather than disband, however, it formed a loose coalition with other leftist groups to protest the growing war in Vietnam. This development paralleled a commitment by SDS to seize leadership of the inchoate antiwar movement. The Gulf of Tonkin Resolution in August 1964 had given President Johnson unlimited authority to wage war against North Vietnam and the Vietcong. The early months of 1965 brought bombing of the North and a vast escalation of US military forces in the South.[15] Even before these developments, SDS had resolved to make opposition to the war its top priority and to sponsor a "March on Washington" in April. This was the beginning of a sustained antiwar movement, but it also brought a crystallization of New Left ideology. Revulsion against the war was broadened to encompass the entire evil "system." SDS president Paul Potter blamed the system for "a war in Vietnam today or a murder in the South tomorrow or all the incalculable, innumerable more subtle atrocities that are worked on people all over—all the time." He asserted that the demonstrators were united with the "people of Vietnam. ... All our lives, our destinies, our very hopes to live depend on our ability to overcome that system." How to overcome the "system," soon dubbed "corporate liberalism" by another SDS president? Their answer was to "build a movement." Thus, as early as 1965 building a *movement* to oppose the *system* became the overriding objectives of SDS, transcending specific issues of war, racism, imperialism, or alleged "university complicity" in all of the above.[16] These particular issues nonetheless were crucial for illustrating the iniquities of corporate liberalism (which had otherwise brought unprecedented prosperity for most Americans) and mobilizing students for the *movement*.[17]

This strategy not only met with some initial success, it refocused SDS on students and campuses. The March on Washington had a far greater impact than originally anticipated. It was followed by the influx of a new generation of SDS recruits. Less intellectual, innocent (at first) of Old Left ideological squabbles, they seemed motivated by pure alienation from the middle-class American establishment. Todd Gitlin (first-generation SDS) described them as "instinctive anarchists, principled and practiced antiauthoritarians."[18] They sported longer hair and blue work shirts, and they indulged in marijuana and anti-establishment rock-and-roll. Their appearance would seem to mark a significant change in the Zeitgeist. Above all, the American hypocrisy that the *PHS* had identified in 1962 resonated as glaring reality to this generation—the racial violence of die-hard segregationists, now depicted on the nightly news; the fulminations of Cold War zealots; and the escalation of the Vietnam War by the "peace" candidate, President Lyndon Johnson. For every committed SDS member, many fellow students shared some degree of this disillusionment and alienation. These sympathizers might participate or not in the emerging protests, but they rarely criticized the radicals, no matter how hyperbolic the rhetoric. They too felt that there was something terribly wrong with the *system*.

This state of mind was soon exacerbated by three kindred developments: the rise of Black Power, the seductive images of Third World Revolution, and the pervasive spread and influence of the Counterculture. All of these far transcended the universities, but nonetheless had a powerful influence on campuses.

The Civil Rights Movement achieved the legal emancipation of Blacks in the segregated South with passage of the Civil Rights Act of 1964 and the Voting Rights Act of 1965. Just five days after the latter act was signed into law, the Black section of Watts, Los Angeles, erupted in a prolonged, destructive riot. Racially based riots ensued in inner cities across the country, culminating in the summer of 1967 with devastating riots in Newark and Detroit. Civil rights did little to ameliorate the oppressive conditions endured by urban Blacks outside the South. The riots documented another failure of American society and, for many, underscored the Left's indictment. Nor did violence by segregationists abate in the South. There SNCC abandoned interracial cooperation by expelling all Whites. Its new leader, Stokely Carmichael, demanded Black Power in tirades that resounded across the country.[19] In Oakland, California, the Black Panther Party for Self-Defense demonstrated its defiance by carrying unconcealed firearms and spouting simplistic communist slogans. The New Left admired and supported militant Black nationalism, often conceding leadership to the "black brothers" and adopting Black vernacular, such as referring to police as "pigs." However, Black Power quickly migrated to campuses, where recently recruited Black students would soon press demands for separatism and special programs.

The seeds of Third-World romanticism were present in the *PHS*, but mounting frustration with the Vietnam War caused them to hypertrophy into a fanciful identification with guerillas and revolution anywhere in the developing world. Prophets were readily found in the writings of Franz Fanon and Regis Debray, the revolutionary icon Ché Guevara, and Chairman Mao Zedong, then leading the Cultural Revolution. Ultimate adulation went to North Vietnam and the National Liberation Front. The New Left and Third World

Revolutionaries had the same enemy—the government and the *system* of the United States. Third World objectives soon were included in student demands, sometimes in conjunction with Black Power and other times calling for Third World Studies.

The Counterculture became all pervasive by the late 1960s.[20] Students expressed their rejection of bourgeois American society with long hair, working-class clothing (or not much clothing at all), obscene language, anti-establishment rock-and-roll, widespread use of marijuana and occasionally harder drugs, and sexual license. Closely related to these affectations was a visceral abhorrence of all forms of hierarchy and authority, particularly as found in universities. That is, countercultural attitudes rejected the hierarchical authority of universities as formal organizations and also the intellectual authority embedded in the curriculum. Anti-intellectualism was inherent in the emphasis on feelings—enhanced by sex, drugs, and rock-and-roll. A natural affinity existed between countercultural rejection of bourgeois norms and New Left condemnation of the *system*.[21] Of course, many hippies sought personal emancipation by dropping out; and truly dedicated radicals took the opposite approach by working in the movement. However, hippies generally supported demonstrations or protests that opposed straight society, whether for Black Power, Third World Revolution, opposition to the war, or transformation of the university.

By the summer of 1966 the leadership of SDS was frustrated: its membership was growing, but tactics such as draft resistance were ineffectual. Nationally, the antiwar movement was a singular issue that was making no headway; and civil rights had been eclipsed by Black Power. The leadership (most of whom were no longer students) resolved to shift its organizational energies to universities and students. It specifically sought to exploit local issues on individual campuses:

> *Not* to change the educational system on campus, *not* to achieve academic reforms, *not* even to get more power in the hands of students within the university setting. It did so because it saw among American studentry the possibility of creating a generation of committed radicals, and thus to change the entire political and social structure of the country.... Never lost was the cardinal idea that students should be agents for *social* change.[22]

This fundamental strategy of the SDS National Office is key to understanding the escalation of the number and severity of campus protests in the following years. Issues were chosen chiefly in order to manipulate—they would say mobilize—students for this larger purpose. Efforts to block armed forces recruiters were intended to expose university complicity in the war and American imperialism; protests against university rules were meant to reveal the authoritarian nature of establishment institutions.

For the next academic year, SDS organizers from the national office and local chapters sought to inflate campus grievances into confrontations that would gain recruits and demonstrate university complicity with corporate liberalism. Most major universities experienced protests over administrative authority, parietal rules, or required curricula. On some campuses, radical students gained control of student government in order to make far-reaching demands. SDS was responsible for staging protests against armed forces recruiters and corporate symbols, especially Dow Chemical, the manufacturer of napalm. Berkeley led the way in raising the intensity of protest when students blocked access to a Navy recruiter. Arguing self-righteously that the university had allowed the Navy to use space reserved for students, radicals were able to escalate this confrontation into a five-day strike. Harvard SDS achieved notoriety by temporarily blockading Secretary of Defense Robert McNamara. Henceforth, administration officials could expect harassment whenever they set foot on campus. By the spring of 1967, protests had increased in frequency and intensity; the challenge for SDS was to utilize these protests to generate "revolutionary consciousness": "we need to move from protest to resistance; to dig in for the long haul; to become full time, radical, sustained, relevant. In short, we need to make a revolution."[23]

The organization now dedicated to fomenting an American revolution consisted of a national office with about a dozen full-time workers, eight "regional travelers" who spread the gospel to campuses, and a national membership of 6,400. More impressive were SDS chapters on 250 campuses with a total membership near 30,000. One survey found almost two-thirds to be students—40 percent undergraduate and 25 percent graduate. Of other with known status, 20 percent were non-students and 10 percent were in high school. Internally, all shades of leftist ideologies were represented, including varieties of communists, socialists, and anarchists. A contingent from the Maoist Progressive Labor Party was a growing (and unwelcome) presence. However, all were pretty much united in opposition to the war, support for Black Power, infatuation with Third World Revolution, and condemnation of university complicity. In these positions they could count on the sympathies of thousands more inside and outside of universities. Despite the existence of numerous antiwar groups or mobilization committees, SDS was the largest and best organized student group. The leadership characterized its members as 85–90 percent shock troops—mostly young students "completely turned off by the American system … anti-intellectual … morally outraged." Intellectuals made up perhaps 5–10 percent, mostly graduate students who theorized and strategized but made fairly tepid protesters. Just 5 percent were "organizers," who kept the chapters running, actively recruited members, and attended regional and national meetings. In this loose structure, linkage between the national office and the chapters was tenuous. Protest activities on individual campuses depended on the strength and radicalism of SDS chapters, their allies, and the receptivity of the local environment.[24] The national office and the national officers lived in an ideological cocoon in which revolution seemed a realistic objective. But then so had Lenin. However, in 1917 Lenin inherited a true revolution, while SDS sought to foment an academic Armageddon.

Academic Armageddon, 1967–1970

Confrontations in the fall of 1967, far exceeded all previous protests. By one count, 60 large campus protests took place, two-thirds against recruiters, half of those from Dow Chemical.[25] SDS was responsible for turning Dow into a symbol of corporate–university complicity, and the company reported that one-third of their campus visits (113 of 339) experienced harassment. Nearly half of the recruitment demonstrations involved violence, and universities called in police in at least 20 of them. A particularly "successful" confrontation was orchestrated at the University of Wisconsin. Hundreds of students blockaded a Dow recruiter and, in the new spirit of resistance, refused to disperse. The university brought in reinforcements from the Madison police, and a bloody melee spilled out of the building and onto the campus in a confused mixture of tear gas and rock throwing. Campus outrage against the police assault was expressed in a mass rally the next day and a five-day strike. The strategy of resistance had succeeded in banishing the Dow recruiter, closing the university, provoking alleged police brutality and, perhaps for some, raising revolutionary consciousness.[26]

The same week at Berkeley a coalition of radical groups that now included SDS assumed the role of aggressor in attempting to shut down the draft induction center in Oakland. After being repulsed on Tuesday, they returned in greater force on Friday to stage a riot that succeeded in preventing the center from operating that day.[27] These violent clashes set an unfortunate precedent for both sides: radicals imagined that resistance was succeeding, that they could impose their will through physical confrontation; and the authorities concluded that decisive physical force was imperative to prevent that from happening.

These escalating protests in the fall of 1967 set the stage for the most prolonged, violent, and destructive confrontations of the *1968 Era*. The following accounts describe the protests that received most media coverage, most affected public opinion, and inflicted greatest disruption on their respective institutions. Each of these episodes was a discrete event, unique in terms of actors, issues, and outcomes; but all were conducted as if there were well understood rules for student class warfare.[28]

Columbia University: April 23–30, 1968

Columbia University in 1968 was a loose collection of 16 schools and three affiliates—Barnard College (for women), Teachers College, and Union Theological Seminary. Just 6,000 of its 20,000 students were undergraduates, nearly half enrolled in Columbia College.[29] The SDS historian likened the development of the Columbia chapter to "the history of many SDS chapters of the time, writ larger ... but in essentials the same."[30] Formed in 1965, it began staging aggressive confrontations over university complicity in the 1966 school year, but also suffered from periodic lapses of energy. By 1968 it consisted of perhaps 50 core members and 100 earnest hangers-on. Columbia had begun recruiting Black students seriously in 1964, and the following year they formed the Society of Afro-American Students (SAS) largely for social support. Radical activists were a minority among Columbia undergraduates, and substantial numbers of students, later organized into the "majority coalition," opposed the disruptions.

SDS was divided between an older faction focused on education and base-building and an "action faction" led by Mark Rudd that advocated direct struggle. In March 1968, Rudd established his reputation by throwing a pie in the face of a Selective Service colonel. He was promptly elected chapter chairman on a promise "to Get the SDS Moving Again and Screw the University." Increasingly audacious confrontations, in violation of university prohibitions, were overlooked by the administration in the hope of avoiding negative publicity. Meanwhile, SDS sought to mobilize students by exploiting two university issues. For some eight years Columbia had pursued a dubious project to build a gymnasium in adjoining Morningside Park for use by Columbia College students and residents of neighboring Harlem. By 1968 both city officials and the Black community had soured on the project, but the university broke ground nonetheless to prevent their permits from expiring. The alleged perfidy of this project purportedly illustrated the university's inherent racism. The second issue aimed to dramatize Columbia's complicity in the war by focusing on its membership in the Institute for Defense Analysis (IDA). The IDA was a think tank that provided Defense Department access to university expertise, scarcely a malevolent activity; but the national office had targeted such university affiliations as symbolic of participation in the war effort. Rudd would later brag, "we manufactured the issues," as events soon revealed.[31]

On Tuesday, April 23, Rudd gathered yet another rally, on this occasion combining both SDS and SAS, to protest these iniquities. After stoking their indignation, a crowd of about 200 set out to vent their anger at a suitable symbol of authority. Unable to enter the administration building, the mob proceeded to the inactive Morningside construction site. Finding it guarded by police, they returned to campus and entered Hamilton Hall, seat of Columbia College, and continued the demonstration. They remained in the building at the end of the day, turning the rally into a building occupation and the college dean into a hostage. At midnight, the SAS caucused and, in the spirit of Black Power, resolved to expel the White demonstrators. SDS complied, but asked what their role should now be: "get your own building" someone suggested. Rudd led his followers to the main administration building and occupied the president's office, fully expecting to be forcefully removed. When that did not happen, another building was taken over, and soon two more. At this point, and for the next days, the occupations themselves became the only "issue" that mattered.

The administration contemplated forcefully removing the occupiers, but was fearful of provoking the Blacks in Hamilton Hall and imagined sympathizers in nearby Harlem. Any decisive university action was then paralyzed by the attempts of concerned faculty to mediate. They wished, above all, to prevent bringing the police onto the campus. They proposed terms that would have met almost all radical demands—ending the Morningside project, withdrawal from IDA, and, most importantly, disciplinary arrangements that amounted to virtual amnesty. But Rudd summarily rejected terms and negotiations, galvanizing the occupiers to remain until forcefully removed. For the opposition, such terms were tantamount to capitulation and enraged the many student anti-protesters and unsympathetic professors. The faculty's fruitless measures occupied most of five days and, for faculty and administration, caused enormous anguish. Finally, after eight days, the inevitable police bust took place—fully covered by the New York media. The Blacks in Hamilton Hall exited peacefully into police vans, and the most radical pockets of SDS resisted. Charges of police brutality abounded, but no serious injuries occurred. However, the administration was discredited; the university community divided and devastated. Mark Rudd had won the battle, if not the war.

Accounts in newspapers and journals were devastating. Conservatives accurately characterized Columbia's actions as pusillanimous; liberals sympathized with the ostensible goals and alleged sufferings of the demonstrators. An ensuing strike was only pre-empted by suspending classes. President Kirk resigned within three months, and his provost and heir apparent was passed over for the succession. Criminal charges against the protesters were dropped, and university discipline brought only letters of admonition. IDA was abandoned, and Columbia took further steps to forbid classified research and scrutinize relations with outside agencies. As a bonus, the successful Navy Reserve Officer Training Program was scuttled. The ill-starred Morningside Park project was terminated as well. The SAS dissociated from SDS and presented its own list of demands to enhance the Black presence at Columbia. Although sometimes extravagant, their specific objectives were largely granted in subsequent negotiation. The number of students of color in the next year's class almost doubled.

SDS and Mark Rudd clearly overreached with a second occupation of Hamilton Hall in May. Forcibly ejected that evening with accustomed violence and vandalism, this time they received no sympathy from the former coalition. The university remained badly divided over different approaches for rebuilding. A Faculty Executive Committee was formed and became the de facto voice of the university. Over the next 12 months, it laid the basis for restructuring the administration and beginning the rebuilding process. Just one year after the crisis, the university voted overwhelmingly to create a University Senate that would set policy on university-wide matters. The lasting damage to the university was nevertheless severe. Some of the most illustrious professors departed; others withdrew from active roles. Promising younger faculty also left for more congenial settings. Columbia's financial situation was tenuous in 1968, but exacerbated afterward by the crisis. Columbia's difficulties were not all caused by the crisis of April 1968. However, the crisis had exposed inherent weaknesses in its governance and structure, and it would take another decade before the university "bottomed out," in the judgment of the university historian.[32] The unique strength of Columbia—its august stature in American intellectual life—was far more difficult to reclaim.

State University of New York at Buffalo: August 1968–June 1970

The private University of Buffalo was incorporated into the State University of New York in 1962. Formerly focused on engineering and medicine, SUNY Buffalo was designated to become a full-fledged "university center," which prompted an expansion that was breathtaking even for that era. In the next four years enrollment rose from 7,000 to 21,000, and 400 additional faculty were hired. A new department of political science, for example, hired 27 members in three years. A magnificent new campus was planned. In 1966, Martin Meyerson became president, lured from UC Berkeley with a vision of creating "a Berkeley of the East." Meyerson's charm, enthusiasm, and plans for a new design for academic excellence lured top academics to this ambitious work-in-progress. He emphasized building the almost non-existent liberal arts, hiring an especially distinguished (and leftist) group of writers and critics for the English Department. Excellent students were attracted as well. The number in the top 10 percent of their graduating classes rose from 10 to 80 percent (1958–1968). A substantial portion of the new students came from the New York City area, and were no doubt familiar with radical and antiwar rhetoric. The City of Buffalo's population, in contrast, was heavily ethnic and strongly Catholic, with a history of racial clashes and latent anti-Semitism—a population with little sympathy for the new academia of the 1960s or the New Left.[33]

The Buffalo chapter of SDS was formed in 1965 and immediately began antiwar protests. They were opposed, often physically, by conservative pro-war citizens, the Buffalo police, and an active FBI unit. Frustrated, the antiwar movement became more radical in 1966 and joined forces with the Marxist-Maoist "Youth Against War and Fascism." Meyerson inherited a fractured campus. Conservative faculty in engineering and medicine demanded and were given permission to conduct research for the Defense Department, despite his better judgment; and a student referendum actually supported cooperation with the Selective Service. Escalating antiwar protests intensified the polarization—between liberal arts and the conservative faculties, and between the university generally and the city. Meyerson became increasingly unpopular with Buffalonians, especially after he froze construction on the new campus over racial discrimination in union hiring; but he was soon reviled equally by radicals.

The confrontations at Buffalo assumed more violent form after August 1968. Draft resisters took refuge in a local Unitarian church, supported by more than 200 demonstrative sympathizers. After several days, a violent police bust produced nine arrests. Henceforth celebrated as the Buffalo Nine, their trials provided further occasions for agitation. From this point a virtual state of war existed between the campus and the community. For the next two years confrontations became more prolonged and destructive. SDS claimed 500 members and issued far-fetched, non-negotiable demands. Physical attacks were launched against the construction site for a defense project and the offices of Air Force ROTC. University operations were compromised by the substantial numbers of radical faculty and students. SDS effectively took over student government by mobbing its meetings. Meyerson's new design had decentralized academic control to constituent colleges, several of which assumed radical guise. Three of the colleges were dominated by radical/Counterculture students and faculty. They offered courses on New Left subjects in which everyone received "As"; one named itself "Rosa Luxemburg College."

All this was prelude to two weeks of a campus-police riot and student-faculty strike in February–March 1970. Crowds of more than 1,000 rampaged against the usual targets and directly battled equally infuriated police. The campus suffered more than $200,000 in damages; 125 students, faculty, and police were hospitalized; and in the denouement 45 faculty were arrested for an illegal sit-in.

When passions finally cooled the dreams of an academic Berkeley of the East were a distant memory. Meyerson had taken leave in the fall of 1969, and gladly accepted the presidency of the University of Pennsylvania. His successor in July 1970 was Robert Ketter, who represented the old University of Buffalo. The star faculty recruited by Meyerson soon departed, and those who remained opted for a faculty union. Ketter imposed a more traditional academic structure but chafed against the SUNY bureaucracy. He sought to mend relations with the Buffalo community, but enrollments declined nonetheless. SUNY Buffalo survived and eventually moved to its new campus with only memories of the scars and the promise of the *1968 Era*.[34]

San Francisco State College: November 1968–March 1969

San Francisco State became part of the California State College system when it was reorganized under the Master Plan in 1961. Formerly oriented toward adult education, it chafed under the yoke of the system bureaucracy. In liberal San Francisco, the college was soon beset with antiwar protests, including physical confrontations. A Black Student Union (BSU) was organized in 1963, and it assumed a posture of Black nationalism after a SNCC organizer arrived in 1966. Other students of color organized a parallel Third World Liberation Front. Their chief objective was a Black Studies Program, toward which the college was sympathetic but slow to organize. San Francisco State was permissive toward its students. Disciplinary action, if any, was determined by a student board; students controlled invitations to campus speakers; and an Experimental College was created for student-organized courses. Black students used the latter to establish an entire Black Studies curriculum, emphasizing Black nationalism and adopting the Black Panthers' logo.[35]

The White-run student newspaper became loudly critical of what it called Black racism. The resulting conflict intensified until a group of Blacks invaded the paper offices and assaulted the editor in November 1967. Several attackers were subsequently arrested, including George Murray, a tutor in Black Studies and a Black Panther. In the next months, several buildings were occupied to protest disciplinary actions against the Black students. Murray nonetheless continued as a student and tutor, but also inflamed the situation. He traveled to Cuba (about the same time as Mark Rudd) and attacked the United States in a fiery antiwar speech that was reported in national media. Back home, he advocated that students carry guns to protect themselves against racist administrators. Outrage against the retention of Murray as an instructor and the continuing turmoil on campus finally led the Chancellor of the State System to demand that Murray be suspended. The BSU countered that suspension would trigger a strike. On November 1, the president succumbed to the pressure and suspended Murray, and five days later the campus was engulfed in a strike.

The BSU issued ten "non-negotiable" demands that included the creation of a Black Studies Department under their control with 20 full-time faculty positions; the admission of all Black students who wished to attend; and of course the retention of Murray. The Third World Liberation Front added demands for a School of Ethnic Studies with 50 faculty slots. The "Third World Strike" soon forced the closing of the campus. When the president and faculty suggested a (hopefully) peaceful resolution through university-wide discussion of the issues, the president was fired. Linguistics professor S. I. Hayakawa became the college's third president of that year. A hard-liner toward student protest, his awkward but earnest efforts at times disarmed the strikers. Still, with all sides enraged, violent clashes continued into the spring. The college was willing to establish a Black Studies Department, but not to reinstate Murray. When Murray was arrested and jailed on weapons charges, that issue became moot. San Francisco State reopened on March 21 after the longest college disruption of the *1968 Era*. The BSU achieved a Black Studies Department under its control, which now meant under the influence of the Black Panthers. Its extremist teaching almost cost the college its accreditation. The conflict also launched the career of S. I. Hayakawa as an icon of resistance to student radicalism, and prompted legislation giving universities far greater powers over obstreperous students, although most institutions were scarcely willing to use them.

Cornell University: April 1969

The crisis at Cornell also drew inspiration from Black Power but raised deeper issues of university integrity. Cornell President James Perkins (1963–1969) epitomized the enlightened liberalism of the early 1960s. Much like his good friend Clark Kerr, he envisioned a university committed to addressing and ameliorating challenges facing American society. He was the first major university president to implement aggressive recruitment and special programs for disadvantages Black students, raising their numbers from eight to 250 by 1968. An Afro-American Society (AAS) was formed in 1966 and soon became increasingly militant under the influence of Black Power. By no means all Black students supported the radicals, but moderate Blacks were threatened for not doing so. An active SDS chapter played a secondary role, assisting the AAS and supporting their demands.[36]

Racial animosity passed a threshold in spring 1968, when AAS accused an economics professor of racism and pressed their demand for his dismissal by occupying the economics department. Terminating even a visiting professor on the basis of an AAS interpretation of his teaching would be an egregious violation of academic freedom. This situation was rationalized by charges of "institutional racism." According to this newly invoked theory, historically White institutions unconsciously committed subtle forms of racism. In effect, anything that gave offense to Black students could be viewed as evidence of institutional racism. Given the prevalence of liberal guilt, exacerbated by a handful of actual anti-Black incidents, many faculty, administrators, and President Perkins sympathized with this view, at least in part. They acknowledged a responsibility to modify their speech and behavior to avoid giving offense. In this atmosphere, academic freedom and the enforcement of campus laws and regulations, let alone civil behavior, were subordinated to the appeasement of Black sensibilities—as defined by the AAS. As the administration largely ignored increasing provocations, Black militants became more paranoid in identifying ubiquitous institutional racism and more strident in their demands.

The centerpiece of those demands was creation of a Black Studies program. After relenting on an original demand for a separate college, the chief point of disagreement became the extent of student control. After prolonged negotiations an agreement was reached in early April, largely on the president's insistence, that accorded Black students an unprecedented role in determining curriculum and selecting faculty. Militant Blacks were nonetheless frustrated by the lengthy process and had begun to buy rifles for "self-defense," like the Black Panthers. The crisis was precipitated by the decision of the judicial board to reprimand three AAS activists for previous disruptive acts. The AAS responded by occupying a campus building, Willard Straight Hall. Feeling threatened, they smuggled rifles into the building that evening. The next day, facing armed students and a potential catastrophe, university negotiators capitulated to all of the AAS demands, including nullification of the student reprimands. The occupiers then marched out of the building brandishing their rifles and giving the Black Power salute for the national news media and all the world to see. Still, the university's humiliation was not finished.

The next day the faculty repudiated the administration agreement as a capitulation to force and an abandonment of academic integrity. SDS then joined in by organizing a huge demonstration, accompanied by explicit threats of violence from the AAS. Under great pressure, the faculty acceded to this intimidation and reversed its vote, approving the administration's agreement. However, the reaction to this surrender was also intense. Several professors resigned immediately, including Black Economics Professor Thomas Sowell, who charged that Black students were not being held to the same standards. Others formally protested the abdication of academic freedom at Cornell. President Perkins was soon gone; and the Cornell Africana Studies Center became one of the most politicized units of this type. At Cornell, well-meaning liberal efforts to rectify racial inequality resulted instead in compromising basic university values of academic freedom, equal treatment, and critical inquiry.

Stanford, Harvard, and Berkeley: April–May 1969

Besides Cornell and San Francisco State, at least 83 other colleges and universities experienced Black protests in 1968–1969.[37] But other issues also animated activists in the manic spring of 1969. At Stanford University growing opposition to classified research came to a head in April, when antiwar activists occupied the Applied Electronics Laboratory for nine days, eventually leaving peacefully under threat of expulsion. Protesters had two targets. Electronics research had helped raise Stanford to the top ranks of American research universities, but much of this was for the Pentagon and much of that classified. The university also sponsored the Stanford Research Institute (SRI), a nonprofit institution originally founded to perform research for local industry. By the 1960s SRI had become largely a contractor for the Defense Department. Classified military research received little sympathy from Stanford's liberal faculty and students, although it was the livelihood of more than 1,000 employees. The occupiers were generally applauded on campus, increasing pressure on the university. The faculty senate voted to end all classified research on campus, and the trustees soon followed by cutting ties with SRI, making it an independent nonprofit research institute. No classified research was actually terminated, but it no longer was performed under the Stanford aegis. With this issue removed, support for disruptive actions by the core of radical students gradually waned.

Harvard had one of the largest chapters of SDS, and its chief focus was opposition to the war.[38] As elsewhere, it adopted more confrontational tactics from 1967 onward, as frustration with the war grew among students and faculty. In 1968–1969 the existence of the Reserve Officers Training Corps (ROTC) was the issue chosen to exemplify university complicity. The administration effectively eviscerated the program, but SDS used the lack of immediate cessation as a pretext to occupy the administration building. Harvard '69 was in some ways a reprise of Columbia '68. Student revolutionaries cared little for the ostensible issues. Once in control of University Hall, the occupation itself became the chief issue—and the resort to a police bust two days later the principal controversy. Liberal faculty could show their antiwar bona fides by criticizing the use of police, and moderates who blamed the students found themselves on the defensive. Harvard, however, was a far stronger university and community than Columbia, and neither the occupation nor the bust caused irreparable damage. Two years later, Law School Dean Derek Bok—a critic of the bust—became the new president of Harvard and an exemplar for the management of obstreperous students (below).

At Berkeley the battle of People's Park became the *reductio ad absurdum* of student protest. Confrontations between dedicated radicals and authorities escalated during 1968–1969. The Regents' refusal to allow Black Panther Eldridge Cleaver to teach a course led to a building take-over, vandalism, and a violent bust. In the spring, the Third World Liberation Front attempted to close the campus with a strike. In May, in an effort to mobilize the large, local Counterculture population, activists decided to turn an unused piece of university property into a "People's Park." An eclectic collection of hippies, radicals, students, and others fashioned a park of sorts. This strangely constructive effort struck the fancy of the community. A student referendum favored the park by six to one. However, the park had no legal standing, and it was adamantly opposed by the Regents and Governor Ronald Reagan. They ordered the park to be fenced off, but to do this against local opposition required state police protection. Supporters stoked their indignation at a large rally, then marched on the park, setting off a full-scale riot. Protesters actively fought with police, and police fired shotguns seemingly indiscriminately at rioters, killing one (an unconnected riot tourist). The National Guard had to be mobilized to restore order and occupy the park. Ironically, the battle of People's Park and its aftermath tended to unite hippies, radicals, and the Berkeley community against the police and the Governor; but in fact it signaled the eventual demise of large-scale student protest at the university.[39]

Kent State University: May 1–4, 1970

President Nixon's invasion of Cambodia (April 30, 1970) provoked exasperation, frustration, and rage at campuses across the country. Kent State had a fairly small radical community. Protests the previous year had been dealt with harshly, jailing demonstrators and banning SDS. Cambodia provoked an angry but peaceful rally on Friday, May 1. That night crowds in the downtown bars turned ugly, starting a riot, defying local police, and vandalizing businesses. The town declared a state of emergency and requested the National Guard. The next night a protest rally turned into a defiant mob that set fire to the ROTC building and celebrated as it burned. From this point the National Guard and its mission to restore and enforce order became the chief source of resentment. The situation deteriorated until the morning of May 4, when an unplanned gathering of students confronted the assembled soldiers. At least some students behaved outrageously, hurling stones and epithets at the Guard, but presenting no physical threat. For reasons that have never been determined, the Guard opened fire—61 rounds that randomly killed four and wounded nine students.[40]

After Armageddon

After the killings at Kent State the era of violent student protest effectively ended.[41] The tragedy at Kent State, and the killing of students by police at Jackson State soon afterward, seemed to underline the fact that events were spinning out of control. Universities admitted as much by suspending classes and terminating the spring semester. When students returned in the fall of 1970, their politics were no different, but the illusion that direct action would have any effect was replaced by sullen resignation and pervasive cynicism. Moreover, the most radical leaders, advocates of resistance who had been responsible for the most damaging confrontations of the *1968 Era*, were largely missing—dropped out, suspended, or gone underground.[42] Shell-shocked universities, for their part, were prepared to appease any remotely feasible student demand in order to avoid confrontation. What then were the consequences of these and all the other confrontations?

Considering the extreme demands forwarded by protesters, there was never any chance for fulfillment. However, in other respects, the protesters achieved some degree of success. Insofar as Mark Rudd was determined to "screw the university," he delivered. Blacks at Cornell took down a liberal president in ignominious fashion. And Harvard radicals had the satisfaction of forcing the university into the embarrassment of calling in the police and alienating its largely liberal constituency. Whatever short-term gratification these triumphs may have brought, they certainly appear hollow in a longer-term perspective.

Campaigns against defense research and ROTC achieved some success. Columbia was willing to concede on these issues. Stanford curtailed defense research and divested SRI. MIT likewise moved its huge weapons R&D operations into a separate organization, the Draper Labs. Congress reacted to the controversy over defense research in universities with the Mansfield Amendment, which forbade the Department of Defense from funding research not directly related to its mission. Weapons research thus continued in the same buildings by the same people, only now under new, non-university management. However, basic research not related to weapons, which the Department had formerly supported, was now eliminated—just at the time that federal support for academic research generally was being scaled back.

Black students obtained many of their objectives in terms of recruitment of students and faculty, special living arrangements, and Black Studies programs largely under their control. Universities had been willing, if not eager, to grant most of these items as part of commitments to ameliorate racial inequality in higher education, often derided as liberal guilt. Demonstrations by militant Black students burnished the ideology of Black Power and succeeded in obtaining more far-reaching measures than universities considered prudent or academically legitimate.[43] These concessions were often achieved at some cost to their respective institutions. Harvard was acutely embarrassed by ceding control of its Black Studies program to students, but soon rectified this anomaly. The capitulation at Cornell was a stain on the reputation of the university for years to come, and Black students have continued to defend their gains with the same belligerent tactics.[44] And, San Francisco State's surrender to the BSU for a time undermined the academic credibility of the entire university.

Elsewhere, the direct results of the confrontations of the *1968 Era* were largely negative. SUNY Buffalo perhaps suffered the greatest long-term damage. While it seems unlikely that it could have become the Berkeley of the East within the confines of the SUNY system, the destructive fury of its demonstrators and their adversaries doomed its once promising bid for academic distinction, or even academic leadership within SUNY. At Berkeley, and Madison too, the academic core largely weathered the turmoil and destruction of these years. At Berkeley much violence was deflected off campus, although that was not true for Madison, where the 1970 bombing of the Army Mathematics Research Center by antiwar terrorists killed one victim and caused extensive damage. Some of these scars would heal, but the *1968 Era* brought permanent changes to American universities.

The Legacy of the *1968 Era* for American Universities

The United States in the 1960s experienced a cultural revolution.[45] The *ancien régime* in this revolt was the conservative 1950s, dominated by a pervasive ideology that idealized an "American Way of Life," centered on family, church, country, and expanding economic prosperity. It culminated in the events of 1968 and afterward—the *1968 Era*—in an intense polarization of insurgent and conservative forces. This upheaval affected all of American society, but the most radical challenges tended to be cultivated and implemented, at least initially, on the nation's college campuses, and indeed the universities may have been the institution most deeply affected by this legacy.

Volumes have been written on the student rebellion the 1960s, but its impact on American society is less easily chronicled.[46] Most accounts tend to focus on the dramatic events that shook American politics and society in this era. Principal campus actors—Tom Hayden, Jerry Ruben, or Bill Ayers—soon pursued the social revolution beyond university campuses. Even when the focus is trained on higher education, causation can be problematic.

The most distinctive feature of the *1968 Era* was the total rejection of the American government, institutions, and society by student radicals, symbolically expressed in their spelling of *Amerika*. The previous sections have described how these extreme positions evolved in the New Left, and how concepts they sponsored like corporate liberalism, university complicity, and the *system* permitted a wholesale condemnation of the foundations of American society. No social movement of comparable dimensions in American history adopted such an unredeemed negative view of the country, nor drew such apocalyptic conclusions. As radicals contemplated strategies appropriate to this view, they resurrected and embraced the basic tenets of revolutionary Marxism, with all its doctrinal rigidity, hair-splitting, and schisms. The radical Left, in Todd Gitlin's phrase, "imploded"—isolated in its own fantasies and oblivious to the real world. Thus, the disintegration in 1969 into antagonistic splinters, each pursuing its own ideological strategy, was a likely if not foreseeable outcome.[47] These radicals nonetheless had been largely responsible for the major confrontations of the *1968 Era*. That they were tiny in numbers and delusional in dreams of revolution is beside the point: far larger numbers, especially within universities, sympathized with their critique of America and their interpretations of unfolding events. And, events after 1970s provided considerable evidence to sustain this critique.

Omnipresent since 1965 was the Vietnam War. A strategic blunder, a tactical disaster, a public relations fiasco, as well as a moral swamp—Americans of all stripes recognized the war as a colossal mistake that the government would not acknowledge and seemingly could not terminate. Daily reports of bombings and body counts reinforced the tremendous frustration felt by much of the population. This frustration translated into an intense hostility toward the military in general, and other branches of government that sustained this misguided effort.

No less disturbing was the issue of race. During the 1960s Americans became acutely aware of the centuries of mistreatment endured by Black Americans and the continuing discrepancies in their education, employment, habitation, and representation. Despite real progress, these issues remained highly divisive. Black Power alienated many Whites, as did measures intended to improve conditions for Black Americans, like school busing to achieve racial integration and affirmative action. White opposition was interpreted on the Left as the residual racism of American society and blamed for thwarting efforts to overcome Black inequality.

Given the polarization created by these two issues, additional issues could readily be added to the lists. A romantic view of developing nations idealized anti-American partisans and demonized all attempts by the United States to influence these countries or intervene on their behalf. The long-standing distaste for capitalism among the Left remained prominent. American business interests were assumed to be driving American foreign policy toward developing countries, supporting pliant dictators, and suppressing popular revolution. Discriminatory hiring practices by business were held responsible for the downtrodden condition of Blacks. And business allegedly sustained the permanent war economy through their lackeys in Congress.

Lifestyles provided an added dimension by which members of the student movement and their sympathizers continued to express alienation from bourgeois society: long hair, bell bottoms, workshirts for men; beads and long dresses for women comprised the "antiuniform."[48] Freedom to smoke marijuana was sacrosanct, as was sexual liberation, communal living, and rejection of authority. Students expressed their most vitriolic hatred toward law enforcement, a sentiment largely reciprocated. In less extreme forms, disparagement of bourgeois stereotypes became a staple of the entertainment industry.[49]

The loss of legitimacy of mainstream America spread far beyond those students who participated in demonstrations. The late 1960s saw the largest proportion of students majoring in liberal arts in the modern era, and a corresponding avoidance of studies or careers in business. Student disdain for mainstream America was widespread and found alternative outlets in graduate school or countercultural pursuits. Perhaps most powerful was the determination to avoid any compromise with the Establishment—any suggestion that Black demands were unreasonable; any criticism of the tactics of antiwar demonstrators; any restraint against the freedom to smoke dope—all were interconnected and backsliding on any issue was tantamount to fraternizing with the enemy.[50]

By the end of the *1968 Era*, the student Left and many academic sympathizers had evolved a Manichaean view of the world: the war, the Establishment, the military, the police, and mainstream American society were irredeemably evil; the antiwar movement, anti-Americanism, Black nationalism, and the countercultural lifestyle were the true bearers of redemption. This view, in a milder dosage, pervaded a sizable portion of the American population, although not enough to elect George McGovern in 1972, or even come close. Rather, the campuses of the country's selective colleges and universities provided its most enduring refuge. It scarcely commanded a majority even there. However, it dominated the outlook of the most politically active students, and was tacitly endorsed by large numbers of others who did not wish to be tainted by association with the discredited Establishment. As these views became endemic on campuses, changing in form and content in the 1970s and 1980s, what had formerly been the New Left morphed into the Academic Left, while still preserving the essential Manichaean dichotomy.[51]

Thus, the first major legacy of the *1968 Era* was persistence of the ideological critique of American society and its crystallization into a self-conscious Academic Left. Inseparable from this development was the second major legacy—the emergence and, soon, dominance of identity politics on campus. The path to identity politics was blazed by Black students and their successful demands for separate programs during the *1968 Era*. These steps paralleled developments on the national level, where the original ideal of the Civil Rights Movement for a color-blind society was displaced by the preferential arrangements of affirmative action, deemed necessary to overcome intractable conditions. The embrace of minority preferences and their extension to women and other officially recognized groups was not a coup by the Left: it occurred during the Nixon administration with widespread support across the political spectrum.[52] In higher education a similar commitment was made voluntarily by university administrations to extend preferential recruitment to official minorities in undergraduate, graduate, and professional programs. However, this movement in effect established the preconditions for the institutionalization of highly partisan identity politics, which stemmed directly from the student movement. This connection can be seen most clearly in the rise of women's studies.

The women's movement owed its origins neither to universities nor the New Left.[53] The ideological blinders of student radicals, besides their blatant sexism, long prevented them from seeing how an accommodation with feminism would contribute to their crusade against American society. Although many women participated in the student movement, the New Left insisted that capitalism was the problem, not male chauvinism.[54] A study of this generation of future leaders of women's studies found that they abandoned the movement as it self-destructed. They then "drifted" into graduate schools with little direction or purpose, but with radical convictions intact. There they discovered in a left-leaning feminism a translation of the 1960s critique into its own distinctive critique of American society.[55] Campuses became the strongest bastions of feminism, and "feminism … maintained the fire of sixties radicalism" for decades afterward.[56] "Women's Liberation" was as revolutionary as SDS had been (at least rhetorically) in its rejection of patriarchal society (i.e., American society) and all its entrenched institutions and culture.

In demanding their own curricula, programs, degrees, and faculty, women were "brilliantly practical." The number of women's studies programs mushroomed in the 1970s—from the first degree-granting program in 1970 to 500 in 1980. Almost immediately, they became the template for other officially designated minorities to establish their own culture studies programs. For universities, succumbing to these pressures was not just the path of least resistance, they had no plausible defense. In the multiversity, the capacious curriculum encompassed topics of significance to all manner of groups and interests.[57] Objections to culture studies came chiefly from academic traditionalists—now discredited and despised by the new polity. For Todd Gitlin, the connection with the "late New Left politics of separatist rage" was direct:

> Graduate students and young faculty ... carried ... "the politics of the Left" into the academy and institutionalized (or interred) it there. Identity politics became an organizing principle among the academic cohorts who followed, whose political experience, if any, began in the late 1960s or thereafter. Politics for them was the politics of interest groups—however laced with revolutionary rhetoric.[58]

Administrators appeased the new Academic Left by adopting the posture of what Harvard President Derek Bok called the "socially responsible university," which "must constantly address moral issues and ethical responsibilities in all [its] relations with the outside world."[59] A significant remnant of politically active students was the chief goad, and the issues they emphasized were consistent with the Manichaean worldview. Students supported the unionization of migrant workers against agribusiness corporations. To protest apartheid in South Africa they also targeted US corporations, demanding that universities divest holdings of companies that operated there.[60] Environmentalism was a movement that almost everyone could embrace. The accomplishments of the environmental movement during the 1960s took place entirely outside of universities, but the organization of Earth Day in 1970 made it a popular and enduring student cause. A kind of Counterculture rally, it featured anti-corporate rhetoric on campuses. Among the Academic Left it assumed a millenarian stance in which the only recourse to ecological disaster was a reconstruction of society.[61]

The legacy of 1960s radicalism became institutionalized in a delimited part of the university—literary studies, history, religion, sociology, and especially cultural studies. These partisans now regarded the university as an ivory tower, its social responsibility being to criticize society. But they were increasingly in a minority. After the early 1970s, enrollments in these areas plummeted as undergraduates sought employment credentials in business or professional fields. Students identifying themselves as liberal fell from 35 to 18 percent (1971–1981). Freshmen considering it "very important" to become "very well off financially" grew from near 40 percent in the 1960s to over 70 percent by 1985.[62] After 1980, especially, science and engineering began to cultivate closer relations with industry, much to the disgust of the Academic Left.

In fact, the trends after 1975 undermined the causes of 1960s radicals. The new generation of students was predominately politically moderate (or uninterested) and culturally materialistic. The struggle for social justice was now waged in legislatures and courts. Experiments in community organization had ended badly more often than not. Third World romanticism was belied by the behavior of Marxist dictators—in Cuba, North Vietnam, and especially Cambodia.

Dedicated academic Marxists attempted to keep the theoretical flame of radicalism alive in classrooms.[63] However, the dismal record of communism became an increasing embarrassment after revelations of the Gulag and the rise of Solidarity in Poland. With events undermining cherished beliefs, the Left found refuge in literary theory and academic politics.

By the 1980s, the Academic Left had become entrenched and dominant in literary and cultural studies. They had also become influential in the administration of universities through networks of interested groups and true believers. Their worldview still held the critique of American society to be axiomatic, but political action was now confined to the university and directed inward. From the security and insularity of their academic posts, they now assumed more aggressive intellectual positions,[64] especially in three areas: abstruse literary theory intended as critique of the Western tradition of rational inquiry; efforts to exert influence through identity politics; and attempts to mold student beliefs through required courses and restrictive speech codes. However, this was the Reagan Era in American politics. As Gitlin put it, "while the Right was occupying the heights of the political system, the assemblage of groups identified with the Left were marching on the English Department."[65] Now, efforts by the Academic Left to exploit its power base began to be resisted by conservative opponents in what became known as the Culture Wars.[66] These controversial issues can scarcely be given adequate treatment here. However, they stem from the values and outlook that emerged from the *1968 Era*.[67]

If the Culture Wars represented new applications of the Manichean worldview, they also served to obscure the ironies of the legacy of the *1968 Era*. The campus Left that once championed free speech now sought to impose restrictive speech codes. Having once stood for freedom against institutional authority, it now demanded that students be required to take classes purveying correct views of diversity. Having once imagined that it stood on the side of reason and knowledge, it now condemned rationality and objectivity as "male modes of thought." What endured was the dichotomous view of the world—in one camp a racist, sexist, homophobic, imperialist, capitalist society; in the other the forces of virtue (or self-interest) seeking to overcome these evils. However, although the campus Left once sought to claim the mantle of democracy, there were always many more people in the opposing camp. In frustration, the Left put politics above principle, seeking by whatever means seemed feasible to achieve their ends.[68] For a time, in the 1960s, during an unpopular war and a looming racial crisis, large numbers of sympathizers found their worldview plausible—indeed, aspects of these views compelling. However, that movement destroyed itself through intolerance of the realities of American society and delusions of revolution. Its legacy was taken up by special interest groups and fashioned into an effective strategy of identity politics. The revolution—and it has been a true revolution—that occurred over the subsequent generation in the place of women and minorities in American society was the work of once despised liberals, who applied the muscle of the state to achieve these ends[69]—not the ideologues of the Academic Left. The latter created a congenial and insular place for themselves and their worldview on university campuses, where they might still be found.

Notes

1 For negative interpretation, e.g., John Patrick Diggins, *The Rise and Fall of the American Left* (New York: Norton, 1992); Kenneth J. Heineman, *Put Your Bodies upon the Wheel: Student Revolt in the 1960s* (Chicago: Ivan R. Dee, 2001); for positive, Terry H. Anderson, *The Movement and the Sixties* (New York: Oxford University Press, 1995); and, internationally, Arthur Marwick, *The Sixties: Cultural Revolution in Britain, France, Italy, and the United States, 1958–1974* (New York: Oxford University Press, 1998). For at least a decade after the *1968 Era*, a multitude of studies sought to identify and analyze the inherent causes of student rebelliousness, historically and internationally; however, this literature became far less relevant when students largely ceased rebelling.
2 The following description of the development of SDS draws from Kirkpatrick Sale, *SDS* (New York: Random House, 1973); Todd Gitlin, *The Sixties: Years of Hope, Days of Rage* (New York: Bantam Books, [1987] 1993).
3 Tom Hayden, *Reunion: A Memoir* (New York: Random House, 1988), 25–72.
4 The *Port Huron Statement* has been reprinted many times. I have used copy downloaded from Hayden's website: page numbers are from this edition. The iconic status of the PHS among the contemporary Left is memorialized in Howard Brick and Gregory Parker, eds., *The New Insurgency: The Port Huron Statement and Its Times* (Ann Arbor: Maize Books, 2012).
5 Kevin Mattson, *Intellectuals in Action: The Origins of the New Left and Radical Liberalism, 1945–1970* (University Park: Pennsylvania State University Press, 2002), 187–228.
6 Ibid., 43–96.
7 The charge of hypocrisy, in retrospect, appears to be harbinger of deep cultural change: the recognition that the truisms of the prevailing cultural *mentalité*, the "American way of life," were in fact not true.
8 The political issues of the 1960s are explicated in G. Calvin Mackenzie and Robert Weisbrot, *The Liberal Hour: Washington and the Politics of Change in the 1960s* (New York: Penguin, 2008); James T. Patterson, *Grand Expectations: The United States, 1945–1971* (New York: Oxford University Press, 1996); cultural issues in David Steigerwald, *The Sixties and the End of Modern America* (New York: St. Martin's Press, 1995).
9 Ironically, the years 1964–1966 saw the greatest tide of liberal legislation in the history of the Republic, which was ignored by the New Left: Mackenzie and Weisbrot, *The Liberal Hour*.
10 Joy Ann Williamson, "'Quacks, Quirks, Agitators, and Communists,' Private Black Colleges and the Limits of Institutional Autonomy," *History of Higher Education Annual* 23 (2004): 49–81.
11 Hayden, *Reunion*, part 3; Steigerwald, *The Sixties*, 129–131.
12 Especially valuable for understanding the Free Speech Movement are: Clark Kerr, *The Gold and the Blue: A Personal Memoir of the University of California, 1949–1967*, vol. 2 (Berkeley: University of California Press, 2003); Robert Cohen, *Freedom's Orator: Mario Savio and the Radical Legacy of the 1960s* (New York: Oxford University Press, 2009); and Mark Kitchell, *Berkeley in the Sixties* (San Francisco: California Newsreel, 1990). A variety of perspectives are presented in, Robert Cohen and Reginald E.

Zelnik, *The Free Speech Movement: Reflections on Berkeley in the 1960s* (Berkeley: University of California Press, 2002).
13 Kerr offered a comprehensive theory of worldwide industrial development in: Clark Kerr, John Dunlop, Frederick Harbison, and Charles Myers, *Industrialism and Industrial Man* (New York: Oxford University Press, 1960); Paddy Riley, "Clark Kerr: From the Industrial to the Knowledge Economy," in Nelson Lichtenstein, ed., *American Capitalism: Social Thought and Political Economy in the Twentieth Century* (Philadelphia: University of Pennsylvania Press, 2006), 72–87.
14 Hal Draper, *The Mind of Clark Kerr: His View of the University Factory and the New Slavery* (Berkeley: Independent Socialist Club, October 1964); Cohen, *Freedom's Orator*.
15 James T. Patterson has shown how 1965 was the pivotal year of the 1960s revolution: *The Eve of Destruction: How 1965 Transformed America* (New York: Basic Books, 2012).
16 Complicity joined corporate liberalism and the system in the New Left vocabulary of catch-all condemnations whose content did not require explication.
17 Gitlin, *The Sixties*, 177–188.
18 Ibid., 186.
19 Stokely Carmichael and Charles V. Hamilton, *Black Power: The Politics of Liberation in America* (New York: Vintage Books, 1967).
20 Popular usage of the term is attributed to Theodore Roszak's account of the ideas employed to rationalize this phenomenon: *The Making of a Counter Culture: Reflections on the Technocratic Society and Its Youthful Opposition* (New York: Doubleday, 1969; first published in the *Nation*, March–April 1968). The phenomenon was well-established and commercialized by that late date. For example, the "Human Be-In" of January 1967 was the high point of the Bay area Counterculture. See also Peter Braunstein and Michael William Doyle, *Image Nation: The American Counterculture of the 1960s and 1970s* (New York: Routledge, 2002), 5–14.
21 The linkage between the Counterculture and the New Left is best described by Gitlin, *The Sixties*, 195–221.
22 Sale, *SDS*, 295–296.
23 Ibid., 336. The theoretical rationalizations for embracing violence, or "resistance," drawn from Franz Fanon, Herbert Marcuse, and others, are traced in Steigerwald, *The Sixties*, 135–140.
24 Ibid., 271, 351–355. After the 1968 riots in Chicago protesting the Democratic National Convention, SDS added at least 100 new chapters and many new members.
25 Protests against recruiters were all planned by radical groups, usually SDS, and hence tactical in nature.
26 Sale, *SDS*, 369–383; Tom Bates, *Rads: The 1970 Bombing of the Army Math Center at the University of Wisconsin and Its Aftermath* (New York: HarperCollins, 1992), 81–92.
27 Kitchell, *Berkeley in the Sixties*.
28 Knowledge of actions on different campuses was widespread through the many underground publications, including SDS's *New Left Notes*, and SDS "travellers" who circulated among campuses.
29 For a succinct and balanced account: Robert A. McCaughey, *Stand Columbia: A History of Columbia University in the City of New York, 1754–2004* (New York: Columbia University Press, 2004), 423–489; the official account: *Crisis at Columbia: Report of the Fact-finding Commission Appointed to Investigate the Disturbances at Columbia University in April and May 1968* (New York: Random House, 1968).
30 Sale, *SDS*, 430.
31 McCaughey, *Stand Columbia*, 485. Mark Rudd in his memoir appears oblivious to any serious consideration of political issues and chiefly concerned with action, as well as what was then called an "ego-trip": *Underground: My Life with SDS and the Weathermen* (New York: HarperCollins, 2009).
32 McCaughey, *Stand Columbia*, 528–531.

33 Kenneth J. Heineman, *Campus Wars: The Peace Movement at American State Universities in the Vietnam Era* (New York: New York University Press, 1993); Warren Bennis, *The Leaning Ivory Tower* (San Francisco: Jossey-Bass, 1973), 126.
34 Patricia A. Malony, "Presidential Leadership, Change, and Community: SUNY Buffalo from 1966 to 1981," in John B. Clark, W. Bruce Leslie, and Kenneth P. O'Brien, eds., *SUNY at Sixty* (Albany: SUNY Press, 2010), 144–158; Roger L. Geiger, "Better Late than Never: Intentions, Timing, and Results in Creating SUNY Research Universities," in John B. Clark, W. Bruce Leslie, and Kenneth P. O'Brien, eds., *SUNY at Sixty* (Albany: SUNY Press, 2010), 171–183.
35 Fabio Rojas, *From Black Power to Black Studies* (Baltimore: Johns Hopkins University Press, 2003), 45–92.
36 Donald Alexander Downs, *Cornell '69: Liberalism and the Crisis of the American University* (Ithaca: Cornell University Press, 1999): possibly the best case study of the *1968 Era*.
37 Ibid., 65.
38 In early 1967 SDS was dismayed by the result of a debate on the war with the UN Ambassador, and rejected "mere correctness or rationality" if they do not advance "political effectiveness": Morton Keller and Phyllis Keller, *Making Harvard Modern: The Rise of America's* University (New York: Oxford University Press, 2001), 308.
39 Kitchell, *Berkeley in the Sixties*; W. J. Rorabaugh, *Berkeley at War: The 1960s* (New York: Oxford University Press, 1989).
40 *Report of the President's Commission on Campus Unrest* (Washington, DC: GPO, 1974).
41 Heineman, *Campus Wars*, 257–266: antiwar protests persisted through 1972, often using civil disobedience, but generally eschewing the violence advocated by *1968 Era* extremists.
42 Sympathizers have blamed the demise of the student movement on repression led by the federal government, especially the FBI's COINTELPRO, which included agents provocateurs; and the fragmenting effect of the women's liberation movement, which diverted women to their own special cause: Caroline Rolland-Diamond, *Chicago: le moment 68: Territoires de la contestation étudiantes et repression politique* (Paris: Éditions Syllepse, 2011), 331–336.
43 E.g., Joy Ann Williamson, *Black Power on Campus: The University of Illinois, 1965–1975* (Urbana: University of Illinois Press, 2003). Some writers praise these confrontations in terms of results achieved rather than the means employed: Martha Biondi, *The Black Revolution on Campus* (Berkeley: University of California Press, 2012); Ian Wilhelm, "Ripples from a Protest Past: In 1969, an Armed Occupation by Black Students Roiled Cornell's Campus. Here's Why It Still Matters Today," *Chronicle of Higher Education* (April 17, 2016).
44 Glenn C. Altschuler and Isaac Kramnick, *Cornell: A History, 1940–2015* (Ithaca: Cornell University Press, 2014), 290–296.
45 Steigerwald, *The Sixties*.
46 Todd Gitlin, *The Twilight of Common Dreams: Why America is Wracked by the Culture Wars* (New York: Metropolitan Books, 1995); Heineman, *Put Your Bodies upon the Wheels*: a concise bibliography, 227–233.
47 At its last annual meeting, SDS expelled the Maoist Progressive Labor faction, and the rump, known as the Weathermen, went underground to pursue revolution.
48 Gitlin, *The Sixties*, 215.
49 James Livingston, *The World Turned Inside Out: American Thought and Culture at the End of the Twentieth Century* (New York: Rowman & Littlefield, 2010).
50 Alan Sica and Stephen Turner underline the difficulty "to recall truthfully the bitter, even murderous dislikes of the era: between Veterans of Foreign Wars and longhairs or peaceniks; between radicalized blacks and conservative whites": Alan Sica and Stephen Turner, eds., *The Disobedient Generation: Social Theorists in the Sixties* (Chicago: University of Chicago Press, 2005), 7.

51 John Patrick Diggins, *The Rise and Fall of the American Left* (New York: Norton, 1992), 279–306; Paul R. Gross and Norman Levitt, *Higher Superstition: The Academic Left and Its Quarrels with Science* (Baltimore: Johns Hopkins University Press, 1994), 1–15.
52 John D. Skrentny, *The Minority Rights Revolution* (Cambridge, MA: Harvard University Press, 2002).
53 Alice Echols, *Daring to Be Bad: Radical Feminism in America, 1967–1975* (Minneapolis: University of Minnesota Press, 1989).
54 Gitlin, *The Sixties*, 362–376.
55 Patricia J. Gumport, *Academic Pathfinders: Knowledge Creation and Feminist* Scholarship (Westport: Greenwood Press, 2002).
56 Jeremy Rabkin, "Feminism: Where the Spirit of the Sixties Lives On," in Stephen Macedo, ed., *Reassessing the Sixties: Debating the Political and Cultural Legacy* (New York: Norton, 1997), 46–81, quote p. 47.
57 David P. Baker, *The Schooled Society: The Educational Transformation of Global Culture* (Stanford: Stanford University Press, 2014), 99–121.
58 See discussion of identity politics in Gitlin, *Twilight of Common Dreams*, 141–150.
59 Derek Bok, *Beyond the Ivory Tower: Social Responsibilities of the Modern University* (Cambridge, MA: Harvard University Press, 1982), 299.
60 Philip G. Altbach and Robert Cohen, "American Student Activism: The Post-Sixties Transformation," *Journal of Higher Education* 61, 1 (January–February 1990): 32–49; Robert A. Rhoads, *Freedom's Web: Student Activism in an Age of Cultural Diversity* (Baltimore: Johns Hopkins University Press, 1998).
61 Gross and Levitt, *Higher Superstition*, 149–178; Mackenzie and Weisbrot, *The Liberal Hour*, 223–226.
62 Roger L. Geiger, "Demography and Curriculum: The Humanities in American Higher Education from the 1950s to the 1980s," in David A. Hollinger, ed., *The Humanities and the Dynamics of Inclusion since World War II* (Baltimore: Johns Hopkins University Press, 2006), 50–72.
63 Diggins, *Rise and Fall*, 279–298. Bertell Ollman declared wishfully, "a Marxist cultural revolution is taking place in American universities" and sought to demonstrate that proposition with three volumes of *The Left Academy: Marxist Scholarship on American Campuses* (Bertell Ollman and Edward Vernoff, eds. [New York: McGraw-Hill, 1982], I, 1). Perhaps a more accurate assessment is given by Eric Olin Wright: "in the late 1960s, Marxism was the only game in town … if you were a serious intellectual and really wanted to develop theoretical grounding for radical critique of the status quo.… Beginning in the mid-1980s and accelerating in the 1990s, Marxism became increasingly marginal to academic life and intellectual debate." Sica and Turner, *Disobedient Generation*, 341–342.
64 E.g., the National Women's Study Association constitution states its overriding political aim: "Women's Studies, then, is equipping women … to transform the world to one that will be free of all oppression" (quoted in Rabkin, "Feminism," 78, n.30); "Black studies programs … saw the postsecondary experience as serving an openly political purpose and as an instrument with which oppressed peoples could learn to change society": Williamson, *Black Power on Campus*, 30.
65 Gitlin, *Twilight of Common Dreams*, 148.
66 The conservative soldiers in the Culture Wars linked the politicization of universities directly to the student radicalism of the 1960s, but their case was flawed. William Bennett sought to restore a curriculum based on Western heritage that had scarcely existed previously, that was in fact more a straw man (the "canon") for the literary Left; Alan Bloom, a faculty refugee from Cornell '69, exaggerated in holding universities responsible for the cultural excesses of the 1960s; and Roger Kimball's indictment of "tenured radicals" of the literary Left missed the key role of the succeeding generation in promoting identity politics, as noted by Gitlin.

67 The Culture Wars transcended university campuses: Andrew Hartman, *A War for the Soul of America: A History of the Culture Wars* (Chicago: University of Chicago Press, 2015).
68 Donald Alexander Downs, *Restoring Free Speech and Liberty on Campus* (New York: Cambridge University Press, 2015).
69 Skrentny, *Minority Rights Revolution*.

Contributors

Editors

Roger L. Geiger is Distinguished Professor of Higher Education Emeritus at the Pennsylvania State University and an editor of *Perspectives on the History of Higher Education*. His latest book is *The History of American Higher Education: Learning and Culture from the Founding to World War II* (Princeton University Press, 2015).

Nathan M. Sorber is Assistant Professor of Higher Education, Director of the Center for the Future of Land-Grant Universities at West Virginia University, and an editor of *Perspectives on the History of Higher Education*. He is co-editor of *Land-Grant Colleges and the Reshaping of American Higher Education* (Transaction Press, 2013), and the author of *The Morrill Act in Yankeedom: A History of the Origins and Early Years of the Land-Grant Colleges* (Cornell University Press, forthcoming).

Christian K. Anderson is Associate Professor of Higher Education at the University of South Carolina. He teaches and does research on the history of higher education and comparative higher education.

Contributors

Timothy Reese Cain is an Associate Professor in the Institute of Higher Education at the University of Georgia. He writes and teaches about the history of higher education, the faculty, student activism, and learning outcomes assessment.

Julianna K. Chaszar is a Lead Academic Adviser in the College of the Liberal Arts at the Pennsylvania State University and works with undergraduates pursuing studies in Spanish, Italian, French, and Portuguese. She completed her Ph.D. in Higher Education at Penn State in 2008.

Charles Dorn is Associate Dean for Academic Affairs and Professor of Education at Bowdoin College. His work has appeared in the *American Journal of Education*, *Diplomatic History*, *Teachers College Record*, and *History of Education Quarterly*. He is the author of *American Education, Democracy, and the Second World War* (Palgrave Macmillan, 2007) and *For the Common Good: A New History of Higher Education in America* (Cornell University Press, 2017).

Adam Laats is Associate Professor of Education at Binghamton University (State University of New York). He is the author of *Fundamentalist U: Keeping the Faith in American Higher Education* (Oxford University Press, forthcoming).

W. Bruce Leslie is a SUNY Distinguished Service Professor in the History Department at The College at Brockport. He is the co-author, with Prof. Kenneth O'Brien, of *Sixty-Four Campuses One University: The Story of SUNY*, the first history of the nation's largest system of higher education.

Kenneth P. O'Brien is currently a Faculty Fellow in the SUNY Provost's Office and a member of the Department of History at The College at Brockport. His most recent publications include *SUNY at Sixty* (SUNY Press, 2010) co-edited with W. Bruce Leslie and John Clark, and "Education Markets in English and American Universities," co-authored with John Halsey in *Higher Education in the UK and the US* (Brill, 2014).

INDEX

Page numbers in *italics* denote tables, those in **bold** denote figures.

AAS *see* Afro-American Society (AAS), Cornell University
AAU *see* American Association of Universities (AAU)
AAUP *see* American Association of University Professors (AAUP)
academic freedom: and anti-racist activism 186, 187; and collective bargaining 118, 119, 123, 124, 126, 135, 137; University of South Florida 51, 61, 62, 65
Academic Left 192–3, 194–6
academic majors: state teachers colleges 41–2; University of South Florida 58
Advanced Placement Program 13, 84, 103
affirmative action programs 51, 67–9, 193
affordability of higher education 8, 10, 30
AFL *see* American Federation of Labor (AFL)
African-American students 5, 6, 54, 146; and affirmative action 51, 67–9, 193; anti-racist activism 158–62, 163, 173, 177, 181–2, 185, 186–7, 190, 191; Black Studies programs 68, 162, 185, 186, 187, 190; and faculty transfers 117, 127–30; honors education 95–6; state teachers colleges 28, *28*; University of South Florida 51, 65–9; Wheaton College 160–1
Afro-American Society (AAS), Cornell University 186–7

AFT *see* American Federation of Teachers (AFT)
Alexander, John 160, 161
Allen, John S. 11, 50–1, 52–3, 55, 59, 70–2; and affirmative action program 67–9; and Johns Committee 51, 61–5; and liberal arts education 11–12, 51, 56–8
Alumni Association, Brockport State Teachers College 33
American Association of Universities (AAU) 7, 82
American Association of University Professors (AAUP) 16, 61, 62, 65, 117, 119, 122, 123, 124, 125–7, 130–6, 137–8
American Association of University Women 63
American Civil Liberties Union 123
American Federation of Labor (AFL) 16, 118, 120
American Federation of Teachers (AFT) 116, 117–18, 119, 121, 131, 132, 137, 138
American Oxonian, The 80
Anderson, Florence 100
anti-communist activities 51, 60–5, 84, 118, 173–4
anti-intellectualism 178
anti-racist activism 158–62, 163, 173, 177, 181–2, 185, 186–7, 190, 191

anti-slavery evangelical activism 158–9
anti-war movement 15, 69–70, 123, 147, 151–2, 153, 154, 176, 178, 183–5, 191
anti-war terrorism 190
Armerding, Hudson 155, 160–1, 162, 164, 165
arms race 173
Army General Classification Test 5
Association of American Universities 6
Association of Urban Universities 9
athletics, college 32–3, 58
Aydelotte, Frank 14, 79, 80–3, 85
Ayers, Bill 191

Ball State Teachers College 10
Barth, Karl 150
Belleville Junior College 16, 117, 119, 130–6, 137, 138
Belleville News-Democrat 136
Benca, Otto K. 128
Bestor, Arthur 36
Bible institutes 148
Biola College 151, 154–5
Bish, Charles 95
BJU *see* Bob Jones University (BJU)
Black and Puerto Rican Students of Wheaton College 160
Black Panthers 127, 177, 185, 188
Black Power/nationalism 67, 170, 177, 178, 179, 181–2, 185, 186–7, 190, 191
Black Student Union, San Francisco State College 185, 190
Black Studies programs 68, 162, 185, 186, 187, 190
Blanchard, Charles 147–8, 149, 155
Bob Jones University (BJU) 148, 150, 151–3, 164
Bogan Junior College 129–30
Boger, Ernest 66
Bok, Derek 188, 194
Braukman, Stacy 65
Brave Son 156, 157, 158, 159, 161
Breaking the Academic Lock-Step 82
Brockport State Teachers College 9–11, 24–46; change to comprehensive college 10–11, 40–4; curriculum 36–9, 40–2, 45; enrollment growth 31, 34, 35, 41, 42–4; liberal arts education 10–11, 36–9, 40–4, 45; student life 10, 30–6, 45; students 26–30, *28, 29*; teaching careers after college 39, *40*; veterans 31–2, 34; women's roles 34–5
Broucek, Dave 153

Brown, Albert W. 41, 42, 45–6
Bruckner, Molly 129, 130
Bryan, Ned 95
Bryan, William Jennings 148
Bryan University 148
Buck, Paul 6
Buffalo Nine 184
"Building an Honors Program" 94, 106
Buswell, James O., III 159, 161
Byse, Clark 132

California State Colleges 9, 184–6
Calvin College 151
Cambodia 188–9
Cambridge University, UK 79, 80
Campbell, Barbara 58
campus newspapers: Biola College 154; Brockport State Teachers College 33–4; Moody Bible Institute 153–4; San Francisco State College 185; University of South Florida 58, 62, 70; Wheaton College 156–8, 159, 161, 164
campus rebellion *see* student protest movement in the 1968 Era
Cardozier, V. R. 23
Carmichael, Stokely 177
Carnegie Commission on Higher Education 11, 12–13, 18
Carnegie Corporation 6, 89, 91–2, 93, 94, 95, 97, 98, 100, 101
Carnegie Foundation 59
Carr, Robert 136
Castro, Fidel 173–4
Catholic colleges 45
Catholic upward mobility 45
CCCTU *see* Cook County College Teachers Union (CCCTU)
CCCU *see* Council for Christian Colleges and Universities (CCCU)
CFHE *see* Commission on Financing Higher Education (CFHE)
Changes and Experiments in Liberal Arts Education 82
Chicago Federation of Labor 121
Chicago Federation of Men Teachers 120
Chicago Federation of Women High School Teachers 120
Chicago State College 116, 117, 123–7, 137–8
Chicago Teachers Federation 120
Chicago Teachers Union (CTU) 120–1, 127, 137
Chimes, The 154

Chronicle of Higher Education, The 58–9
CIA 173–4
CIC *see* Committee on Institutional Cooperation (CIC)
Citizens Schools Committee 120
City Colleges of Chicago 116, 119, 121–2, 123, 126, 131–2, 137, 138
City University of New York 119
civil disobedience 175
civil liberty violations 60
Civil Rights Act (1964) 177
civil rights movement 15, 51, 117, 123, 173, 174, 175, 177, 193; affirmative action programs 51, 67–9, 193; evangelical and fundamentalist colleges 146, 158–62; and faculty transfers 117, 127–30; University of South Florida 65–9
Clark, Burton 81
Clark, Dan 48n22
Clark, Felton 95
Clearwater Christian College 164
Cleaver, Eldridge 188
Cobb-Roberts, Deirdre 65–6
Cohen, Joseph 14, 79–80, 83–91, 93, 94, 95, 96–8, 100–1, 102, 105–6
Cohen, Lizabeth 57
Cold War 13, 36–7, 50, 52, 84, 172, 173–4, 177
collective bargaining in Illinois 15–16, 116–39; American Association of University Professors (AAUP) 16, 117, 119, 122, 123, 124, 125–7, 130–6, 137–8; American Federation of Labor (AFL) 16, 118, 120; American Federation of Teachers (AFT) 116, 117–18, 119, 121, 131, 132, 137, 138; background and context 117–19; Belleville Junior College 16, 117, 119, 130–6, 137, 138; Chicago State College 116, 117, 123–7, 137–8; Chicago Teachers Union (CTU) 120–1, 127, 137; City Colleges of Chicago 116, 119, 121–2, 123, 126, 131–2, 137, 138; Cook County College Teachers Union (CCCTU) 117, 121–2, 123–30, 137–8; faculty transfers 117, 127–30; Northeastern Illinois State College (NISC) 116–17, 123–7, 137–8
college athletics 32–3, 58
College of Basic Studies, University of South Florida 57–8, 60
College of Business Administration, University of South Florida 58

College of Education, University of South Florida 58
College of the Liberal Arts, University of South Florida 58
college preparatory tracks 13
collegiate life: state teachers colleges 10, 30–6, 45; University of South Florida 58
Collier, Troy 69
colloquia 83, 85, 88, 94
Columbia University 17, 99, 180–3, 189
Commission on Financing Higher Education (CFHE) 4, 6–7, 8
Committee on Academic Freedom in Illinois 123
Committee on Institutional Cooperation (CIC) 105
community colleges 5, 16, 42–3, 53; *see also* Belleville Junior College; City Colleges of Chicago
commuter institutions 54–5
commuter students 9, 10, 20n19, 69; Brockport State Teachers College 30, 36; University of South Florida 50, 56, 58, 69
comprehensive colleges 10–11, 18, 40–4, 45–6
comprehensive examinations 79, 80, 81, 82
Conant, James Bryant 38–9, 48n30
Conference on the Representation of Economic Interests (1964) 119
conservative evangelical education *see* evangelical and fundamentalist higher education
Cook County College Teachers Union (CCCTU) 117, 121–2, 123–30, 137–8
Cooper, Russell M. 55, 60, 62
Cooperative Education Program, University of South Florida 59–60
Cornell Africana Studies Center 187
Cornell University 146, 186–7, 189, 190
costs of attendance 8, 10
Council for Christian Colleges and Universities (CCCU) 16–17
Counterculture 178, 188, 192
Crane College 127–8
Craven, Wes 146, 156–7, 164
Critique 157
CTU *see* Chicago Teachers Union (CTU)
Cuba 173–4, 185
Culbertson, William 153
cultural revolution 18, 170–1

Culture Wars 195, 199n66
Cunningham, Sean 54

Daley, Richard 12
Daley, Richard J. 120, 121, 122, 137
dance program, Brockport State Teachers College 41
Darley, Ward 87
D'Arms, E. F. 85, 86–8, 89, 90
Davis, Bertram 133, 134
Davis, Jerome 61, 63, 65
Daytona Beach Evening Times 64
Debray, Regis 177
Dedman, Wayne 40, 46n8
defense research 181, 182, 183–4, 187, 188, 189–90
demand for higher education 8–9; *see also* enrollment growth
denominational colleges 147, 148, 149
departmental honors programs 82–3, 85, 86, 88, 94, 102–3, 104–5, 107n5
desegregation 127–30
Dewey, John 5, 36, 38
dictatorial regimes 173–4
doctoral programs 43, 44
dormitories 30, 31, 34, 55
Dow Chemical 179, 180
draft resistance 178, 180, 184
Draper, Hal 175–6
Draper Labs 189
Dunham, Alden 43

early marriage 99
Earth Day 194
Economic Research and Action Project 174
Edgar Stern Family Fund 100
Edman, V. Raymond 151, 155, 156, 157, 158, 159, 161–2
education for citizenship 11–12, 51, 56–8
Edwards, D. C. 133, 134
Eisenhower, Dwight D. 172, 173
elementary education programs, state teachers colleges 26, 28, 37–9
Elementary Teachers Union 120
Eliot, Charles 80
enrollment growth 8–9, 51–2, 53; evangelical and fundamentalist colleges 149, 150; state teachers colleges 31, 34, 35, 41, 42–4; University of Colorado 93; University of South Florida 58
environmentalism 194
equality of opportunity 6–7

ethnicity of students 27–8, *28*, 45
Eurich, Alvin 95
evangelical and fundamentalist higher education 17, 18, 146–66; anti-racist activism 158–62, 163, 165; campus newspapers 153–4, 156–8, 159, 161, 164; evangelicalism 17, 150, 151; faculty divides 161–2; free speech movement 146, 155–8, 163, 165; fundamentalism 147–50, 163–5; fundamentalist/evangelical split 150–1; protests and counter-protests 150–5
evangelical reform 150–1
evangelical social activism 158–62
excellence in education 84
extracurricular life *see* collegiate life

faculty transfers 117, 127–30
faculty unionization *see* collective bargaining in Illinois
faith-based colleges 16–17; *see also* evangelical and fundamentalist higher education
Fanon, Franz 177
Federal Highway Act (1956) 55
federal investment in higher education 5–6, 52
fees *see* costs of attendance
Feminine Mystique 34, 35
feminism 193
Fewkes, John 120, 121
Financing Higher Education in the United States 6
Finkin, Matthew W. 134
first-generation students 10, 11, 27, 44–5, 56
Fischer, Herman 157
Fisher, Margaret E. 67
Fisk University 118
Fleming, Denna Frank 62
FLIC *see* Florida Legislative Investigating Committee (FLIC)
Florida 53–5; *see also* University of South Florida (USF)
Florida Board of Control 55, 61, 62, 64–5, 66
Florida Board of Regents 68
Florida Legislative Investigating Committee (FLIC) 51, 60–5
Ford Foundation 12, 84
Franke, Walter 133
Franklin, John Hope 96
Fraser, James 44, 47n9

free speech movement 17, 146, 155–8, 163, 165, 174–6, 195
Freedom Now 160
Friedan, Betty 34, 35
Fuller, David Otis 164
Fuller Theological Seminary 150
Fund for the Advancement of Education 84, 86, 95, 100
fundamentalist higher education *see* evangelical and fundamentalist higher education

general education 3–7
General Education in a Free Society 4–5, 8
General Elementary Education curriculum, state teachers colleges 28, 37–9
general honors programs 13–15, 18, 85, 89, 93–4, 102, 104, 106, 108n19
Georgia State University 12
"Get-Out-The-Vote" campaigns 66
GI Bill 1, 31, 48n22, 52, 83
Ginsberg, Allen 65
Gitlin, Todd 177, 191, 194, 195
golden age portrayals 51–2
Goldwater, Barry 173
Gordon College 162
Gould, Samuel 41, 46
graduate education 44
Graduate Record Examination 86, 88
graduate school attendance 99, 103
Graf, Otto 105
Great Society 15
Grebstein, Sheldon N. 65
Grede, John F. 121, 122
Grubb, W. Norton 57
Guernsey, Bob 154
Guevara, Ché 177
Gulf of Tonkin Resolution 176

Haber, Al 171
Haberaecker, Hugo J. 131, 134, 135
Haley, Margaret 120
Hamilton, Michael S. 149
Hampton, Fred 127
Harvard 18, 80, 188, 189, 190
Harvard Red Book 4–5, 8
Hawkins, Virgil D. 66
Hawthorne, Gerald 158
Hayakawa, S. I. 185
Hayden, Tom 171, 173, 191
Heald Commission 39, 40
Health and Physical Education programs, state teachers colleges 26, 28–9, 31, 35, 37, 38
Health and Physical Education programs, state teachers colleges, state teachers colleges 41
Henry, Carl 149–50
Henry, David Dodds 12, 13
high schools 103
high-ability students 8, 13–15; *see also* honors programs
Higher Education Act (1965) 12, 69
Higher Education for American Democracy 4, 5–6, 53
Hofstadter, Richard 84
Hollinshead, Byron 6
Homecoming, Brockport State Teachers College 33
Hommes, Jack 157–8
homosexuality 60–5
Honors Courses in American Colleges and Universities 85
honors programs 13–15, 18, 79–107, **102**; departmental honors 82–3, 85, 86, 88, 94, 102–3, 104–5, 107n5; general honors 13–15, 18, 85, 89, 93–4, 102, 104, 106, 108n19; Inter-University Committee on the Superior Student (ICSS) 14, 18, 80, 88–9, 91–106; interwar period 14, 80–3; and Joseph Cohen 14, 79–80, 83–91, 93, 94, 95, 96–8, 100–1, 102, 105–6; recruitment and retention of students 103, 105; spillover effects 104; state teachers colleges 39
House Un-American Activities Committee 60, 173
Howard University 116, 118
Hoxby, Caroline 14–15
Hurst, Charles 127, 130

ICSS *see* Inter-University Committee on the Superior Student (ICSS)
IDA *see* Institute for Defense Analysis (IDA)
Idzerda, Stanley 96
IFT *see* Illinois Federation of Teachers (IFT)
Illinois *see* collective bargaining in Illinois
Illinois Association of Junior Colleges 126
Illinois Federation of Teachers (IFT) 121, 126
Illinois Public Junior College Act (1965) 121, 130

in loco parentis rules 151, 153–4
Institute for Defense Analysis (IDA) 181, 182
institutional racism 186
Inter-University Committee on the Superior Student (ICSS) 14, 18, 80, 88–9, 91–106
intercollegiate athletics 32–3, 58
Intercollegiate Studies Institute 147
interdenominational colleges *see* evangelical and fundamentalist higher education
interracial marriage 160, 161–2
IQ determinism 8

Jackson, Frederick 89, 91, 93, 95, 97–8, 101
Jackson State University 17, 189
Jaeck, Gordon S. 159
Jefferson, Margaret 61
Jencks, Christopher 16, 17
John Birch Society 173
Johns, Charley 51, 60
Johns Committee, Florida 51, 60–5
Johnson, Larry 65–6
Johnson, Lyndon 15, 176, 177
Johnson, Noel 128–9
Jones, Bob, Jr. 152, 164
Jones, Bob, Sr. 148
Joughin, Louis 122
junior colleges 5, 6, 16; *see also* Belleville Junior College; City Colleges of Chicago

Kaluger, George 26–7
Kappa Delta Pi 35
Kaufman, Michael G. 129–30
Kennedy, John F. 15, 118, 173
Kent State University 17, 71, 152, 188–9
Kerouac, Jack 65
Kerr, Clark 12–13, 15, 41, 52, 172, 175, 186
Ketcham, Robert 164
Ketter, Robert 184
Kim, Dongbin 9, 69
Klotsche, J. Martin 59
Kodon 156–7, 164
Koerner, James 36–7, 38
Korean War 84
Kugler, Israel 132

land-grant universities 12, 89, 95
Larsen, Charles M. 124, 126, 134, 135, 136

Laurel Foundation 100
Lazerson, Marvin 57
League for Industrial Democracy 171
Lee, William 121
Lehman, Herbert 26
Lewis, Todd 154
liberal arts colleges 37, 38, 50–1; *see also* comprehensive colleges; Wheaton College
liberal arts education 3–7, 11–12, 83; state teachers colleges 10–11, 18, 36–9, 40–4, 45; University of South Florida 11–12, 51, 56–8, 63
liberal reform 15
living at home *see* commuter students
Lowell, Abbott Lawrence 80
Lucas, Christopher 37, 48n30
Lynd, Staughton 123

McArdle, Bernard F. 129–30
McCarthy, Joseph 60
McCarthyism 51, 60–5, 84, 173
McCloskey, Matthew 54
McGovern, George 192
McIlnay, Philip 157–8
McNamara, Robert 179
Mahoney, Margaret 100
Malcolm X College 127–8, 130
Mansfield Amendment 189
Mao Zedong 177
Maoist Progressive Labor Party 179
March on Washington 176
marriage 39; early 99; interracial 160, 161–2
Marsden, George M. 147
Marshall, John 87, 91
Martin, Edwin P. 67
Martin, T. T. 148
master's programs 18, 44
Mautz, Robert B. 68
Mayhew, Lewis B. 55–6, 57, 59
MBI *see* Moody Bible Institute (MBI)
Mead, Margaret 99
Methodist colleges 149
Meyerson, Martin 183–4
Michigan Daily 171
Michigan State University 89, 96
middle classes 8–9
military research *see* defense research
Millett, John 6
Milligan, Jan 132, 134
Mills, C. Wright 172
Milwaukee Technical Institute 118

MIT 189
Mitterling, Philip I. 101, 105
Monroe, Charles R. 128
Moody Bible Institute (MBI) 150, 151, 153–4
Moody Monthly 150
Moody Student 153–4
Mormino, Gary 54
Moser, Alvin 159
Murk, James 159, 161
Murray, George 185

National Association for the Advancement of Colored People (NAACP) 66
National Collegiate Honors Council 18, 79, 101–2, 104
National Education Association (NEA) 16, 95, 118, 119, 130, 137
National Guard 152, 188, 189
National Labor Relations Board 137
National Merit Scholarship Program 13, 84, 103, 105
National Mobilization Committee to End the War in Vietnam 70
National Opinion Research Center 99
National Research Council 81–2
National Science Foundation (NSF) 100, 101
Native American students 28, *28*
Nature and Needs of Higher Education 6–7
NEA *see* National Education Association (NEA)
Nelson, Richard J. 125, 126, 138
New Evangelicalism 150
New Frontier 15
New Left *see* student protest movement in the 1968 Era
New Mobilization Committee to End the War in Vietnam 70
new vocationalism 58–60
New York Federation of Newman Clubs 28
New York State Board of Regents 25, 26, 31, 46n5
New York State Normal School, Albany 25
New York Times 44
Newman Clubs 28, 45
Nicholson, R. Stephen 128
Niebuhr, Reinhold 150
NISC *see* Northeastern Illinois State College (NISC)
Nixon, Richard 18, 188

normal schools 25–6, 30–1, 46n5
Norris, J. Frank 148
North Central Association of Colleges and Secondary Schools 95
Northeastern Illinois State College (NISC) 116–17, 123–7, 137–8
Novar, Leon 128–9
NSF *see* National Science Foundation (NSF)
nuclear weapons 173

occupational education *see* vocational education
Ocean Hill-Brownsville 117, 138
Ohio 11
Ohio State University 89, 96
One-to-One, University of South Florida 66–7
Oracle, The 70
orthodox education *see* evangelical and fundamentalist higher education
Oxford University, UK 79, 80, 81

parental education 27, 47n13, 47n14
parental occupations 26–7
participatory democracy 171–2
Patin, Henry A. 117
Patterson, James T. 15
peace movement 173; *see also* anti-war movement
Pennsylvania 26–7, 47n12
People's Park 188
Pepperdine College 147
Perkins, James 186, 187
Pittsburgh Forgings Company Foundation 100–1
Playground Teachers Union 120
Podhoretz, Norman 65
Port Huron Statement 170, 171–4, 177
post-Sputnik criticism 36–7, 48n29
Potter, Paul 176
Potter, Ron 161
President's Commission on Higher Education 4, 5–6, 8, 53, 83
professional education courses, post-Sputnik criticism 37, 38, 48n29
professional-oriented education *see* vocational education
progressive education, post-Sputnik criticism 36–7, 48n29
Protestant evangelical education *see* evangelical and fundamentalist higher education

pro-war stance 152, 153, 154; *see also* defense research

Quint, Howard 93
Quonset huts 31, 34

racial and ethnic minority students 5, 6, 54, 146; and affirmative action 51, 67–9, 193; anti-racist activism 158–62, 163, 173, 177, 181–2, 185, 186–7, 190, 191; Black Studies programs 68, 162, 185, 186, 187, 190; and faculty transfers 117, 127–30; honors education 95–6; state teachers colleges 28, *28*; University of South Florida 51, 65–9; Wheaton College 160–1
Reagan, Ronald 188
religious affiliation 16–17; *see also* evangelical and fundamentalist higher education
religious identity of students 28, *29*, 45
Reserve Officers Training Corps (ROTC) 184, 188, 189
residential accommodations 30, 31, 34, 55
Reuther, Walter 120
Rickover, Hyman 36
Riesman, David 16, 17
Riley, William Bell 148
Rilling, Paul M. 68
riots 177, 180, 184, 188, 189
Rockefeller, Nelson 40
Rockefeller Foundation 6, 86–8, 89, 91, 100
Romney, George 41
ROTC *see* Reserve Officers Training Corps (ROTC)
Roth, Herrick S. 118
Ruben, Jerry 191
Rudd, Mark 181–2, 189
Rupprecht, Arthur 161
Rury, John L. 9, 69

Sachs, Jerome 125
St. John's University 118, 119
St. Petersburg Times 64
San Francisco State College 184–6, 190
Sarasota Herald Tribune 64
Savio, Mario 146, 175, 176
Schoenherr, Charles 163, 164
SCLC *see* Southern Christian Leadership Conference (SCLC)
SDS *see* Students for a Democratic Society (SDS)

secondary schools 103
segregation 54, 127, 171, 173, 177
seminaries 148, 149
seminars 81, 83, 85, 94, 104
Serviceman's Readjustment Act (1944) *see* GI Bill
sexism 193
Shabot, Oscar 128, 129, 130
Shircliffe, Barbara 66
sit-in protests 128, 173, 184
SNCC *see* Student Nonviolent Coordinating Committee (SNCC)
Snider, Genevieve 131, 132–3, 134
social class 6–7, 8–9, 26–7, 35, 36, 44–5
social mobility 27, 44–5
social prestige of higher education 57
Society of Afro-American Students, Columbia University 181–2
Southern Christian Leadership Conference (SCLC) 66
Southern University 95–6
Sowell, Thomas 187
specialist programs, state teachers colleges 26, 28–9, 31, 35, 37, 38
specialization 3–4
Sputnik satellite 13, 36, 50, 52, 84, 103, 173
Stanford Research Institute (SRI) 187, 189
Stanford University 187, 189
state teachers colleges 9–11, 18, 23–4, 44–6; post-Sputnik criticism 36–7, 48n29; *see also* Brockport State Teachers College
State University of New York (SUNY) 10, 12, 24, 40, 44, 46n5; Buffalo 183–4, 190; *see also* Brockport State Teachers College
Statement on Government of Colleges and Universities (1964) 124
Steering Committee of Teacher Welfare Organizations 120
Stenholm, Gilbert 164
Strasser, Rose 41
strikes, by faculty 117, 118–19, 121–2, 125, 126, 129, 136, 138
Strong, Edward 175
student activism 52; anti-racist activism 158–62, 163, 173, 177, 181–2, 185, 186–7, 190, 191; evangelical and fundamentalist colleges 146, 150–8, 163, 165; and faculty transfers 117, 127–30; University of South Florida 66–7, 69–70, 71; *see also* anti-war

Index

movement; student protest movement in the 1968 Era
student life: state teachers colleges 10, 30–6, 45; University of South Florida 58
student lifestyle rules 151, 153–4
student newspapers *see* campus newspapers
Student Nonviolent Coordinating Committee (SNCC) 171, 173, 174, 177, 185
student protest movement in the 1968 Era 17–18, 170–96; Berkeley 171, 174–6, 179, 180, 188, 190; and Black Power/nationalism 67, 170, 177, 178, 179, 181–2, 185, 186–7, 190, 191; Columbia University 17, 180–3, 189; Cornell University 186–7, 189, 190; and Counterculture 178, 188, 192; free speech movement 17, 174–6, 195; Harvard 188, 189, 190; inception 171–80; Kent State University 17, 71, 152, 188–9; legacies of 190–6; San Francisco State College 184–6, 190; Stanford University 187, 189; SUNY Buffalo 183–4, 190; and Third World Revolution 177–8, 179
Students for a Democratic Society (SDS) 17, 70, 155, 170, 171–4, 176–7, 178–80, 181–2, 183–4, 186, 187, 188
Students for Peace and Freedom 69–70
Stumpf, Wayne 136
Stylus, The 33–4
Sumberg, Albert 135–6
Sunbelt 53–5; *see also* University of South Florida (USF)
SUNY *see* State University of New York (SUNY)
Superior Student in American Higher Education, The 101
Superior Student, The 93, 94–5, 97–8, 99, 101, 102, 106
superior students 8, 13–15; *see also* honors programs
supply of higher education 9–13
Sutherland, Samuel 154–5
Swarthmore College 14, 79, 80–1, 82, 83
Swenson, Norman 121, 124, 126, 128, 138

Taft, William 71
Talbot Seminary 154–5
Tampa Bay area, Florida 53–4, 55; *see also* University of South Florida (USF)

Tampa Times University of South Florida Campus Edition 58, 62
Tannenbaum, Abraham 103
Tennessee Temple College 151, 164
Tenney, Merrill C. 161–2
Thelin, John 44
Third World Liberation Front 185, 188
Third World Revolution 177–8, 179
Time magazine 13, 14, 15
Tower, Donald 31, 41
Tri-State College 118
Truman Commission *see* President's Commission on Higher Education
tutorial system 81, 82
two-year colleges 9, 52

unionization of college faculty *see* collective bargaining in Illinois
United Federation of College Teachers 118
United Federation of Teachers 138
United States Steel Foundation 100
University of California 12, 15, 41, 172; Berkeley 52, 146, 156, 171, 174–6, 179, 180, 188, 190
University of Colorado 79–80, 84–5, 86–8, 89–90, 91, 92, 93
University of Colorado Libraries 102
University of Florida 66
University of Georgia 96–7
University of Illinois 12, 97, 116, 130, 133
University of Michigan 105, 171
University of Minnesota 148
University of North Carolina 89
University of South Florida (USF) 11–12, 50–72; background and context 53–5; civil rights and affirmative action 51, 65–9; constitution 70–1; Cooperative Education Program 59–60; curriculum 11–12, 51, 56–8, 63; and Johns Committee 51, 60–5; liberal arts education 11–12, 51, 56–8, 63; student activism 66–7, 69–70, 71; students' educational objectives 51, 56, 57, 58–60
University of Tampa 66
University of Tennessee 96
University of Toronto 82
University of Washington 89
University of Wisconsin 59, 60, 97, 146, 148, 180
university-based research 12–13, 52
Upward Bound program, University of South Florida 67

urban universities 9, 11–13; *see also* University of South Florida (USF)
urban-grant universities 12–13
US Office of Education 99, 101
US Supreme Court 66
USF *see* University of South Florida (USF)

Van Ek, Jacob 87
Van Waes, Robert 132
veterans 1, 31–2, 34, 48n22, 52, 83
Vietnam War 15, 69–70, 147, 151–2, 153, 154, 176, 177, 191
violent student protest *see* student protest movement in the 1968 Era
vocational education, students' preference for 11–12, 51, 56, 57, 58–60
vocationalism 3–4, 58–60
Voget, Lamberta 159
Voting Rights Act (1965) 177

Walker, Glenwood 86
Washington Post 64
Watts, Glen 156
Wayne University 12
weapons research *see* defense research
Webster, Daniel 46
Weil, Oscar 121, 126, 130
Weir, Walter D. 91, 93, 101

Wert, Robert 89
Wheaton College 17, 18, 146–8, 155–66; anti-racist activism 158–62, 163, 165; campus newspapers 156–8, 159, 161, 164; evangelicalism 17, 150, 151; faculty divides 161–2; fall in applications 163–4; free speech movement 155–8, 163, 165; fundamentalism 147–8, 149, 163–5
Wilson Junior College 128–9
Winter, David 159
Wipf, Don 153–4
women: graduate school attendance 99; honors education 99–100; marriage 39, 99; post-war enrollment growth 52; state teachers colleges 34–5, 39, *40*; teaching careers 35, 39, *40*
women's movement 193
women's studies programs 193, 199n64
work experience 59–60
World Christian Fundamentals Association 147
Wynn, Dudley 104

Yale University 123
Young Americans for Freedom 147
Youth Against War and Fascism 183